S0-BRG-843

DogLife 🐾 Lifelong Care for Your Dog®

DOBERMAN PINSCHER

tfh

Liz Palika

DOBERMAN PINSCHER

Project Team
Editor: Mary E. Grangeia
Copy Editor: JoAnn Woy
Indexer: Elizabeth Walker
Design: Angela Stanford
Series Design: Mary Ann Kahn, Angela Stanford

TFH Publications®
President/CEO: Glen S. Axelrod
Executive Vice President: Mark E. Johnson
Publisher: Christopher T. Reggio
Production Manager: Kathy Bontz

TFH Publications, Inc.®
One TFH Plaza
Third and Union Avenues
Neptune City, NJ 07753

Printed and bound in China

11 12 13 14 15 16 1 3 5 7 9 8 6 4 2

Library of Congress Cataloging-in-Publication Data

Palika, Liz, 1954-
  Doberman pinscher / Liz Palika.
    p. cm. -- (Doglife)
  ISBN 978-0-7938-3614-7 (alk. paper)
  1. Doberman pinscher. I. Title.
  SF429.D6P348 2012
  636.73'6--dc23

                    2011025339

This book has been published with the intent to provide accurate and authoritative information in regard to the subject matter within. While every reasonable precaution has been taken in preparation of this book, the author and publisher expressly disclaim responsibility for any errors, omissions, or adverse effects arising from the use or application of the information contained herein. The techniques and suggestions are used at the reader's discretion and are not to be considered a substitute for veterinary care. If you suspect a medical problem consult your veterinarian.

Note: In the interest of concise writing, "he" is used when referring to puppies and dogs unless the text is specifically referring to females or males. "She" is used when referring to people. However, the information contained herein is equally applicable to both sexes.

The Leader In Responsible Animal Care For Over 50 Years!®
www.tfh.com

CONTENTS

INTRODUCTION

INTRODUCING THE DOBERMAN PINSCHER

The faded black-and-white photographs in the Palika family photo album portray the wonderful relationship between a boy and his dog. In one photo, a cute, blond, curly-headed toddler is hanging on to the collar of a black and tan Doberman Pinscher, the dog appearing very patient as the toddler tries to walk. In another photo, the dog is sitting upright, looking alert and watchful, as the toddler snoozes on a blanket in the grass.

The toddler in those photos is my husband, Paul Palika. Many of his first memories as a child were of the Doberman Pinschers in his family. "There was always a dog within reach," he says, "Although I know the dogs had to leave my side sometimes, I don't remember that. I just know a dog was always nearby, and I remember getting a sense of comfort from that."

The dog who was Paul's first companion as a child was Fritz. In the photos of Paul as a toddler, Fritz was a long, lanky, and gangly puppy. Other photos from the family album show Paul growing from a toddler into a child as Fritz grew from an adolescent into a handsome, mature dog. His mother, Edith Palika, showed their Doberman Pinschers in conformation dog shows and obedience trials, but most importantly, the dogs were treasured family pets and companions.

IN THE BEGINNING

Researchers have long debated where, when, and how dogs became domesticated. The most widely held theory is that wolves came to human encampments to eat leftovers from the animals people butchered. Wolves eventually looked for these convenient sources of food and grew accustomed to people, gradually coming closer and closer. However, although the wolves became familiar with humans, they'd never become tame companions solely by visiting their camps to scavenge.

Another theory is that people took in orphaned wolf cubs and raised them, as people do today with puppies who have lost their mother. Anyone who has raised a wolf, or even a wolf hybrid, can attest to the difficulties this entails. Wolves are not domesticated animals, and even pups raised by people still grow up to be wild animals.

Many researchers now believe that the canines people adopted and eventually domesticated were different from wolves—especially different from the gray wolves we are familiar with today. Archaeological

Although the true roots of the breed remain unknown, it is believed the Doberman Pinscher originated in Germany around the late 1800s.

evidence shows that the early canines who eventually became our domesticated dogs actually made an evolutionary split from wolves long before they began hanging around people, perhaps as many as 100,000 to 135,000 years ago. These unnamed canines continued to evolve until they interacted with humans some 10,000 to 15,000 years ago.

It's hard to tell exactly why these early dogs were domesticated; fossil records from that long ago often aren't clear. However, life at that time was difficult.

Although companionship was probably part of the relationship, dogs—mankind's first domesticated species—also must have performed some jobs that made mankind's survival easier. Most historians agree that the first dogs most likely assisted with hunting to find and run down game or herd it to a specific location. Warning of the approach of other predators or unfamiliar people may also have made them useful companions. Something as simple as snuggling up with the children to help keep them warm could have also aided in the family's survival.

No matter what occupations these early dogs had, it was obvious that their relationship with humans was mutually beneficial. As needs changed over thousands of years—both for people and dogs—the jobs dogs were asked to do also changed. Sighthounds chased down fast game, while scenthounds tracked it. Some dogs developed herding skills, while others became more protective. Selective breeding produced dogs with specialized skills and abilities, as well as unique body conformation and appearances.

Today, many dogs still work alongside human partners. Apart from their traditional roles working on farms and ranches, they act as guide dogs, hearing assistance dogs, and other service dogs assisting their disabled partners. Military and law enforcement dogs risk their lives to protect us on a daily basis. They function in professional capacities helping to find lost people, household pests, contraband items, and any number of things that would be difficult for people to otherwise locate. There are many jobs dogs perform to make life easier for people. But dogs are most valued as companions, friends, and occasional confidants; there are currently more dogs living with people as pets than at any other time in our shared history.

THE DOBERMAN PINSCHER IN GERMANY: A BREED CREATED WITH A SPECIAL PURPOSE

Karl Friedrich Louis Dobermann, known as Louis, lived in Apolda, Thuringa, Germany in the mid-1800s. He held a variety of jobs during his adulthood, including work as a butcher, night watchman, tax collector, and dog catcher. It was his job as tax collector that became problematic, however, as he often carried money. Wanting a dog for protection and apparently not happy with the dogs available to him, Louis decided to create a unique breed that would suit his purposes.

Historians have said that Herr Dobermann wanted a dog large enough to be imposing to robbers yet not too large to handle and care for. He wanted a short coat for easy care and a minimum of grooming. He also wanted an intelligent dog who was easy to train, yet alert, protective, and aggressive when necessary. In other words, when he began creating his breed, he had very specific requirements in mind.

The Doberman Pinscher is named after Karl Friedrich Louis Dobermann, who developed the breed.

The early Doberman was bred to be a working dog who was alert, protective, and aggressive when necessary.

Unfortunately, Herr Dobermann didn't keep very good records. Although choices for the development of his new breed were made carefully, its true origins remain unknown. As dog catcher, he had access to all the stray dogs of the region, giving him easy access to a variety of breeds.

Historians have identified several breeds available in Germany at that time that were either known to have been used or appear to have been used in the creation of Herr Dobermann's new dog. They include:

- **German Pinscher:** Herr Dobermann initially envisioned a large terrier-like dog, and the German Pinscher had the alertness, aggressiveness, and persistence he required.

- **Manchester Terrier:** This breed provided a short, shiny coat, elegant appearance, refinement, and black and tan coloring.

- **Beauceron:** This hard-working breed provided size, substance, intelligence, working ability, and a desire to please.

- **Weimaraner:** This breed (known then as the Weimer Pointer) added scenting abilities, retrieving skills, and also had the short coat he required.

- **Rottweiler:** The Rottweiler contributed size, stamina, intelligence, and working abilities, as well as black and tan coloring.

In addition, some believe an old German sheep herding breed (not the German Shepherd of today) was added to the mix to further enhance physical soundness and a strong work ethic. Often called Thuringian Shepherds, these dogs also were prized for their intelligence and bravery. Some histories of the Doberman Pinscher mention Great Danes, German Shorthaired Pointers, and other breeds in their ancestry.

When Herr Dobermann's health began to fail in the late 1800s, he left his dogs in the care of Otto Goeller, who continued Dobermann's vision for the breed. At one point, Greyhounds were added to the mix for added height and speed, but historians differ as to when this occurred. Some say it was during the time Herr Dobermann was creating the breed, while others feel that Herr Goeller brought in the Greyhound later. However, without records, it's really hard to tell exactly what went into the creation of the modern-day breed.

Early Dobes were heavy-set, with heavier heads, more like Rottweilers than the Dobermans of today. The coat was coarse, tended to be wavy, and was of medium to short length. And, as with mixed-breed dogs, there was considerable variation among individual dogs.

Herr Dobermann's vision for the breed was that of a working dog. He wanted an intelligent, alert, protective, and aggressive dog, and that's what he and Herr Goeller achieved. The Dobermann Pinscher of that time was not bred to be a household pet, but a hardcore law enforcement or military dog, and a very effective one at that.

National Dobermann Pinscher Club

In 1899, The National Dobermann Pinscher Club was formed in Germany. Herr Goeller and other Dobermann Pinscher enthusiasts created a breed standard outlining exactly what this new breed should look like. In addition, temperament and character were addressed.

The German Kennel Club recognized the breed soon after its name officially became Dobermann Pinscher. Varying during the early years, it was initially known as Dobermann's Dogs, and then as Thuringian Pinschers. When the breed began working with law enforcement and military personnel, it became known as Soldatenhunds, or Soldier Dogs. By 1899, the National Dobermannpinscher Klub was formed in Germany, and a year later the breed standard was accepted. Less than a year after that, Doberman Pinschers were recognized by the German Kennel Club. Along with the second "n" in Dobermann, *Pinscher*, which translates to *terrier*, was dropped from the breed name in most parts of the world as it was felt that *terrier* was not an accurate designation for these dogs.

THE DOBERMAN PINSCHER IN THE UNITED STATES

The first Doberman Pinscher was imported into the United States by E.R. Salmann in 1908, although existing records don't tell us anything about who this person was or who his dog was. That same year, the first Doberman was registered with the American Kennel Club (AKC). He was a black and tan male named Doberman Intelectus, bred by Doberman Kennels and owned by Carl Schulyheiss. He was sired by Doberman Bertel out of Doberman Hertha, both German imports. Ch. Ferry v Raufelsen of Giralda was the first Doberman to win Best in Show at the Westminster Kennel Club show in 1939, and his line was responsible for producing seventeen American champions.

Although both World War I and II had a devastating effect on the breed in Europe, this motivated its development in the United States. During World War I, so many people were starving that families could not afford

The Doberman Pinscher breed has evolved over time, becoming more refined in appearance and more docile in temperament.

to feed their dogs. Even dedicated Doberman breeders saw their animals starve to death or had to put them down because of imminent starvation. Two factors saved the breed during this period: the breed's use by military and police units, and the exportation of the best dogs to America, both to initiate America's breeding programs but also to save the dogs from their questionable fate in Europe at that time. With help from American breeders, the Doberman breed began to recover its numbers. However, World War II again threatened its stability. During this era, all dog clubs in Germany were overseen by the Nazi party, which meant the breeding and exportation of dogs was controlled by the government and the German military. Germany used dogs effectively in the military, and so their

exportation was severely restricted—not just to the United States—but to any country.

Again, the breed's survival was boosted by the United States' official use of military service dogs during World War II. The Marine Corps was the first to establish a Corps War Dog training facility at Camp LeJeune, North Carolina. The dogs were trained for several duties, including sentry, scout, messenger, and mine detection work. Some dogs were also taught to carry packs and to pull weight, such as a sled. Sydney Moss, then President of the Doberman Pinscher Club of America (DPCA), promised to help recruit dogs for the war effort. Many other DPCA members volunteered their time and money to help find, screen, and recruit potential military service dog candidates. More than 90 percent of the dogs used by the Marines in World War II were Doberman Pinschers. Nicknamed "Devil Dogs" by the Marines, most were often volunteered by their families.

Dobermans also served admirably in Korea and Vietnam. Wray Stout, who served with the US Coast Guard in Korea, recalls a Doberman Pinscher who made a lasting impression on him, "I wasn't trained for ground combat; I was trained for shipboard work. So when we arrived in Korea, and I was handed a rifle and told to get off the ship, I was scared. Really scared. However, I just happened to be in formation behind a dog handler and his big black and tan Doberman. That dog scared me,

too, but I knew he was on my side."

Dr. William Putney, a retired veterinarian who served with the Marines and their dogs in World War II, wanted to honor all of the "Devil Dogs" who served and gave their lives so their Marines could live. "Those dogs saved hundreds of lives in the battle of Guam," he said. A monument honoring all the war dogs who served, as well as those who gave their lives, was established at the US Naval Base in Orote Point, Guam. A life-sized bronze statue of Kurt, a Doberman who served with distinction, was placed at the memorial that bears the inscription "Always Faithful."

The first Doberman Pinscher was registered with the American Kennel Club in 1908.

In 2010, the Doberman Pinscher was ranked the 14th most popular breed registered with the AKC.

The Doberman Pinscher Club of America

The Doberman Pinscher Club of America (DPCA) was formed in 1921 by George Earle III, an American politician who later served as the president's special emissary to the Balkans during World War II. The club adopted the German breed standard because, during this time in history, quality Dobes were being imported from Germany as well as Holland and Russia.

DOBERMAN PINSCHER POPULARITY

Popularity emerged slowly for Doberman Pinschers. Although prized by military and law enforcement units, the breed was looked upon by the general public as potentially dangerous, as dogs who were loose cannons ready to blow

up. The phrase, "Dobes turn on their masters," summarized the prevailing attitude that people had toward the breed at one time.

Some of this was deserved. Early in their development, Dobes were bred to be aggressive; Herr Dobermann's vision of the breed's occupation was that of working dog and protector. The breed's success in World War I and II, as well as in the Korean War and Vietnam, shows how well suited for that role the dogs were. In addition, some military war dogs were rehomed without being given a transition from military life to civilian life. For these dogs, who today we would say were suffering from post-traumatic stress disorder, that adjustment was difficult. Behavioral problems, including too much aggression for civilian life, were not uncommon.

In addition, in the 1960s, there were several

highly publicized incidences of Dobermans attacking small children. The children were hurt and, in a few cases, killed. The media grabbed onto these incidences, and the breed was labeled "dangerous." The media, of course, didn't report on the details of these cases and what led up to the attacks.

However, American breeders were already working on changing the breed's temperament. Although still alert, the dogs were watchful and protective without undue aggression. This wasn't enough to change the perception of the breed in many peoples' minds. In fact, when portrayed in the popular media, the Doberman is usually the bad guy. These two recent films are examples of this:

• *Beverly Hills Chihuahua* (2008): In this film starring Drew Barrymore, a Doberman character named El Diablo is portrayed as evil.

• *Up!* (2009): In this film starring Ed Asner, a Doberman named Alpha is a bully and the leader of a gang of bad dogs.

The popular media needs bad guys, and to many, Dobes are still a common choice.

But efforts to soften the Dobe's temperament and image are working, and registration statistics show that. In 1999, the breed was ranked at number 23 in popularity as compared to other registered AKC breeds. By 2004, the breed had moved up to number 22; by 2008, to number 18; and by 2010, Dobes were the 14th most popular breed registered with the AKC.

Celebrity ownership encourages a change in the public's perception of the breed, too. William Shatner—actor and famous *Star Trek* starship captain, director, and avid horseman— has owned several Doberman Pinschers. A photo of his black-and-tan female Dobe, Charity, is prominent on his website www. williamshatner.com and shows Charity licking

his face. Mariah Carey owned Princess, a Dobe who was prominent in one of her videos and accompanied her to interviews.

Popularity is a dual-edged sword, however. Whenever a breed is highlighted in a movie, on television, or in other media, a demand is created for that breed. The most famous example of this is the popularity of Dalmatians after Disney's 101 Dalmatians. When people want a breed, whether it be Dalmatian or Doberman, indiscriminate breeders will pop up hoping to make a substantial profit satisfying that demand. Unfortunately, these individuals don't understand that indiscriminate breeding can create physical, health, and temperament flaws in their dogs.

Nevertheless, positive changes in the breed's temperament are now seen in other ways. Although Dobes have been used for a number of years in the Pilot Dog, Inc., guide-dog program, which provides assistance to the visually impaired, they are now also being used in other service dog programs. Dobes are also serving as wonderful, affectionate, and caring therapy dogs, visiting people of all ages in hospitals, nursing homes, care facilities, and retirement homes.

Doberman Pinschers are competing in many canine sports, including agility, flyball, competitive obedience, and rally. But don't think the breed has become too soft; many are still competing successfully in working dog sports, including Schutzhund.

The Doberman Pinschers my husband grew up with were treasured family pets and companions, handsome show dogs, and well-trained obedience competitors. They were watchful and protective without being aggressive. He says, "I have fond memories of those dogs. They were always by my side, ready for a hug or a cuddle; and always ready to play."

PART I

PUPPYHOOD

CHAPTER 1

IS THE DOBERMAN PINSCHER RIGHT FOR YOU?

Doberman Pinschers have elegance, intelligence, loyalty, athleticism, and so much more. Does this make a Dobe the perfect dog? Well, some people who have shared their lives with this breed think it is pretty close to perfect—at least, for them. They also agree that this is not the right breed for everyone. When making a decision as to whether the Doberman Pinscher is a good breed choice, people should take into consideration that these dogs are often slow to mature. Most experts don't consider the breed mentally and physically developed until the age of 2 years, with some individuals maturing even later.

TEMPERAMENT AND PERSONALITY

Many people are drawn to the breed because of its temperament and personality. Melissa C. Wilkins, a volunteer for Dobie-Rescue. org, says, "Doberman Pinschers are amazing, loving, and loyal companions. They seem to instinctively know what you want or need from them. I love the devotion they give to their human companions." Wilkins, of Enterprise, AL, adds, "The intuitiveness of the Doberman is unmatched by any other breed."

During the initial formation of the breed under the guidance of Herr Dobermann and Herr Goeller, and then as working dogs in World Wars I and II, Korea, and Vietnam, Doberman Pinschers were not bred to be pets. Today, the breed retains the alertness and watchfulness of its early ancestors, but breeders have softened its temperament through selective breeding.

Temperament

"All the Dobermans I have shared my life with have had terrific temperaments," says Carol A. Byrnes, a certified pet dog trainer from Spokane, Washington. "They love to work. They want to be with you, and they love attention but aren't 'needy' or groveling."

Temperament is normally defined as a set of innate traits; in other words, traits that the dog is born with rather than behaviors he learns. Although every Doberman Pinscher is an individual, there are some temperament traits that are commonly seen in the breed.

- **Dedication and loyalty:** Mary Waugh Swindell, the head trainer for Dancing Dogs of Boyd, Texas, says, "I love the breed's focus on the people they love." She adds that there

Provided that the breed is a good match for the owner, Dobes make wonderful pets and companions.

is an intensity about their dedication; there is no doubt that you are loved when a Dobe loves you.

- **Intelligence:** This is a very bright breed. Cheryl Lent, a dog trainer who enjoys engaging in performance sports with her dogs, channels this intelligence in her training sessions with them. She asks her dogs, "Show me something new!" The dog can sit, or down, or spin, or shake his head, but can't repeat a behavior that has already been shown in that training session. It takes a very smart dog to keep this game going.

- **Intuitiveness:** Dobes seem able to read their owners' minds; guessing (or knowing) what is wanted before anything is said.

- **A sense of humor:** When describing the Dobe temperament, many owners mention the breed's sense of humor. Kim Somjen, DVM, of Ringoes, New Jersey, says, "What attracts me most to the breed is its sense of humor. All of my dogs have had a wicked sense of humor, playing jokes on me and the other dogs in the house. They know how to push buttons to get a reaction."

- **Watchfulness and protectiveness:** Although the breed's temperament has been softened significantly from the aggressive dog of the past, these dogs are still watchful and protective. Wilkins says her Dobes are watchful over home and family; no one can approach without them giving an alert.

Originally bred as working dogs, the modern Dobe temperament now allows the breed to wear many hats successfully. In the right household, Dobes make wonderful pets and companions. They are also excellent therapy dogs and service dogs, and they eagerly compete in many performance sports. Dr.

Somjen currently trains and competes in many venues with her Dobermans, including obedience, rally, agility, tracking, flyball, and Schutzhund. Versatility is very much a part of the Doberman makeup.

Personality and Behavior

Temperament and personality are closely related. Whereas temperament consists of traits one is born with, personality can be affected by life's events. For example, a Dobe puppy may be born with the qualities to be smart, loyal, and funny, but lack of socialization or abuse and neglect could cause him to withdraw from people and become fearful and mistrustful.

Admired for their loyalty and intelligence, Dobes require lots of attention, affection, and daily interaction. Their purpose in life is to gain the approval and acceptance of their master.

On the other hand, that same Dobe, if raised with affection, socialization, and guidance, will have a great chance of growing up to become a wonderful family companion.

Behavior, too, is dependent on both temperament and experience. How a dog will react to things that happen around him is based upon his natural temperament, what has happened to him in the past, and how he is feeling about the world around him at the moment.

It's difficult to predict the behavior of an entire breed of dogs, so a certain amount of generalization is necessary. The following, then, pertains to most Dobermans, although a certain amount of variance is to be expected among individuals.

- **Affection with family:** Dobes are very affectionate with their owner and family members. Although not clingy, they are happiest when close to their people. In most instances, expect a Dobe to want to be in the same room with you.
- **Unhappy alone**: A Dobe left alone for too long will be unhappy. This can often translate into destructive behavior, self-mutilation (licking or flank sucking), or barking and howling.
- **Aloof with strangers**: Dobes prefer to share their affection with family rather than people they don't know. On a walk, your Dobe isn't going to want strangers to pet him—even friendly strangers.
- **Protectiveness:** Your Dobe will be alert toward unfamiliar people and exhibit protective behavior, which he will indicate by moving his ears forward and standing on his tiptoes; if permitted, he will likely growl and bark.

Dr. Somjen says, "Dobermans are fiercely loyal and prefer to stick by your side. Their extreme intelligence makes them appropriate for such a close life with their people."

THE ELEGANT DOBERMAN

Each breed of dog is characterized by what's called a *breed standard*. This is a detailed description of the "perfect" specimen of the breed. Although no one—human or canine—is perfect, the breed standard provides a blueprint for those trying to breed better dogs. Breed standards can vary depending upon the club or registry that creates them. When Dobes first came to America and the Doberman Pinscher Club of America (DPCA) was first organized, the breed standard was based upon the document drafted in Germany.

But standards change. For example, let's compare some basic points presented in the American Kennel Club (AKC), Kennel Club (KC), and Federation Cynologique Internationale (FCI) Doberman breed standards.

- In the breed description, the AKC prefers the dog's physical conformation to demonstrate speed and endurance, whereas the FCI doesn't state this.
- The KC wants the dog to express toughness, while the AKC and FCI don't state this.
- The AKC and KC want the iris of the eyes to be uniform in color, whereas the FCI doesn't state this.

Although these may seem to be minor differences—and sometimes the differences are truly minute—a breed standard is what keeps the Doberman Pinscher looking like a Dobe rather than a Greyhound. There's nothing wrong with Greyhounds, but they aren't Dobes. Differences in the standards result in variances in conformation—which determines how the dog looks—from one country to another. Unless otherwise stated, the descriptions provided here are based on the breed standard per the DPCA and the AKC.

Size and Build

Doberman Pinschers are medium-sized dogs. Herr Dobermann wanted to create a breed big enough to do the work he needed done, and yet not so large as to be cumbersome or hard to care for. Males stand between 26 and 28 inches (66 and 71 cm) tall at the point of the shoulders, while females are between 24 and 26 inches (61 and 66 cm) tall. Males tend to weigh between 85 and 95 pounds (39 and 43 kg), while females weigh between 70 and 80 (32 and 36 kg) pounds.

The Dobe's build reflects his athleticism; most notably his speed and agility. He is well muscled, yet not bulky. He should be big enough to be imposing. The Dobe's terrier ancestry gives him agility and quickness, while the Greyhound in his ancestry gives him speed.

There is only one size for Doberman Pinschers, with variation only for sex. For example, there is no such thing as a Miniature Doberman. There is a dog called a Miniature Pinscher, but that is a totally different breed. The terms *Warlock*, *King*, or *Royal* have also been used at various times to label larger than normal Dobes, but there is no breed standard or official recognition for large, extra-large, or giant-sized Dobermans.

Coat Type and Color

The Doberman's coat is short and hard. It is amazingly thick and lies close to the skin. The coat should be smooth and shiny.

Doberman Pinschers are square, medium-sized dogs, with a well-muscled build that reflects their athleticism and agility.

The Doberman's sleek, shiny coat is short, thick, and lies close to the skin.

Once in a while, some of the Dobe's ancestors make an appearance and the dog will have a slightly wavy coat, like that of the Rottweiler or Beauceron. Although this coat type is not correct for the show ring, it does remind us that Dobes had a variety of ancestors in their genetic makeup. Some dogs will also have a slight undercoat on the neck, underneath the shiny outer coat. This is acceptable but shouldn't be visible.

There are four acceptable colors for Doberman Pinschers. They include black, red, blue, and fawn (also called Isabella). All will have clearly defined rust-colored markings:

- One marking will be above each eye, where an eyebrow might be.
- Rust also appears on the muzzle going up to the cheeks. The top of the muzzle is the dog's base color, but the areas on the sides and underneath the muzzle are rust.
- Many Dobes will also have an additional rust spot on each cheek; sometimes connected to the muzzle marking and sometimes as an additional spot. A separate spot, sometimes called a thumbprint, is considered optimum.
- There is usually a rust marking on the upper throat.
- Most Dobes have a rust marking on the front of the chest, usually at the top of each front leg, but often extending across the chest.
- The legs and feet are rust colored. The lower part of the legs, the pasterns, and the backs of the legs are rust colored, but the front of the legs above the pasterns should be the same color as the coat.

- There is usually a small circle under the tail that is rust colored.

Although some Dobermans have a white coat, this is not an acceptable color. The DPCA has studied these albino dogs extensively and found that they are sensitive to light, have vision problems, and are prone to skin cancer. Significant temperament problems have also been noted. There is an ongoing discussion between DCPA and the AKC to impose a breeding restriction on white Dobes. The DPCA has created a tracking system to identify any Dobes that may carry the gene for albinism. These dogs will have a "Z" after their registration numbers so that breeders can avoid putting them into their breeding programs and passing on the trait.

Body and Legs

The neck carries the head proudly, with a strong arch that many people see as horse-like. The shoulders are strong, supporting the neck and front legs. The length of the shoulder blade should equal the length of the upper foreleg. The point of the upper shoulder, called the *withers*, is the highest point of the body.

The back is short, strong, hard, and extends in a straight line from the withers to the base of the tail. The chest is broad. The ribs are not flat but instead are wide enough to provide plenty of room for the heart and lungs. The hindquarters are strong and well balanced with the chest and shoulders. The belly is well tucked up; a waist is evident.

The legs are strong, athletic, and parallel to each other when viewed from the front or back. The paws are catlike and compact, with well-arched toes. The paws face forward, without turning in or out. Dewclaws may be removed.

The Doberman will have balanced movement and a strong reach forward, with the front legs pulling the ground under him as the rear legs drive him forward. In a trot, the rear feet will place themselves in the same spot vacated by the front paws moving forward. He should appear to be moving smoothly with an efficiency of movement.

Head

The Dobe's head is just as elegant as the rest his body. The skull is triangular in shape, like a wedge, broad between the ears, and tapering to the nose. The wedge shape can be seen from above as well as from the side. There is a slight stop (indent and drop) between the eyes, but the top of the muzzle and the top of the skull are parallel and continue the wedge shape. The length of the top of the muzzle from nose to stop equals the length of the skull from stop to the back of the skull. The skin of the head is taut, with flat cheeks and lips that are close to the jaws and teeth.

Muzzle

The Dobe's muzzle is strong without being bulky. It is not as fine as that of the Greyhound or as heavy and wide as that of his Rottweiler ancestor. The lips are tightly fitted to the muzzle and do not droop. The nose is black on black dogs, dark brown on red dogs, dark gray on blue dogs, and dark tan on fawn dogs.

Teeth

The Dobe should have 20 teeth in the upper jaw and 22 in the lower jaw. The teeth are large. The front incisors should meet in a scissors bite, with the upright lower teeth touching the inside of the incisors of the upper jaw. If the upper teeth extend past the lower incisors, this is called *overshot* and is undesirable. If the lower teeth extend past the upper incisors, this is called *undershot* and is also undesirable.

The Dobe's head is just as elegant as the rest of his body. The skull is triangular in shape, broad between the ears, and tapering to the nose.

skull. The AKC official breed standard says the ears should be "normally cropped and carried erect." When carried erect and set high on the skull, the ears provide the alert, regal appearance most people recognize in the breed.

Ear cropping, however, has become quite controversial. In many countries, including Belgium, England, Hungary, Switzerland—to name just a few—cropping is banned. Interestingly enough, in Germany, the Doberman Pinscher's ancestral home, tail docking and ear cropping are banned, and a Doberman with a docked tail or cropped ears cannot compete. The justification for banning these procedures is that they are unnecessary for the dog's health.

Eyes

The eyes are almond shaped (oval) and are relatively close together, especially as compared with many other dog breeds. The eyes are alert and intelligent. The iris should be uniform in color. Black dogs will have medium to dark brown eyes. Red, blue, and fawn dogs will have eyes that match the color of the coat; however, darker eyes are preferred to lighter ones.

Unfortunately, the breed is prone to missing teeth. Although the cause has been blamed on various breed ancestors, it doesn't really matter where it began. Although one or two missing teeth is not looked upon with too much disfavor, a dog with four or more missing teeth cannot compete in AKC conformation dog shows. Teeth are particularly important for a breed such as the Doberman, when the breed's ancestral work is considered.

Ears

The Dobe's ears are positioned so that the base of the ears is level with the top of the

Tail

The AKC requires the tail to be docked at the second joint. As per the discussion regarding ear cropping, in many countries tail docking is looked upon with as much disfavor as ear cropping.

LIVING WITH A DOBERMAN

Doberman Pinschers have come a long way since Herr Dobermann's efforts to create a protective working dog to stand by him as he collected taxes. These once hard-charging, stocky, coarse dogs are now elegant, athletic, intelligent, empathic companion dogs. But even with these changes, this breed is not for everyone.

Environment Requirements

Dobes are quite versatile and can thrive in many different living situations. Mary Swindell says, "My first Dobe lived in an apartment for 5 years. Then we moved to the suburbs, and he finished his life in the country. My husband had his first two Dobes in an apartment." This flexibility with living conditions makes the breed quite adaptable.

Whether a large house or a small apartment or condo, Dobes can be comfortable anywhere. They aren't the type of breed to stretch out and take up all the walking space in the living room, either. They are creatures of comfort and would be content on your sofa—next to you, of course—or in a comfortable dog bed.

Training Tidbit

Determine what the house rules will be before you bring your new dog home, and make sure that all family members abide by them. For example, decide whether your Doberman Pinscher will be allowed on the furniture. Because these dogs love comfort, once you allow your Dobe to cuddle up on the sofa or on your bed, it will be difficult to change his behavior later. If you don't want him on the furniture, provide him with a comfortable bed of his own in each of the rooms in which you often spend the most time.

One thing that potential new owners need to keep in mind is that this is an "indoor" breed. A daily walk or run and time outdoors to play—with the owner participating—is fine and necessary, as are trips outside for the dog to relieve himself. However, Dobes should not be left alone outdoors for long hours every day. These dogs are happiest when they spend time with their owner—and some would be happiest if they could crawl under their skin. Left alone for long hours each day, a Dobe is likely to develop behavior problems.

"We have eight acres now," Swindell says, "and our dogs love to run." She clarifies that statement, "When we're outside with them. If we go inside while the dogs are outdoors, they don't run and play; they stand at the window and look inside at us."

In addition, weather can pose a problem. Although Dobes can go for walks in all sorts of weather—from hot to cold—temperature and weather conditions can affect how long they remain outdoors. Shanna Gardner, of Jacksonville, Florida, says, "These dogs do not have an undercoat and need to be kept primarily indoors." Carol Byrnes says, "My dogs are weenies about the weather—they hate the rain and don't like to be cold."

Every Dobe can be unique, however, and this needs to be taken into consideration when deciding whether the breed is right for you and your family. Melissa Wilkins, who does Doberman rescue, says, "I have been around dozens of Dobes, and their needs are as individual as they are. There is no cookie cutter home for a Dobe."

Exercise and Playtime Requirements

Doberman Pinschers are not an overly active breed; they are not generally referred to as "busy" dogs. However, daily exercise is important, as is some playtime with you. "Dobes need to run on a regular basis," says Swindell, "If left alone too much without exercise, a Dobe can become destructive."

Paulette Bethel, of Fallbrook, California, and the owner, breeder, and trainer of many titled Doberman Pinschers, says, "This breed needs exercise. We throw the ball a lot for the dogs to retrieve. We walk them several miles each day, and we run up and down the stairs throughout the day."

Some recommendations for daily exercise for a healthy adult Doberman could include:
• an hour of brisk walking
• several short play sessions, which may include retrieving a thrown ball or toy
• a training session in trick training, agility, or flyball
• a half-hour run alongside a bicycle

Daily exercise and playtimes are important for any dog's physical and mental well-being.

By the Numbers

Puppies have different exercise needs than do adult dogs. A puppy from 2 to 4 months of age can be introduced to walking on a leash, but the walks should be kept very short, about five minutes at a time. Playtimes should also be kept short, again five minutes at a time. As the puppy grows, gains strength, and coordination, and his attention span increases, exercise and playtimes can be extended.

Dobes are not a good choice for people who tend to be sedentary.

Sociability

Doberman Pinschers are not as reactive, protective, or aggressive as they were many years ago, but even with softening of their temperament, they are not nearly as social as many other breeds, such as Labrador Retrievers or Golden Retrievers. Swindell says, "This breed bonds very tightly with its owner. Most Dobes are very affectionate, although some are loving to their family and aloof with strangers.

The Dobe and Strangers

This working dog was originally bred to be a watchful defender when necessary. Although the role of the Doberman Pinscher has changed significantly since those early years, the breed still has the tendency to be wary of strangers. The degree of wariness can vary, however.

Some people get a Dobe expecting him to be an aggressive guard dog but are then disappointed that the dog doesn't perform as expected. Most Dobes are watchful and wary of strangers, but they are not likely to show aggression toward someone for no reason.

Some Dobes will be standoffish with strangers, yet can also be bribed into interacting. Stillwell says, "Some of my Dobes are mercenaries. If you have something they're interested in—a ball or a treat—then they will become interested in you. If you don't have something for them, they can't be bothered."

There are varying levels of protectiveness within the breed. Dr. Somjen, a veterinarian who competes with her Dobes in performance sports, says the breed's suitability for working dog sports—such as Schutzhund, which requires the dog to show some aggression and a willingness to bite a decoy—is the subject of an ongoing debate. "Many feel the breed has suffered a bit because they consider it to have been 'watered down'—no longer as sharp or aggressive as it once was—to make it more acceptable to the general public."

The Dobe and Children

Dobermans can be very good with children when well socialized with them. Gardner, who volunteers with Dobie-Rescue.org, says, "Dobermans with a sturdy temperament are excellent with children and can be very tolerant. Even my adopted Dobermans, who have experienced past abuse and neglect, are very tolerant of children and truly enjoy their company."

Paulette Bethel says, "My Doberman raised my two sons. When Mick and Rob left for the day, either on their bikes or snowmobiles, Apollo went with them. At first, my parents and friends thought I was certifiable because I dared to trust my children to a 'killer' dog. Yet, within months, they were all converts."

Not all Dobes are safe around children, however. Bethel says, "I have had two Dobermans whom I felt did not have the temperament to be around children."

A lack of socialization to children could cause the dog to feel anxious around them. If the dog grows up in an adult-only household and never meets kids, or if some rowdy kids scare the Dobe during puppyhood, then he may grow up thinking that children are creatures to be feared.

There is no way to say for sure that every Doberman Pinscher will be safe with children. Bethel says, "I don't think any blanket statement is fair or truthful."

The Dobe With Other Pets and Dogs

When well socialized with other pets, most Dobes will live with them quite peacefully.

Multi-Dog Tip

Although aggression issues can occur, Kim Somjen, DVM, says, "With training and socialization, any Doberman should be able to control himself and coexist with other dogs." As socialization and training progresses, however, and to prevent unwanted behavior, she adds, "I don't recommend leaving your Dobe unsupervised while with other dogs or animals."

My husband's mother, Edith Palika, had Doberman Pinschers and Standardbred horses. Paul grew up with the dogs and horses, and doesn't remember any problems between the two species.

Socialization is often the key to good behavior. Stillwell says, "Socialize! Socialize! Socialize! Our Dobes are good with other dogs as well as cats, small animals, and our chickens. They tend to ignore our neighbor's livestock, although one of our dogs, Casanova, loves our neighbor's llama."

"My Dobes live with four cats," says Wilkins, "I've also fostered Dobes headed to or from rescue, but with proper introductions they do very well with other animals." Wilkins also says that her neighbor has horses and hasn't had any problem with the dogs reacting aggressively toward them.

If you have small pets, however, is important to note that the breed's terrier and Greyhound ancestry is still present. Because of this, many—if not most—Dobes have a very high prey drive. If a cat, rabbit, or even a small dog runs away from your Dobe, the chase will be on. Bethel says, "The chase will be on, but it

Dobermans can be very good with children and other pets when well socialized with them.

will be a game." Any game can get out of hand, though, and should the Dobe catch the small animal, the result could be tragic.

Socialization during puppyhood and on into adulthood is also important when it comes to the Dobe's attitude toward other dogs. For the most part, when well socialized, Dobes are fine with other dogs. However, aggression in adult male Dobes toward other male dogs is not unknown. Dr. Somjen says, "Males tend to be okay with other dogs as youngsters. But as they get older and mature, they tend to be less tolerant of other offensive males with poor social skills. Although this is not as common with females, it also does occur."

Training Requirements

Training should be an integral part of every Doberman Pinscher's life. This isn't necessary because these dogs are bad but because they were bred to do a job. Without ongoing activity, training, or a job to do, the Dobe will get bored and may very well get himself into trouble.

"Training should begin the day a Doberman Pinscher joins his new home and should continue until the day he dies," says Dr. Somjen. She adds, "Training is very important to this breed. Not just because the dog has an active mind and needs to work to be fulfilled, but also because an untrained Dobe is a poorly behaved one. These dogs tend to like to push the envelope, and they need to learn boundaries."

Cheryl Lent believes in keeping a Doberman's mind just as busy as his body. She trains and competes in agility and obedience, and has just started tracking with her dogs.

She's even tried herding and says the dogs did well. Cheryl says, "I love the physical beauty of these dogs, but I really love their minds the most. Dobes are easy to train; they're so smart and loving."

Grooming Requirements

Grooming a Dobe is very easy and, in fact, there aren't many dog breeds as easy to keep looking sleek and attractive. Here's all that you have to do:

- Brush the short, sleek coat weekly to keep it clean and healthy; more often if your dog gets dirty.
- If your Dobe starts smelling a little "doggy," give him a bath.
- Clean the ears weekly.
- Clean the teeth a couple of times per week, or daily if possible.
- Trim the toenails weekly, or as needed.

When asked about grooming a Doberman, Paul Palika says, "Easy! Five, ten minutes tops, and the dog looks wonderful."

Health Challenges

Although Doberman Pinschers are generally healthy and hardy dogs, the breed is unfortunately prone to some serious health issues—as are other breeds—and potential

Want to Know More?

For more information on health issues that may affect Doberman Pinschers, see Chapter 8: Health of Your Doberman Pinscher Adult.

owners need to take this into consideration when making their decision. Not only should they query breeders about these concerns when looking for a Dobe, but they must also understand the possible challenges that could impact the dog's life.

Dobermans can suffer from a number of inherited or genetic disorders, including albinism, cardiomyopathy, hypothyroidism, liver disease, active hepatitis, progressive retinal atrophy (PRA), vestibular disease, von Willebrand's disease, and Wobbler's syndrome.

It's always hard to lose a much-loved dog, but it's even harder if the dog is young and lost to a devastating disorder. However, research is ongoing, and responsible breeders test their breeding dogs in the hope of eliminating some of these diseases.

A highly intelligent, working breed, Dobes require daily activity and exercise. Toys and chews provide mental stimulation and encourage positive behavoir.

CHAPTER 2

FINDING AND PREPPING FOR YOUR DOBERMAN PINSCHER PUPPY

A puppy has unlimited potential. He is an exciting link to the future and to all the wonderful things that you and your canine companion will do together. But that excitement needs to be tempered with some logic and common sense. First, you need to find a reputable breeder, choose your new puppy, and make sure you're ready for him before bringing him home. Then, you need to understand that puppies are babies, and so the first few days and weeks may be challenging. Being prepared for what will happen will make it easier on you and your new Dobe.

THERE IS NOTHING LIKE A PUPPY!

Most people, when adding a dog to the family, choose a puppy rather than an adult dog. Carol Byrnes says, "I like to bond early with a puppy. I also want to be a part of the socialization process, as this is especially important with this breed."

When raising a puppy you're in charge of everything, from choosing the right puppy for you, to housetraining him, supervising him to make sure he doesn't get into trouble, socializing him, and training him. It can sound like a daunting task but, at the same time, it's

exciting and rewarding. You can mold this puppy so that he grows up to be a wonderful companion, your next best friend.

Choosing Show Quality or Pet Quality

Before choosing this puppy, though, think about what you want. Obviously, you've decided to get a Doberman Pinscher, but what are your expectations?

- Do you want to enter your Dobe in conformation shows? If so, you'll need to talk to breeders who also show their dogs and make sure they help you choose a puppy who shows potential to compete.
- Do you want to compete in obedience trials? Again, find a breeder who also participates in obedience or performance sports with her dogs. Your Dobe will need to have the potential for this, as well as a sound body.
- Do you want to participate in canine performance sports—agility, flyball, tracking, etc.? These require a Dobe with a sound mind as well as a sound body.
- Do you want to participate in working dog sports such as Schutzhund? These activities require a sharper, tougher dog than many Dobes today. However, there are still good

If you want to add a Dobe puppy to your family, the best source for acquiring one is from a reputable breeder.

working lines. If this is your goal, look for a breeder whose dogs have been successful in these sports.

The most important job, however, is that of pet and companion. And if that's what you're looking for in your dog, that's absolutely fine.

Finding the Puppy of Your Dreams

There are many sources for puppies. You may see a cute little puppy in a box outside of a grocery store and be tempted to rescue him. Granted you may save that puppy's life, but is he going to be healthy and long lived? There's no way to know.

Doberman Pinschers, as a breed, may have some significant health problems. If you want to add a Dobe puppy to your family, the best

source for acquiring one is from a reputable breeder. Although there are no guarantees about future health, a reputable breeder will do everything she can to produce healthy, well-behaved puppies.

So, what qualities define a reputable breeder? There are no set requirements for someone to be labeled a reputable breeder. However, some of the characteristics that may make one breeder stand out over another might include:

- She loves her dogs and is not breeding for financial gain.
- She is continually increasing her knowledge of the breed.
- She keeps herself up to date on health issues, research, and tests for health problems.
- Her breeding dogs are regularly tested for

health problems, and the results of the tests are made available to potential puppy buyers.

- She's a member of local, regional, and/or national breed clubs.
- She knows of and follows the Doberman Pinscher Club of America (DPCA)'s Code of Ethics.
- She participates in dog sports or activities.
- She screens potential puppy buyers to make sure the puppies go to the right homes.
- She is available to puppy buyers after the sale.

You can find a reputable breeder in several different ways. Your veterinarian might have a client who breeds healthy Dobes. You can also go to the DPCA's website for a referral to a breeder at www.dpca.org

Once you have the name of a few breeders in your area, contact them and ask if you can visit the facilities and see the dogs. While on the phone, some good questions to ask are:

- Does she screen her dogs for health problems? If she says her dogs don't have

What to Look for When Visiting a Breeder

The responsible breeder's dogs will look well cared for and happy. The breeding dogs should spend a considerable amount of time indoors and be treated as members of the family. If they spend time in kennels, check these out for cleanliness and amount of space. Ask how the dogs spend a typical day. Aside from good nutrition and health care, all the dogs, both adults and puppies, should receive training, socialization, playtime, and affection daily.

any health issues, thank her and look elsewhere.

- Does she provide a health report on each individual and his or her parents? Ideally, she should share all health records and test results with potential puppy buyers.
- What kind of guarantees does she offer puppy buyers? It is impossible to guarantee that a Dobe will never get sick at any time during his lifetime, but there should be some warranties offered.
- Can you meet the puppies and breeding dogs? The answer should be yes, of course, but at her convenience.

When you talk to the breeder, expect her to ask as many questions as you do. Don't take offense at this. After all, she is going to want to know that her puppies are going to the very best homes possible. Some of these questions may include:

- How much research have you done on Doberman Pinschers? Obviously, she will want to make sure that you know what the breed is like and what to expect.
- Have you owned a dog in the past? Dobes aren't always the best choice for first-time owners because they can be challenging.
- What happened to that dog? The breeder is looking for someone who will keep a dog for his lifetime and not get rid of him if difficulties arise.
- Where do you live? Do you own or rent? Are there any restrictions on pets where you live? Unfortunately, many people live in dwellings where large dogs or certain breeds are not allowed. Many landlords will also have other limitations.
- How often will the dog be left home alone? Dobes are not happy dogs when left alone for many hours every day.
- Are you an active person, or are you naturally sedentary? While Dobes enjoy

snooze time on the sofa, they also need daily exercise, socialization time with other people and dogs, and time to train and play with their owner.

Once you find a breeder you like, don't be surprised if she places you on a waiting list for a puppy. I once waited a year and a half, and although that seemed like a long time, it was well worth the wait.

When it comes time to choose the right individual puppy for you, let the breeder help you. Although many puppy tests are available that can screen the puppies by temperament, they are difficult for potential puppy buyers to do correctly. However, the breeder has been watching these puppies since birth. Let her guide you to the one that she feels will suit you best.

BEFORE YOUR PUPPY COMES HOME

There are some things you need to do before bringing home your new Doberman. When he first arrives, you'll want to get to know him and enjoy him. So, it's better to have more time to help him acclimate comfortably to his new environment than to spend time shopping for him and doing errands. To make the transition easier and less stressful for your puppy, prepare your home for his arrival ahead of time, and have some basic supplies on hand—food, bowls, a crate, toys, etc. The less hectic his first few days are, the better for you and your little Dobe.

Puppy-Proof the House

Puppies are like babies and will explore their world by putting anything into their mouth. They will chew on the most surprising things, including remote controls, cell phones, electrical cords, and more. They will eat socks and underwear, and they will chew on shoes.

Puppies love to raid the cat food dish and get into the cat's litter box. Because so many of these things can be harmful—if not deadly—to a puppy, preventing him from having access to them is important.

Decide where your puppy will spend his time. He shouldn't have free run of the house for quite a while, so think of how you can restrict his freedom so that he remains safe when you cannot supervise him. A crate (often called a travel crate or kennel crate) is a great place for your Dobe to sleep, but he shouldn't spend much time in it during the day. Using an exercise pen (foldable free-standing fence) is a good way to confine a puppy to a particular area, and a baby gate can close off hallways or certain rooms.

Next, in the rooms where your puppy may spend some time with you out of the exercise pen or crate, get down on your hands and knees and look at things from your puppy's point of view. Don't just look at the room from your height, but look at it from his eye level; things look very different down there. What can your pup chew on or mangle? Although Dobes aren't known to be the most destructive

Multi-Dog Tip

When looking at a litter of adorable Doberman puppies, don't be tempted to bring home more than one. Two puppies, especially from the same litter, will bond more strongly to each other rather than to people. If you want more than one Doberman, wait until the first puppy is 2 to 3 years old, mentally mature, and well trained. Then get another one.

Before bringing your new Dobe home, pet-proof your house and yard to ensure his safety.

of breeds, they can easily get into trouble. Carol Byrnes says, "Dobe puppies require supervision to guide their inquisitive minds and mouths." However, if you supervise your puppy and prevent him from chewing on inappropriate things by providing him with appropriate toys, he can be taught what to chew and what not to chew.

It's important to put away anything you don't want your puppy to damage or that might be dangerous for him. In the bathroom, that includes medicines, vitamins, makeup, shampoos, soaps, cleansers, and toilet bowl cleaners. In the kitchen, put away household cleaners and chemicals such as detergents, oven cleaners, floor waxes, drain cleaners, etc. In other areas of the house, make sure your puppy can't find any items that may cause choking hazards or may be toxic if ingested.

As you puppy-proof, don't forget the garage and basement—especially if your puppy is going to be allowed access to these areas. Put away car maintenance products, including oil, gas, and antifreeze. Yard chemicals, including herbicides, pesticides, and fertilizers, can be deadly. Flower and garden care products, including systemic insecticides and sprays, need to be stored out of reach. Snail and slug bait, mouse and rat poison, and gopher poison will kill a dog easily and must be locked up. Extreme care must be taken if these products are used at all—indoors or outdoors.

Puppy-Proof the Yard

Once you've puppy-proofed your house, take a look at your yard, too. A yard can contain and accumulate all kinds of things that can become a problem should your puppy decide to chew on them. Put away all yard and garden chemicals, garden tools, cushions for the lawn furniture, children's toys, pool supplies, and anything else that your Dobe might find appealing.

If you have a pool, is it safely fenced off? A curious puppy could easily fall in and drown. If the pool is not fenced off, you may want to build a dog run so that your Dobe has a safe place to relieve himself. If you have a spa or hot tub, is the cover secure and are all straps tucked in so they don't look like toys? Is the power cord safely tucked away where a puppy can't reach it?

Outdoor lights and sprinkler heads can also be attractive to puppies. Take a look at them and see if they can either be moved or protected in some way. Sprinklers and drip irrigation lines may appear to be toys and need to be kept out of reach.

Fencing also needs to be secure, so check it for loose boards, protruding nails, holes, or gaps at the bottom, or any other weak spots that may cause injury or allow your dog to escape. Make sure your gate locks so it isn't easily opened or can open by accident. An adult Dobe can easily jump a 4 to 5 foot (1.2 to 1.5 m) high fence from a standing start, so it needs to be high as well as secure.

By preventing your puppy from getting into trouble, you can keep him safe until you can teach him what he's allowed to do and what he shouldn't do. Prevention and supervision are the keys to keeping your Dobe safe and sound.

Setting Up a Schedule

If you haven't lived with a puppy before, or if it's been a few years since you've done so, you're going to discover that puppies can create chaos quite easily. Puppies can't care for themselves, so they need constant attention: they need to be fed, they need to be taken outside to relieve themselves, they need playtime, they need quiet time to bond with you, and they need supervision and training. Caring for a young pup can be quite overwhelming.

However, all this can be handled more easily if you establish a schedule that will work for both you and your Dobe. For example, what time do you normally get up in the morning? Do you allow yourself just enough time to get your needs taken care of before leaving for work or getting the kids up for school? If so, then you may have to allow 15 to 30 minutes for the puppy. The important items on your puppy's schedule will include:

- Three meals initially, and then by 4 to 5 months of age, one meal in the morning and one in the evening will suffice.
- Potty breaks to relieve himself after waking up in the morning and after each nap. He will also need to go outside after playing and after eating.
- Two or three short naps each morning and afternoon, and another in the evening.
- Two or three playtimes and a short training session will round out his day. As your

By the Numbers

Puppies younger than 6 to 8 weeks of age have little bowel and bladder control and need to relieve themselves often. However, at about 3 to 4 months of age, their control gets better. For example, a 4-month-old puppy will need to go outside every 2 hours during the day, while a 6-month-old puppy can advance to relieving himself every 3 hours during the day.

puppy gets a little older, he will also need time to attend a puppy class as well as have socialization visits with other people and other friendly, healthy puppies and dogs.

When setting up your schedule, keep it realistic. Your puppy will thrive on a schedule because dogs are creatures of habit. But the schedule also needs to work for you, too.

Shopping for Supplies

When shopping for your pup, you don't need to go overboard; just get the items you'll need for the first few weeks. Then, as you get to know your puppy, you can get additional supplies.

Clothing

If you live in a cold climate and are going to be bringing home your new puppy in the winter, you may want to get him a doggy jacket or sweater. Dobermans don't have a long, thick coat and can get chilled, especially when they're puppies. Although your puppy will be living indoors, a sweater or jacket can help keep him warm on those trips outdoors.

Crate and Doggy Bed

A crate is one of the most important items you'll buy for your Dobe. Aside from being his private den and a safe haven, it also plays a role in training your new puppy—particularly in housetraining him.

The crate serves as a safe haven when your puppy can't be supervised.

Several different types of crates are available. Hard plastic crates, the most common type, come apart so the top can be inverted and stored. Although bulky, they are sturdy, easily cleaned, and dogs appear to get used to them quickly because the solid walls offer privacy. Wire crates, which look more like cages, are also easy to use. They are often heavy, though, but are collapsible and store flat for convenience. You can drape a towel or tarp over the sides for privacy when necessary, just be sure to leave the front uncovered for proper ventilation. Soft-sided nylon crates that look more like carry bags are great for small dogs but are not really useable for Doberman Pinschers who could chew and tear them.

Whether you choose a plastic crate or a metal one is totally up to you. Take a look at the variety of crates at your local pet supply

A collar or harness must be properly fitted for safety and comfort.

with sections that can be slid into place just for this purpose. If your crate doesn't, use a heavy cardboard box to make a back portion of the crate inaccessible.

For the first year or so, your puppy's crate will also serve as his bed, but you may want to make another doggy bed available to him when he spends time with you in other rooms of the house. One in the living room, family room, or your home office will keep him comfortable. Don't get a bed and put it in his crate, though, because your puppy will likely shred it. An old towel will work fine until he matures.

Collar and Leash

A collar and leash are also very important. A break-away collar, quick-release collar, or buckle collar will work fine for daily wear. The collar can be leather, nylon, or cotton; it really doesn't matter as long as it is soft on the puppy's neck. The collar should fit well around the neck but allow enough slack so that if it gets caught on something your puppy can pull his head out of it. Many people prefer break-away collars for this reason. Always supervise your puppy if he isn't wearing a break-away collar to prevent accidents from occurring. You will go through several collars as your puppy grows.

A 4- or 6-foot (1- or 2-m) long leash is suitable for a puppy. Just choose something that's comfortable on your hands. As with the collar, the leash can be leather, nylon, or cotton. In fact, many dog owners like the leash to match the collar.

Food

Find out what kind of dog food the breeder has been feeding your pup so you can have some of the same variety on hand. If the breeder is feeding a homemade diet, raw or cooked, as so many do today, ask for her recipes so you can

store before buying one, and think about your ability to move it, store it, and use it. Most important, choose a crate that will give an adult Doberman Pinscher room to stand up, turn around, and lie down. You aren't going to need to provide this much room for your puppy now, but he's going to need additional space as he grows.

Once you bring the crate home, section off a part of it. Your puppy will need room to lie down comfortably, but if you give him the entire crate, he will relieve himself in a corner of it because he'll have plenty of room to get away from the potty area. Some crates come duplicate them. If you want to change foods, that's fine. Just don't do it right now; you can make some gradual changes once your puppy is settled in and more relaxed.

Food and Water Bowls

While shopping, don't forget to pick up some food and water bowls. Bowls that don't tip are best because many puppies try to play with their bowls—and flipping over a full food or water bowl makes a mess. Stainless steel bowls are both durable and easy to keep clean. It helps to have two sets of each so that you always have clean bowls available, which is necessary for your pup's good health. You may also want to have an additional water bowl outdoors, so that clean, fresh water is available at all times, especially in hot weather.

Grooming Supplies

Keeping a Dobe looking great doesn't require a lot of grooming, so you won't need many grooming supplies. However, you will want a soft, natural bristle brush and either a set of nail trimmers or a nail grinder. You will want to have a bag of cotton balls and some ear cleaner, too, as well as a child's toothbrush or a toothbrush made for dogs. Use baking soda or a doggy toothpaste for cleaning the teeth; never use toothpaste made for people because it can make your dog ill.

Identification

An identification tag can be made prior to bringing home your puppy because the most important information on it is yours. Even if you haven't chosen your Dobe's name yet, your contact information can bring him back home should he accidently become separated from you. Put a cell phone number as well as a home number on the tag. Later, you can have another tag made with your dog's name on it if you like.

There is also another identification option. When you bring your new puppy to the veterinarian for his first exam, ask about microchipping him. This is easy to do, and it is a relatively painless procedure. A small microchip the size of a grain of rice is inserted under the skin at the shoulder. If your puppy becomes lost and isn't wearing a collar, a scanning device is passed over that spot to read the information on the chip. After the microchipping is done, you will be given paperwork and must register the microchip so that your contact information will be available on a database. Of course, this information must always be kept up to date.

Training Tidbit

A puppy needs to gnaw on things because it helps him explore his new world, and it relieves teething discomfort. Having toys available for chewing will also help to keep him entertained and busy. Keep in mind, a bored puppy will find something to amuse himself with, and that might be your brand new shoes! Toys aren't just for fun; you can use them to teach your puppy what is and is not appropriate to chew on. If your Dobe is gnawing on your shoes, your furniture, or other belongings, give him a toy instead. Praise him when he chooses it over inappropriate objects. Give him one or two toys at a time, and rotate them to keep him interested.

Safety Gate and/or Exercise Pen

You may also want to purchase a safety gate or two (baby gates work well for this purpose) and an exercise pen to restrict your puppy's movement in the house. These can keep him close to you and prevent him from getting into trouble when you cannot supervise him.

Toys

Last, but certainly not least, are toys. Dobes have strong jaws, so provide him with some tough, sturdy toys. Nylabones, which are durable nylon bones that come in a variety of types for varied chewing needs, are great for Dobe puppies. Choose a few medium sized-toys and rotate them often. No matter what brand or kind of toy you get, make sure it's safe and strong enough so that your puppy can't chew off small pieces and swallow them.

BRINGING HOME YOUR NEW PUPPY

Your breeder will let you know when your Dobe puppy is ready to come home. Most recommend waiting until 9 to 10 weeks of age so that the pup is mature enough to leave his mother and littermates. In addition, by 9 weeks of age, puppies are past the fearful period of development they go through during this stage of life.

Puppies of less than 8 weeks of age still need their mother and their littermates. Momma dog teaches her puppies about bite inhibition—an important lesson—and the puppies need to play, socialize, and live together to learn many important life skills. Once they reach 8 to 10 weeks of age, they can then move on to the next stage of their lives.

Make an appointment with the breeder to bring home your puppy on a day when you can spend some time with him. If you work Monday through Friday, bring him home on

Be patient with your puppy as he adjusts to his new home.

Friday afternoon, if you can. Then you can spend the next couple of days helping him get used to his new life.

Bring a crate when you go pick up your new puppy, so that he can ride home safely and securely in it. Also bring along a leash and collar, some water, a few toys and treats, and towels to contain any accidents. Before loading him into the crate, make sure he's relieved himself. In fact, let him have one more play session with his littermates so he'll be more likely to sleep on the drive home. Go directly home. Don't stop to shop or to see family or friends. Now is not the time to show off your new Dobe. All the excitement will be a little difficult on your puppy, and he will need some time to adjust to all the changes, especially being separated from his mom, littermates, and the only home he's known. During this transitional time, put his needs first.

WHAT TO EXPECT ONCE YOUR PUPPY IS HOME

Your Dobe puppy is going to bring chaos with him as he joins your household, but because you're ready for him, with a schedule already created and supplies at hand, you'll be fine. Let's talk about what to expect from your puppy over the next few days and weeks so you'll be even more ready for this cute new family member.

Getting Through the First Few Days

It's important to remember your puppy is a baby, and for the first few days he's going to miss his mother and littermates. You're unfamiliar to him, as is your family, your home, and your backyard. Although puppies adapt very quickly, your pup may at times be worried or even afraid. This is normal, and he'll get used to things faster than you might expect.

When your puppy is upset, he'll show it by whining, crying, or barking. Very few Dobe puppies make noise just for the sake of making noise; that's not typical for the breed. So if your puppy is crying, find out why. Here are some possible reasons:

- **He is hungry.** Most Dobe puppies need three meals per day, ideally spread out equally throughout the day.
- **He needs to relieve himself**. If he's just up from a nap, or wakes you out of a sound sleep, or has just eaten or played, then get him outside. Praise him for telling you that he needed to go.

- **He's lonely.** Having just left his mother and littermates, he's alone for probably the first time in his life. Give him some attention or distract him with a toy.
- **He has hurt himself.** Maybe he tripped over his own paws and fell, or he bit his tongue.

Your Dobe puppy will sleep through the night eventually, but he probably isn't going to do so for the first few days. He doesn't have the bowel and bladder control for it yet. To help him make it through most of the night—and so you can get some sleep without having to wake up several times—here are some useful tips:

- Feed your puppy dinner no later than six or seven o'clock in the evening.
- Stop offering your puppy water by about nine o'clock in the evening. If the weather is hot, offer him ice cubes.
- Get your puppy outside to relieve himself before you go to bed. If he doesn't relieve himself then, get him running around a little bit to encourage pottying.
- Set your alarm for half way through the night so you can take your puppy out for a much-needed potty break.
- As soon as you wake up in the morning, take your puppy outside.
- At about 3 months of age, stop setting your alarm in the middle of the night. If your puppy wakes you up, take him outside but wait for him to wake you.

Your Dobe won't be a baby for long; he's going to grow and change rapidly. But be patient with him now.

Teaching Your Puppy His Name

Those first few days after your Dobe joins the family are the best time to teach him his name. Some people have a name all picked out before they bring home their puppy, while others want to get to know the puppy first to see what

Let your puppy get to know you and your family before introducing him to other people and new places.

name will fit him best. Neither method is right or wrong; it's a personal decision.

When choosing a name, however, keep a few things in mind. First, choose a name that will be suitable for your dog's entire lifetime. He may be a puppy now, but will you be happy calling him Puppers when he's 10 years old and a majestic, adult dog? Also, choosing tough aggressive names aren't always a good idea. A Doberman named Killer won't do your dog or the breed's reputation any good. Choose a name that fits your dog, yet is going to be suitable for his lifetime.

Name Training

Teach your puppy his name by saying it in a happy tone of voice, just as you might say, "Ice cream!" This joyful tone of voice teaches him that his name is a good thing. Then, after saying his name, pop a treat in his mouth, pet him, and smile at him.

Say his name in a happy tone of voice whenever you play with him, when he brings you his toy, or even if he just looks at you. You can even make a noise, like tapping your fingers on the table, and when he looks at you, say his name and praise him, "Buster! Good boy, Buster!" Do not say his name if you're unhappy with him or are interrupting bad behavior. Always use his name only when reinforcing a positive association to it.

Sticking to a Schedule

Remember puppies (and dogs) are creatures of habit and do better when there's some routine to their lives. Hopefully, the schedule you prepared prior to your puppy's arrival will work well for both of you.

Start implementing the schedule right away. Teach your puppy that meals come at certain times, as do potty breaks, walks, playtimes, and bedtimes. Now, that doesn't mean there can't be some flexibility. If you will normally take your puppy for a walk and playtime at noon, that doesn't mean you can't do it earlier or later. Just try to keep meals and sleep times the same every day to facilitate housetraining reliability.

If you've tried to implement a schedule for several days and it doesn't seem to be working—for any number of reasons—feel free to change it. After all, it has to work for you and your puppy. It may take a little bit of tweaking before you discover what will suit your lifestyle best.

Giving Your Puppy Some Space

Puppies are adorable and everyone loves to hold, hug, and play with them. Although this is wonderful and a great way to form a relationship with a new puppy, it can be overwhelming for him at first.

Make sure your puppy has quiet time to get accustomed to his new surroundings and family members. Let him spend some time in his crate or exercise pen with a toy or chew bone, or give him lots of time to retreat to it and nap. Alone time will also help him to become independent. If your puppy is constantly with someone, he may panic when he's eventually left alone after you return to your normal routine and are back at work or school during the day. He may cry and bark, or try to escape from his crate or pen. He needs time to learn that being alone is okay.

Getting to Know Others

Let your new puppy get to know you and your family before introducing him to other people and new places. That means, during his first weekend (or first two or three days) with you, refrain from taking him out to meet your friends and neighbors or inviting anyone over to your home to meet him—regardless of how adorable he may be!

Sometime later in the week, let your puppy meet one or two new people at a time. It is important to introduce him to people of different ages and ethnic backgrounds. Keep these encounters calm and controlled. Don't let anyone rough-house with your puppy, though. You want him to learn that people are kind, loving, and trustworthy. If people don't listen to you and insist on getting too aggressive with him—even in fun—take your puppy and walk away. After all, it is your responsibility to protect him and socialize him properly.

Want to Know More?

For more detailed information on how to socialize your puppy, see Chapter 4: Training Your Doberman Pinscher Puppy.

CHAPTER 3

CARE OF YOUR DOBERMAN PINSCHER PUPPY

Your Doberman Pinscher puppy cannot care for himself, so he is completely dependent on you for everything he requires. Dr. Shawn Messonnier, DVM, of Plano, Texas, says, "Our dogs have some specific needs, including good food and clean water. They need regular brushing and bathing. Regular dental care is also needed, and of course, veterinary care."

FEEDING YOUR PUPPY

Your breeder probably gave you recommendations as to what feed your puppy before you brought him home. In fact, she may well have sent some food home with you. Because this is a good-quality food, you may decide to continue giving it to your puppy. However, many options are available, from commercial kibbles to home-cooked or raw-food diets. Deciding which type of food is best can be overwhelming, but your main priority is to feed a wholesome, well-balanced diet that will provide your pup with all the nutrients he needs to develop into a healthy, long-lived adult.

Diet Options

Your Doberman Pinscher puppy, like all dogs, is a carnivore. That means his teeth, jaws, mouth, and digestive tract are all designed to eat meat. Wild carnivores will hunt prey animals for food, and the prey animals will vary depending upon where the carnivore lives and hunts. When a carnivore is unsuccessful in a hunt, he will often eat other foods if he's hungry. These may include tubers (the enlarged roots of plants) and fallen fruits. Eggs are also often a part of a wild carnivore's diet.

But your Doberman isn't a wild carnivore; he's your treasured new puppy. Choosing what to feed him is difficult and the choices are many. We're constantly bombarded with advertising on the Internet, in magazines, and on television, all of which expounds upon the benefits of certain commercial dog foods.

To start, there are two basic feeding choices: commercial puppy food, or meals you can prepare at home. But there are more decisions to make beyond this. Commercial foods vary widely in quality—from inexpensive to very expensive and from foods made with uncertain ingredients to high-quality foods made from human-grade ingredients. The choices available in commercial pet foods are innumerable.

Unfortunately, manufacturer and US Food and Drug Administration (FDA) recalls involving commercial pet food products are far too common. In December 2010, for example, massive recalls were ordered by two major pet food makers. One was because too much vitamin D was incorporated into the foods. The other was because of mold contamination in some of the food ingredients used. Unfortunately, both of these problems resulted in pets becoming very ill and dying.

But homemade diets can vary in quality, too. Raw-food diets, using only raw ingredients, including raw meats and bones, may carry bacteria that are normally destroyed in the cooking process. Likewise, the nutritional content and quality of homemade diets will vary according to the quality of ingredients you use to make up the puppy's diet, just as with commercial diets.

It's tough for puppy owners to know what to do. Christie Keith, a well-known advocate for animal health issues, says, "There are a number of reasons why dog owners need to become wise consumers regarding their pets' health. One is that, unlike people, most dogs eat nothing but processed foods. If those foods are nutritionally inadequate or excessive, or if the company uses manufacturing processes or ingredients that are questionable, or if any contamination affects the food, the impact of even a minor incident is amplified."

Keith is only one of many advocates for change in the pet food industry and for rethinking how we feed our pets. Lucy Postins, a canine nutrition specialist and the founder of The Honest Kitchen pet foods, says, "We humans would never expect to achieve optimum, long-term health if we ate nothing but a 'complete and balanced' breakfast cereal for every meal of our entire lives. The same is true for animals. They need fresh, minimally processed, and varied foods as well."

The best thing you can do for your puppy is to become a wise consumer. Read as much as you can. Several very good books are available, written by pet nutrition experts. Several blogs are also very educational, including Pet Connection at www.PetConnection.com and YesBiscuit! at www.yesbiscuit.wordpress/category/home-prepared-pet-diets/com.

Be aware of pet food recalls. Unfortunately, these occur on a far too regular basis, and if you're feeding a commercial pet food that has developed a problem, such as contamination, you want to know about it. Many blogs, including those I just mentioned, post pet food notices as soon as they find out about them.

If you have questions about a particular food, call the pet food company and ask questions. Be direct, "Where does your meat come from? Is it imported or domestic? Where do your dry ingredients come from? Are they tested for contaminants?"

Last, but certainly not least, become an activist. Keith says, "The louder pet owners clamor for transparency, label changes, and other important consumer safeguards, the sooner pet food companies will realize, if they want us to buy their products, they'll need to give us the information we're asking for."

When to Feed Your Puppy

Most veterinarians recommend feeding puppies at set meal times rather than free

---

Want to Know More?

For more detailed information about proper canine nutrition, see Chapter 7: Feeding Your Adult Doberman Pinscher.

feeding them (leaving food available all the time). Feeding at established times makes housetraining significantly easier because a puppy normally has to relieve himself after eating. In addition, should your puppy get sick, one of the first questions the veterinarian will ask is, "How was your puppy's appetite today? Did he eat his breakfast this morning?" If you free-feed, and your puppy nibbles throughout the day, it's difficult to know how much he is consuming.

Young puppies need three meals daily, with the meals spread out throughout the day. At some point, usually between 4 and 6 months of age, you can switch to a morning and evening feeding. When to do this depends on the individual puppy. If your puppy doesn't eat all of his noon meal, you know it's alright to eliminate it. Otherwise, ask your veterinarian for some guidance.

How Much to Feed Your Puppy

The amount you feed your Dobe puppy will vary. Every commercial food will have feeding guidelines listed on the container. However, this is just a guideline for the average dog. But what is an average dog? You'll need to find an amount that fills your Dobe's tummy, provides enough food for his activities and proper development, yet doesn't make him fat. Finding that same balance will also apply to feeding a raw diet or a home-cooked diet. However, things may happen throughout the day that will increase or decrease your dog's food needs. For example, if your puppy went to puppy class one day and had a lot of training treats, he will need slightly less food at his next meal. But if he had an energetic play session with your neighbor's puppy, he may need more food at his next meal because he'll be hungrier than normal.

Dobe puppies go through some tremendous growth spurts, too, and those are fueled by good food. These spurts aren't consistent, though. A noticeable increase in appetite— puppies usually become ravenous at this time— is usually a good indication that your pup is about to undergo more physical changes.

Just keep an eye on your Dobe, and you'll be able to tell if you're feeding the right amount. He should have some meat on his ribs; you should be able to feel them but they shouldn't appear too prominent. He should have a waistline—even short stocky puppies should have at least some waistline. Your puppy's eyes should be bright, his coat shiny, and he should have enough energy for growth and play.

Where to Feed Your Puppy

Feed your puppy in a place that isn't too busy. You may put his bowl in a corner of the kitchen where people are not always walking past, or in another room. Many people find that feeding the puppy in his crate works well for them. The puppy isn't distracted, he can eat all of his meal without being interrupted, and he isn't pushing his food bowl all around the kitchen floor.

Multi-Dog Tip

If you have more than one dog, don't feed them from the same bowl. Doing this could cause the dogs to squabble over their food, or worse yet, one dog may guard the food and not allow the other to eat. Each dog needs his own bowl.

Besides keeping your puppy healthy, grooming provides a good way to build a positive relationship with him.

GROOMING YOUR PUPPY

Keeping a Dobe puppy groomed is easy. In fact, it's probably one of the easiest aspects of keeping him healthy. But even though your puppy's grooming needs are quite basic, it's still necessary to groom him regularly to keep him looking and feeling his best.

Grooming not only gets your puppy used to the brushing, bathing, ear and teeth cleaning, and nail trimming he will require as an adult, but it's also a good way to build a positive relationship with him. By spending time with your Dobe as you teach him to accept gentle handling, he learns you can touch him without causing him harm. The whole process can be a good bonding exercise.

In addition, grooming can offer an effective way to keep track of your puppy's health. As you groom him, check for any potential health problems, including fleas and ticks, cuts and scrapes, lumps and bumps, and anything else that might appear out of the ordinary.

Introducing your puppy to grooming at a young age will ensure that he's comfortable with these procedures for the rest of his life. This is important because you don't want to have to struggle to groom him when he's all grown up.

Grooming Supplies

Keeping a Dobe looking great doesn't require a lot of work, so you won't need many grooming supplies. The basics include:

- soft, natural bristle brush
- ear cleaner and cotton balls
- toothbrush made for dogs or a child's toothbrush
- canine toothpaste or baking soda
- nail trimmers or a nail grinder
- canine shampoo that's safe for puppies

These supplies will get you started. However, as you get used to the grooming routine, you may want to try some other products. For example, a hound's glove—which, as the name implies, you wear on your hand—is a great tool to use on short coats. It has soft rubber tips on the palm that help to remove dead hair while gently massaging the skin. Something else you may want to try is a dry shampoo. This is rubbed or sprayed onto the coat and wiped off. There's no need to get your dog wet or to rinse him off, yet when you're done, he smells nice and clean.

Getting Your Puppy Used to Grooming

Before you begin grooming your puppy—and before introducing any grooming tools—he must learn to accept handling and to enjoy a gentle massage. Once he is comfortable with these exercises, teaching him to accept grooming will be easy.

Handling Exercise

Sit down on the floor in a spot where you can be comfortable, perhaps against a soft chair or sofa. Invite your puppy to cuddle close to you, or if possible, climb into your lap. Without forcing him into any specific position, begin stroking him gently with long, slow strokes. Be calm and move your hand from his shoulders to his hips. Remember, long and slow strokes; if you move your hands fast, he'll think you want to play—you want him to remain calm and relaxed. When he relaxes, he may turn over so you can rub his belly; that's fine. Just keep the strokes slow and gentle. Ideally, he should fall asleep as you stroke him.

Try to do this at least once per day for a week. If you can make the time to do it twice a day,

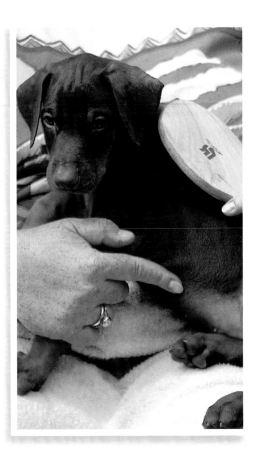

Introducing your puppy to grooming at a young age will ensure that he's comfortable with these procedures for the rest of his life.

that's even better. This will give your puppy time to learn to really enjoy being handled and to trust the process. After a week, begin massaging your pup in the same way—once he is relaxed, move your hands to his head, gently stroking his muzzle, skull, ears, and ear flaps. Then massage his neck, shoulders, chest, and back.

Continue this light massage until you have touched every part of your puppy's body, from his nose to his tail, and everything in between. By doing this, he gets used to the idea that you can handle him everywhere and that you will be calm and caring when you do so.

If your puppy has a problem with the massage at any point, talk to him in a soothing voice and go back to the slow, stroking massage. When he's relaxed again, work back to the part of his body that he didn't want touched. Repeat as needed.

Grooming Tools Exercise

After a couple of weeks of massage, begin to introduce grooming tools. Use the same technique to relax your puppy, but now use grooming tools. Before actually using a tool, let your puppy see and smell it. This will help him to feel more secure about it. During the exercise, gently touch him with each of the tools—a brush, nail clippers, and other pieces of grooming equipment he'll need to learn to trust.

Have a handful of treats in one hand and a grooming tool, such as the brush, in your other hand. Call your puppy to you and give him a treat. Then hold one of the tools out, such as the brush, and encourage him to sniff it. If he's leery of the tool, hold a treat behind it so he has to move around it to get the treat. When he touches the tool, praise him, "Good boy, yes!" and give him the treat. Repeat the exercise several times, until he's comfortable with that particular grooming tool.

Repeat the entire exercise with all of your grooming tools. If you're using a tool with moving parts or one that makes noise, such as nail clippers or nail grinders, let your puppy first get to know it while it is turned off and quiet, and then turned on and making noise.

If your puppy is worried about or frightened by the nail grinder because it vibrates and is noisy, make the introduction gradual but enthusiastic, "What's this? Good boy to be brave!" Perhaps offer extra-special treats in this case. Let your puppy investigate the grinder while it is turned off, and give him a treat and praise, "Good boy!" Then turn the motor on and off, and again offer praise and treats. Touch him gently on the side with the handle of the grinder so he can feel the vibration and offer him treats as you do this. You want him to think that the grinder equals praise and treats from you. Later on, when it's time to trim his nails, he will already have learned not to be fearful of the grooming tool.

Training Tidbit

If your puppy is really worried about nail trimming, give him a spoonful of peanut butter while he's on your lap and then trim his nails while he's still trying to eat it. It's hard for puppies to concentrate on two things at once! Plus, the peanut butter can become a special treat associated with this routine, one that he may come to accept with a bit of happy anticipation.

Before actually using a tool, let your puppy see and smell it. This will help him to feel more secure about it.

A Basic Grooming Session

Again, begin each grooming session with a gentle massage. This, after all, relaxes your puppy. By now you've learned what your puppy normally feels like as you massage him and can notice any problems, often even before you see them. When you and your puppy are both relaxed, begin the grooming routine.

Brushing

A soft-bristled brush can be used to brush your puppy from head to tail. Brush the coat in the direction the hair grows, and clean the hair out of the brush often; even short hairs can clog up the bristles of the brush. Dobes have a short coat, but it does shed quite a bit. Carol Byrnes says, "Dobes shed a lot all year round. I always laugh when someone says, 'It must be nice to have a shorthaired dog who doesn't shed.' White pants and white furniture are not found in the same house as a Doberman."

Cleaning the Ears

Use cotton balls and ear cleaner to keep your puppy's ears clean and healthy. Dampen a cotton ball with ear cleaner just enough so that it is damp but not dripping wet. Holding your Dobe's head still, gently clean the inside of the ear as well as the ear flap. Use a clean, moistened cotton ball for the other ear. Pat each ear dry with a clean, dry cotton ball.

Nail Clipping

Begin by relaxing your puppy and placing him on his back in your lap. Massage one paw gently but firmly. If he accepts this handling, give him a treat and praise. Next, hold nail clippers in one hand and one toe of his paw in the other hand. Touch him with the clippers. If he accepts this, give him a treat and praise. To begin trimming, look for the wider solid base of the nail and then a narrower tip. Just cut off the tip of the nail as you speak softly to your puppy. Praise him, and then repeat this with the other nails, giving an occasional treat and lots of praise for good behavior. If you happen to cut the quick of the nail and it begins to bleed, apply some styptic powder, or if you don't have any, scrape the nail across a bar of soap. Keep your puppy on your lap until the nail clots. Then, next time, take off less nail. If your pup becomes stressed at any time during this procedure, stop and try again later.

If you use a nail grinder instead of clippers, as many dog owners do, follow the directions that came with the product because each brand is slightly different. Again, make sure you get your puppy used to the sound and feel of the grinder before using it.

Many puppies, and even adult dogs, fight nail clipping, but it doesn't have to be a battle

When brushing your puppy's teeth, use a toothbrush and toothpaste specifically made for dogs.

be used with Dobe puppies. You'll also need a doggy toothpaste because those made for humans can make your puppy ill. Although baking soda is fine, many flavored toothpastes are available for dogs, often beef- or chicken-flavored. But again, many puppies think toothpaste is a treat and will keep getting their tongue in the way while you try to brush. As with all training, if you begin this procedure slowly and gently, your puppy will learn to accept it—and some may even like it!

Make a paste using a teaspoon of baking soda and a little water. Dip the toothbrush in the paste and gently brush or just touch some teeth with it. (If you don't use baking soda paste, apply doggy toothpaste to the toothbrush.) Don't worry too much about actual brushing right now; just touch the brush to the teeth in various parts of your puppy's mouth. Offer treats and praise if he cooperates nicely. If he is worried about this, make sure you do it gently and keep the session short. Over several sessions, gradually increase how many teeth you touch, and when your puppy is comfortable with this, start brushing his teeth more thoroughly. Always end the session on a positive note with a treat and lots of praise.

Establish a Routine

Dobes don't need nearly as much grooming as do so many other breeds. Once your puppy is used to the equipment and the procedures for grooming, establish a regular once-a-week routine that can last for your dog's lifetime. Mary Swindell says about her dogs, "I have a weekly grooming session. I grind their nails, clean their ears, and brush them."

Don Hanson, owner of the Green Acres Kennel Shop, which provides professional grooming to its clients, says, "For puppies, I recommend weekly grooming at home, not always because they need it but because it's

and it shouldn't be. When done gently and carefully, nail trimming doesn't hurt. If you don't feel comfortable doing this yourself, your veterinarian or a professional groomer can do it for you or show you how to do it properly.

Brushing the Teeth

Initially, introducing a toothbrush can be difficult because most puppies try to eat it. After all, everything that's put in the mouth should be eaten, right? If you don't have a doggy toothbrush, a child's toothbrush can the best way to acclimate a puppy to a necessary process."

How to Bathe Your Puppy

Although Doberman Pinschers are clean dogs, your puppy needs to be introduced to baths because he will need them throughout his life. Taking the time to make baths a positive experience now will be well worth the effort later because wrestling a full-grown Dobe into the bathtub is no easy chore!

First, change into some clothes that you don't mind getting wet—a bathing suit is great—because you're going to get as wet as your puppy. Run the tap until you have just a few inches (cm) of comfortably warm water in the bottom of the tub, just enough to cover your pup's feet. Put a cotton ball in each of your puppy's ears to keep water out. Have all your supplies and some towels set out and ready to go. Then gently place your puppy in the tub; if you like, climb into the tub yourself.

Holding your puppy and using a hand-held sprayer or plastic cup, get your puppy wet, but be careful not to get water or soap into his eyes or ears. Talk to your puppy, laugh, and keep things fun so he doesn't get scared. Shampoo

Special Care for Newly Cropped Ears

Caring for cropped ears requires professional instruction and dedication. Trainer and Dobe owner Mary Swindell describes the process in detail: "Our breeder has the veterinarian crop the ears when the puppies are about 8 weeks old. The pups are anesthetized for the procedure. The uncut edge of the ear is taped to a Styrofoam cup (or a similarly shaped lightweight object). The cut edge remains exposed so it can heal. The healing edge is kept clean and treated with antibiotic ointment. The breeder keeps the puppies with her during the healing process. Once the edge heals, the ears are taped upright, and then re-taped every three to five days."

Puppies can usually go to their new homes at this point, as long as the owners know how to continue proper ear care. Swindell continues, "The ears remain like this through teething but are unwrapped briefly to breathe while we take a walk. This encourages the pups to work the ear muscles and hold the ears up. At the first sign of drooping, they are taped again. By 7 to 8 months of age, most puppies are done healing, and the ears are firm and up. However, the longer the ear leather, the longer it typically takes for them to stand erect."

If you buy a puppy from a breeder and the ears have recently been cropped, she will show you how to care for them correctly. The length of the ear trim, the heaviness of the ear leather, and the shape the breeder is trying to accomplish will all affect how the ears should be taped and shaped. Wrapping and taping the ears takes some practice; after all, few puppies of that age want to sit still and be fussed over.

Ear cropping is a very personal and controversial decision. Although breeders take great care to make sure their puppies' ears are done correctly, more people are requesting Doberman Pinschers with natural ears.

him gently, then rinse him thoroughly. Towel him off and take him out of the tub. Tell your Dobe puppy what a brave dog he is and make a big fuss over him. End the bath with a yummy treat.

HEALTH CARE FOR YOUR DOBERMAN PINSCHER PUPPY

Caring for your Dobe puppy also includes his health care requirements. These consist of annual veterinary visits, vaccinations, deworming, and a variety of other sometimes less than pleasant issues. There are also a host of diseases and medical problems that you'll hopefully never need to deal with, but it's important that every responsible owner become educated about them in order to offer the best possible care to her pet.

Finding a Veterinarian

Finding the right veterinarian is essential. She (or he) will be a vital partner in maintaining your dog's well-being and longevity. You need to be comfortable with her experience and expertise so that the two of you can make important decisions regarding your dog's care.

To find a veterinarian, ask friends and relatives for recommendations. If you have friends who have Dobermans, their input is even more important because the breed does have some specific health issues. When you have three or four referrals to local veterinarians, call and ask if you can talk to the veterinarian or schedule an appointment (even before you get your puppy). Be prepared to pay for an office visit. Granted, you don't have a dog with you, but you are taking up the vet's time and she deserves to be paid. Then ask some questions:

- Are you comfortable with Doberman Pinschers? Some people are afraid of the breed, so you want to make sure she and her staff are not concerned about handling your dog.
- Are you familiar with current health issues in the breed? Obviously, this is important.
- Do you have any specialties? Ideally, a vet who is a good diagnostician and surgeon is a plus.
- When do you refer clients to specialty clinics? This can be good to know should your dog need special care.
- What are your office hours? The office hours should suit your schedule, or this may cause problems.
- What are your policies regarding after-hour needs or emergencies? Do you send your clients to a local emergency clinic?
- What type of payment do you accept? Do you offer a payment plan? Do you accept credit cards? If so, which ones? Do you accept pet insurance?

While you're at the clinic, take a look around. Is it clean? Is the staff friendly? Do the clients appear happy with the service? Although

By the Numbers

A healthy puppy's temperature is between 100° and 102.5°F (38° and 39°C). However, your puppy may be worried about the visit to the vet (which will make his temperature rise) and frightened by the thermometer. By staying calm yourself, petting your puppy, and talking softly to him while his temperature is being taken, you can keep him calm.

Your Dobe's first visit to the veterinarian should be scheduled soon after you bring him home.

the veterinarian is the most important consideration, her clinic and staff are also vital to your dog's overall care.

The First Visit to the Vet

Your Dobe's first visit to the veterinarian should be scheduled soon after you bring him home. Most veterinarians and breeders suggest having him examined within the first couple of days to make sure he is healthy and has not developed any problems that may have gone unnoticed.

Bring with you any information the breeder gave you, including vaccination and deworming records. Bring a stool sample as well, so that the vet can test for internal parasites.

This initial checkup will be quite thorough. After all, the vet doesn't know your puppy yet and will want to be sure everything is fine. She will also create a patient file so that your puppy's development can be charted as he matures. Things like his weight, size, and temperature will be notated at each visit.

The vet will examine your puppy's mouth to see if his teeth are straight and intact. She will look at the gums to make sure they are pink and healthy. She will look at the rest of the mouth, too, including the throat, just to check for any problems.

She will examine the eyes, eye lids, ears, and ear flaps to check that everything looks normal. She will feel for the glands in the neck and

Your veterinarian will recommend which vaccinations your Dobe requires based on your lifestyle and where you live.

health or development, or what you should expect, this is the time to talk with your veterinarian. Don't be embarrassed about asking questions.

All About Vaccinations

Your dog's immune system is what protects him from disease. When he was born, his mother's immunities were passed on to him and protected him during the early months of his life. But around 6 to 8 weeks of age, his mother's immunities began to fade as his own immune system developed.

The immune system protects the body by producing antibodies, which are substances that defend it against invaders—bacteria or viruses, for example. Each individual type of invader must have a specific antibody to deal with it. Puppies (or people) develop antibodies to every bacteria or virus they encounter. If the body can react quickly enough to produce these antibodies, the puppy will be protected and won't get sick.

Vaccinations work by giving the puppy a very small weakened or killed dose of a particular germ so that he can develop the right antibodies without the risk of getting sick. A modified live virus vaccination contains a live virus that has been altered to decrease its threat to the body. There is always a risk of the puppy getting sick from a modified live vaccine, but it's also more effective at stimulating the body to produce antibodies. A vaccination that contains killed virus is considered safer.

Not all vaccinations are needed by every puppy. The American Veterinary Medical Association (AVMA) recommends that veterinarians consider the pet's lifestyle and disease risks when formulating a vaccination program. For example, if the puppy's owners enjoy camping and hiking, the Lyme disease

run her hands down the neck to the shoulders and then over the body. She will listen to your puppy's heart and lungs, and will palpate the abdomen.

She'll stretch and then fold the front legs to see how they move and whether the shoulder is healthy. She'll do the same thing with the back legs, checking on the knee and hip joints. The paws will be examined, including the toenails and between the pads.

By the time the veterinarian finishes examining your puppy, the stool sample will have been processed. If the stool sample contains any parasite eggs, she can explain what they are and what treatment is needed.

If you have any questions about your puppy's

vaccination may be more important than it would be to a pet who resides in a city where Lyme disease is not prevalent.

Puppies who will be attending a group puppy socialization class may need additional vaccines, too, as will puppies who will be staying at a boarding kennel while their owners are on vacation. All of these and other factors need to be taken into consideration. Discuss your lifestyle and future plans for your Doberman Pinscher so you and your veterinarian can make good choices.

Ask your veterinarian what adverse reactions might occur after the vaccination. Some puppies get a little sleepy afterward, while others may be sore at the injection site. Each type of vaccine may produce different side effects, so make sure you know what to watch for. After the vaccination, wait at the veterinary clinic for at least a half an hour. If your Dobe puppy is going to have a serious adverse reaction, it will most likely happen during this period.

Do not vaccinate your puppy if he's not feeling well. Nancy Kay, DVM, a diplomat of the American College of Veterinary Internal Medicine as well as an award-winning writer, says, "Better to let his immune system concentrate on getting rid of a current illness rather than creating a vaccine distraction." Dr. Kay also says to make sure your veterinarian knows of any previous illnesses, especially any autoimmune issues.

Diseases to Vaccinate Against
The following viral and bacterial diseases are those most commonly vaccinated against in puppies today. Your veterinarian will make recommendations on which ones your Dobe may require based on your lifestyle and where you live.

Bordetella
Bordetellosis is a bacterial infection that causes coughing and other respiratory problems. This is one of the diseases classified under the canine cough or kennel cough umbrella. It is very contagious and easily spread from one dog to another through coughing. It is rarely dangerous to healthy dogs, but puppies can get quite sick.

Coronavirus
The first symptom of coronavirus is diarrhea, which can range from mild to severe. Blood may be found in the feces. Puppies are at risk of dehydration.

Distemper
Canine distemper is a virus that's similar to the human measles virus. It can affect many of the puppy's organs, including the skin, eyes, and intestinal and respiratory tracts. The virus can be transmitted through urine, feces, and saliva. The first symptoms are usually a nasal and eye discharge. This is a potentially fatal disease.

Hepatitis
Canine hepatitis is a virus found worldwide. It's spread through nasal discharge as well as urine, usually through direct contact. The virus begins with a sore throat; the puppy will not want to swallow, drink, or eat. It spreads rapidly to other organs and develops quickly; dogs can die within hours of the first symptoms.

Leptospirosis
Leptospirosis is a bacterial infection that affects the kidneys and is passed from the kidneys to the urine. It is transmitted to other dogs when they sniff contaminated urine. Lepto can also be spread to other animals and people, and it

If your puppy seems unusually lethargic or has prolonged bouts of diarrhea, take him to the vet right away.

can be fatal. Symptoms include fever, nausea, and dehydration.

Lyme Disease

Caused by bacteria, Lyme disease is spread through the bites of infected ticks. A fever is the first symptom, followed by muscle soreness, weakness, and joint pain. Severe, permanent joint damage is possible, as is neurological damage if the disease goes untreated.

Parainfluenza

The parainfluenza virus is one of several viruses called canine cough or kennel cough. It is easily spread through coughing, which also happens to be one of the first and primary symptoms. It may turn into pneumonia, but is generally just a cough that goes away in a week or two.

Parvovirus

This virus, often referred to simply as parvo, has killed thousands of dogs, usually puppies, and since the virus continues to mutate and change, it is still a deadly threat. Next to rabies, this virus is often thought of as the most deadly, dangerous, and fatal disease known to dogs. Vomiting, diarrhea, dehydration, and death are common.

Rabies

The rabies virus is almost always fatal once the disease has been contracted. It is transmitted through contact with an infected animal, usually a bat, skunk, fox, or raccoon. The first symptom is usually drooling because of problems swallowing, followed by staggering, seizures, and other behavioral changes.

Vaccination Controversy

Don't let the fear of possible side effects cause you to not vaccinate your puppy. Modern vaccines have saved millions of dogs' lives. However, vaccines shouldn't be taken lightly; there are potential risks, and the side effects are just one potential problem.

Many veterinarians and dog owners are concerned that too many vaccinations are being administered unnecessarily. Although these inoculations prevent disease and, in some cases, fatalities, a larger number of dogs are suffering from immune system disorders and dying from cancers at younger ages than ever before. There is not yet a proven link to vaccination but questions are being asked, as is a demand for more research.

In answer to these concerns, many veterinarians are now recommending that puppy vaccinations be given over a longer period of time throughout puppyhood and that fewer combination vaccines be given. For example, instead of giving one vaccine that includes distemper, hepatitis, leptospirosis, parvovirus, and parainfluenza, this booster shot can be split into three parts, giving the puppy distemper, hepatitis, and lepto in one shot, parvovirus in a second, and parainfluenza in a third.

If you have any doubts about the vaccinations your Dobe puppy should receive, do some research of your own. Talk to your veterinarian. Talk to your puppy's breeder. Go to the AVMA's website. Get as many facts as possible, then make an informed decision about to how to proceed.

Puppies Get Sick Once in Awhile

Puppies, like human babies, can get sick. Not only are their immune systems just developing, but everything they encounter tends to go into their mouth and get chewed and sometimes swallowed. In addition, because socialization is so important, puppies are often exposed to elements in their environment that may make them ill.

Learning to recognize when there may be a potential health problem is important. Not only do you want to get your Dobe puppy to the veterinarian as soon as possible to prevent the problem from escalating, but knowing whether something is serious or not can give you peace of mind.

Contact your veterinarian if you notice your Dobe showing any of the following symptoms:

- diarrhea that continues for more than 24 hours
- diarrhea that contains blood or mucus
- vomiting that continues for more than a couple of hours
- refusal to eat, and missing more than two meals
- unusual discharge from an eye or the nose
- any eye injury
- an ear that is red, sore, or dirty
- cuts or wounds that are bleeding and gape open, or do not stop bleeding
- refusal to use or put weight on a limb
- tender or distended abdomen
- any potential allergic reaction, including swelling, hives, or rashes
- any potential poisoning, including vomiting, disorientation, tremors, seizures, etc.
- suspected snake bites, spider bites, or bites from other animals, including dogs
- a temperature of less than 100°F (38°C) or more than 102.5°F (39°C)
- seizures, fainting, or loss of consciousness
- trouble breathing or severe coughing

Sometimes, though, your Dobe puppy may not feel good and will not show any symptoms. It's always good to know what's normal for your puppy so that when there is a problem, you can spot the abnormal behavior.

Behavior that might signal a problem may include the puppy hiding, such as under the bed or dining room table, and not wanting to come out. The puppy may also be panting more than normal, especially if it's not hot enough to warrant it. A puppy who is breathing heavily but hasn't been playing hard may have a problem. And finally, a restless puppy who just can't seem to settle down may not be well.

When you call your veterinarian, the receptionist or veterinary technician will ask you several questions. Don't get impatient with her, this is her job. She will compile the information and pass it along to the veterinarian, then get back to you with her recommendations.

Some questions to expect include:

- What is the puppy's problem?
- What symptoms are you seeing?
- What is the puppy's temperature? How did you take the temperature?
- Has the puppy eaten? When? How much? Did he vomit afterward?
- Has there been any diarrhea? What did it look like? How soft? Any blood or mucus?
- Has the puppy raided the trash can recently or chewed on something he shouldn't have?
- Has the puppy attended a puppy class, been boarded at a kennel, or played with other dogs recently where he may have been exposed to something?

Provide any details you think may have bearing on your puppy's illness or injury. Let your veterinarian figure out whether this information is important or not.

Caring for a Sick or Injured Puppy

Once your veterinarian has examined and treated your puppy, you'll need to continue his

---

Make Visits to the Vet Fun

Puppies tend to dislike going to the veterinary clinic because they are usually given a shot, which frightens them because it hurts. Also, the visit itself can be stressful: the clinic smells strange and unfamiliar, there are other nervous animals there, and they are handled by strangers. Unfortunately, if your Dobe learns to dislike visits to the vet when he's puppy, he will often carry that anxiety into adulthood, and that's not good. An adult Dobe who hates the vet clinic can be a problem to handle should he need care.

Ask the staff at the clinic if they would be willing to make a fuss over your puppy whenever he visits. Most people are usually more than happy to do this because they know it makes the experience easier for the animals—and loving animals is a prerequisite for the job anyway! Let them give your puppy kisses and hugs, petting, and yummy treats.

Also, stop by the clinic once in awhile just so your puppy can get some attention from the staff. This way, he won't associate it only with scary things. One of my dogs broke three bones in his paw when he was 3 months of age. Knowing this could traumatize him toward the vet's clinic, I made sure he went in often—not just for splint changes, but also for some love and treats. That dog is now 12 years old and still enjoys visits to the clinic.

Behavior that may indicate your puppy isn't feeling well may include hiding and not wanting to come out.

care at home, and that's where the challenge often occurs. Giving a wiggling puppy a pill or cleaning an infected, sore ear can be tough.

Pills—whether in capsule or tablet form—can be hidden in a piece of cheese or a bit of meat as long as the puppy will eat. If your puppy doesn't have much of an appetite, try some different foods that may be more appealing, such as a piece of hot dog or strongly aromatic cheese. However, if your puppy doesn't want to eat at all, you'll need to put the pill in his mouth and gently get him to swallow it. The easiest way to do this is to reach over your Dobe's head with one hand, pressing the skin of the top lips against the teeth so that he opens his mouth. With the other hand, place the pill at the back of the tongue, getting it as far back as possible. Then close his mouth and rub his throat until you see him swallow.

Giving liquid medication can be messy. If your vet prescribes a liquid medication, ask for a few large syringes. The medication can then be measured into the syringe and put into the puppy's mouth to deliver it between the back teeth. Squirt the medication in a little at a time so your puppy can swallow it. Do not squirt the medication to the back of the throat or the puppy might choke on it.

Eye medication needs to be put into the eye carefully but quickly; if you hesitate, the puppy may jerk or pull away. First, wipe the eye clean with a damp cloth before putting the medication in. Then, holding the puppy close, lift the top eyelid with one hand and put the medication in with the other hand.

Putting medication in an ear isn't as difficult, except that ear infections usually hurt. Again, begin by holding the puppy close to you. Clean

The decision to breed your dog should never be taken lightly. It requires a thorough knowledge of the breed, as well as an ample commitment of both time and expense.

the ear with some ear wipes or cotton balls dampened with ear cleaner. Then place the medication down into the ear canal. Gently massage the base of the ear to distribute the medication.

Follow your veterinarian's advice concerning your puppy's care during his convalescence. Ask if there are special instructions regarding what he's fed, how much activity he is permitted to have, etc. If you have any other concerns or questions, ask. After all, that's what she's there for.

To Breed or Not to Breed?

Not every Doberman Pinscher needs to be bred. Although the best of the best should be bred— such as those Dobes with breed championships, multiple working titles, and those who are

healthy and of sound temperament—many should not be bred. Dogs with certain inherited physical, structural, or other health problems, or those with temperament flaws should not pass along their genetics. Ideally, only the best examples of the breed should be placed into professional breeding programs, as this is how the breed improves.

Breeding dogs is a tough endeavor; not only does it require a thorough knowledge of the breed, including researching and reading pedigrees, but it demands an ample commitment of both time and money. Along with knowing and being up to date on breed genetics, there is the actual breeding, whelping, tail docking, ear cropping, and general care for both the mother and her litter. The breeder must also know what to do in unexpected emergencies, such as complications during the birthing process or the dam not having enough milk. Afterward, she is responsible for finding the best homes possible for the puppies. Breeding dogs—and doing it correctly and with care—is not for the faint of heart.

Spaying and Neutering

Spaying a female dog consists of a surgical procedure called ovariohysterectomy. The ovaries and uterus are removed through a small incision in the abdomen. This is usually done at about 6 months of age. Once spayed, your female Dobe will no longer come into season (will no longer go into heat) and will not be able to reproduce. Recuperation from surgery is usually very easy. Your veterinarian will recommend that your Dobe be kept quiet for a week to ten days; you can do this by keeping her on leash and close to you and putting her in her crate when you can't supervise her.

For males, the surgery consists of a procedure called castration in which the testicles are removed through a small incision forward of the scrotum. As with the females, your veterinarian will tell you to keep your dog quiet for a week to ten days. Again, recuperation is usually very fast; problems may occur if the dog disturbs his stitches or is too active. The scrotum may fill with fluid or the incision may be pulled apart. In either case, contact your veterinarian right away. Most veterinarians use dissolvable stitches so the dog does not need to undergo further discomfort.

Spaying tends to decrease the incidences of mammary gland cancers in females. Removal of the reproductive system also protects against cancers that may have occurred there. There is also a belief that spaying a female reduces female aggression; obviously, a spayed female will no longer come into season twice a year. There are several benefits in neutering males, including a lessening of sexually related behaviors such as fighting with other males, roaming, and other related behaviors. Leg-lifting, marking, and urinating on upright surfaces tend to decrease. Testicular cancer is no longer an issue because the testicles have been removed.

However, spaying or neutering your dog does involve some potential risks and side effects. Surgery and anesthesia always come with possible complications. The dog may bleed during surgery, stop breathing, or even die. Discuss these issues with your veterinarian prior to scheduling the surgery.

Although spaying or neutering your Doberman does stop the chance of unexpected reproduction, this should be a well-researched decision rather than an automatic one. Christie Keith, an administrator for the popular blog Pet Connection and an advocate for pet health, says, "Being intact is in fact normal, even if it's no longer common. I'm increasingly uncomfortable with how few people seem to question or even acknowledge that we're making some pretty significant tradeoffs in terms of our dogs' health."

Some of the potential problems that are seen in spayed or neutered dogs can be serious. For example, both spayed females and neutered males have two times the risk of developing osteosarcoma and hemangiosarcoma cancers as do intact dogs. Spayed females are more likely to develop urinary incontinence later in life, and males are more prone to urinary tract cancers and prostate cancer. Research is continuing on several other possible related problems, including the increased risk of knee injuries. For most dogs not used in breeding programs, however, spaying and neutering are options with noted benefits.

CHAPTER 4

TRAINING YOUR DOBERMAN PINSCHER PUPPY

Your Doberman Pinscher puppy was not born knowing all the things he needs to know concerning living with humans. He's going to chew on anything he can fit into his mouth, which may well include some personal possessions that you don't want him to gnaw on. He will also pull on the leash, jump on people, and relieve himself in the house. Puppies aren't being bad when they engage in these behaviors; they're just following their canine instincts, and they don't know any better. They need your guidance.

Most trainers recommend beginning the training process in early puppyhood. Although you should start training your puppy at home soon after his arrival, he can begin basic obedience training classes after he has received his vaccinations and your veterinarian has given the okay. With positive, consistent training, your Dobe will grow up to be a confident and happy adult who understands what's expected of him.

FINDING A TRAINER

Some dog owners seem to be natural trainers; they are able to communicate with their dog easily and understand how to change his behavior. Most people, however, would do well to have a dog trainer help them through the training process. A trainer can guide both dog and owner through the puppy stage and the challenges of adolescence later on.

Finding a trainer doesn't have to be difficult. If you see some well-behaved dogs in your neighborhood or while out on walks, ask the owners where they went for training. Call several local veterinarians and ask which trainers they recommend. There are also several professional organizations for dog trainers, including the National Association for Dog Obedience Instructors (NADOI), the Association of Pet Dog Trainers (APDT), and the International Association of Canine Professionals (IACP). All three have websites listing member trainers. (See Resources section.)

Don't sign up with the first trainer you find. Instead, find out which trainers are referred most often. You may discover that there are eight or nine trainers in your area, but two are recommended more highly by dog owners and veterinarians. These are the professionals you want to check out in more detail.

Check out the trainers' websites. If you like what they have to say, give them a call. Ask if you can you come by and watch a puppy class.

Obedience training is necessary if you want your Dobe to become a friendly, well-behaved adult dog. Most trainers recommend beginning the training process in early puppyhood.

Is the class well organized? Is good information being shared? Does she handle the dogs well? Is the trainer also a good teacher? Is she able to teach the owners as well as the puppies? Would you be comfortable in this class?

Most puppy classes combine an introduction to the basic obedience commands—all geared toward the puppy's short attention span—with problem prevention and socialization. Part of the class may be discussion followed by a question-and-answer period, while the other part is practicing obedience skills. At some point, the puppies may be allowed to have some free playtime. Every trainer will follow her own individual lesson plans.

Many trainers today, including Kate Abbott, of Kindred Spirits Dog Training in Vista, California, are incorporating the American Kennel Club (AKC) Puppy STAR program into their training curriculum. Abbott says, "This program, which stands for socialization, training, activity, and responsibility, is geared toward socializing the puppies at an age during which it's most effective, as well as beginning the puppy's training. The program also helps steer puppy owners in the direction of becoming responsible dog owners."

As you do your research, you will also find that there are many different ways to train dogs. A standard joke among dog trainers is that if you talk to a dozen dog trainers, each individual trainer will say her method of training is best and the other eleven are wrong. Although this can be confusing, it's also very good because every dog owner is an individual as is each dog, which gives you more options to find a trainer that will best suit you and your Dobe.

The preferred training techniques for Doberman Pinschers—or any dog—are positive ones. They use rewards, such as praise, petting, treats, or toys, to let the dog know when he's done something right. What is important to you is to find a dog trainer and a training method that will be comfortable for you and your dog. So take some time, talk to people, and do your homework.

THE IMPORTANCE OF TRAINING

Training for any dog, especially a Doberman, should be a lifelong process. Bethel says, "Training begins with our puppies from the time they are born—beginning with gentle handling—and continues on through old age."

Training teaches your dog what to do rather than just trying to correct problem behaviors. This is more important than many dog owners realize. If the dog develops bad habits, such as chasing the cat, raiding the trash can, or destructive chewing, for example, these are much more difficult to change once they're established. However, when a dog learns how to behave appropriately from the beginning— from puppyhood—then those bad habits never get a chance to become ingrained.

Mary Waugh Swindell, the Head Trainer for Dancing Dogs in Boyd, Texas, says, "Doberman Pinschers have lots of mental energy and tons of physical energy that needs to be channeled into acceptable outlets. They also have strong personalities, and lots of problems develop when it's not clear what the household rules are and who is running the show."

Kate Abbott says, "Training is not something that is done to the dog; that has such a negative connotation. Instead, think of training as a process that involves both you and your dog. Training is teamwork." Even though training will teach your Dobe puppy household and social rules, the two of you will do this together. Working together toward the same goals and setting your dog up for success is a wonderful way to develop a bond with your dog that builds and strengthens your relationship.

SOCIALIZATION IS IMPERATIVE

Many Doberman Pinschers would be happiest if they lived in a world with only their owner or owners. Bred to be watchful and protective, strangers are often looked upon by them as potential threats. Therefore, to live in our world today, Dobe puppies need to be well socialized.

Socialization is the process of introducing your Dobe puppy to the world around him. He will need to meet people of all ages, sizes, and ethnic backgrounds. For example, if your Dobe lives in a household that contains no children, and he never meets friendly kids in a controlled situation, he may grow up thinking kids are from another planet. He may be worried about them, fearful, or may even react aggressively when he meets a child. The process of socialization, done in a thoughtful and controlled manner, teaches the dog that people other than his owner are okay.

Socialization includes more than just an introduction to people; it also includes exposing your puppy to different sights, sounds, smells, and places. A motorcycle roaring by might be frightening to him initially, but with socialization, he will learn that if you say something is okay, it really is.

Socialization is particularly important for breeds like Dobes, who are naturally wired to be suspicious watchdogs. Although socialization will never cancel out the instinctual behavior a dog might have, it will help him make better choices. Your dog will learn, for example, that the neighbor's child who is yelling while playing is not a problem, but the bad guy jostling you about as he tries to take your purse is a true threat.

The Socialization Process

In his first few days with your family, introduce your Dobe puppy gradually to his new home. Let him explore things while supervised. Show him an object, touch it yourself, and say in a happy tone of voice, "What's this?" When he walks up to the object, praise him, "What a brave puppy! Yes, good boy!"

A big part of the socialization process can be as easy as allowing your puppy to meet new people. Begin by introducing family members who live nearby. Invite them over for a cup of coffee or glass of iced tea. Have them give your puppy a special treat, and then encourage them to pet him gently; do not allow rough play because you want your puppy to enjoy this attention calmly.

Then let your puppy meet some neighbors. Follow the same routine. Let them give your

Socialization begins when your puppy learns to interact with his littermates, but it is a process you must continue throughout his adolescence by introducing him to the world around him.

puppy a treat and then pet him. Just have one or two people meet him at a time; don't let a crowd gang up on him. Keep in mind that your puppy needs to meet babies, toddlers, young kids, teenagers, young adults, middle-aged adults, and senior citizens. He also needs to meet small people and large people. It's also imperative he meets people from a variety of cultures.

Once he's had his shots and clearance from your veterinarian, take your Dobe puppy on some adventures.

He can go to the local pet supply store with you. Not only will he meet new people, but he can be introduced to a strange new environment and meet some customer's friendly dogs. He can also be taught that everything that smells good—dog food, treats, toys and chew bones, are not his.

Another outing could be going back to the veterinarian's office for some petting and treats. Not only will this be good socialization, but it will help teach your puppy that the vet's office is not always a scary place.

Your puppy would really enjoy a visit to the local park. Pack a picnic basket or some snacks and relax while the neighborhood kids play sports. He can hear people cheering for the players and watch while the kids run around. People walking past can pet him.

Go to the local beach and let him sniff the sea breeze. He can try to figure out what the sea gulls soaring overhead are and listen to them squawk.

Take your Dobe out to a variety of places. Just make sure the adventures are fun and not frightening.

Things to Include in the Socialization Process

It's easy to forget that many of the things you use everyday are new to your puppy. You don't

By the Numbers

Although socialization should be an ongoing process from early puppyhood on through adulthood, the most important age to begin introducing your Dobe to the world around him is between 12 and 20 weeks of age. Puppies not socialized during this period often have behavior problems later in life.

think twice about snapping open a plastic trash bag, but that noise can actually scare many puppies. Here are just a few things in your house and yard to which you should introduce your Dobe during puppyhood:

- kitchen appliances (dishwasher, garbage disposal, trash compacter, etc.)
- washer and dryer
- vacuum cleaner
- broom and mop being used
- metal bowl or pan dropped to the floor
- television, radio, computer, phone, etc.
- children's toys, especially those that make noise
- bicycles, skateboards, skates, etc.
- tools moved and used in the garage or workroom
- car engine starting
- lawn mower, leaf blower, trimmers, etc.
- plastic bag blowing in the wind
- crumpled brown paper bag or newspaper
- empty cardboard box

Here are some things to expose your puppy to while away from home:

- walking over different outdoor surfaces, such as dirt, concrete, asphalt, metal manhole covers, gravel, bark, sand, etc.

- walking in a meadow, field, or forest
- walking over a wooden footbridge
- walking on carpet, tile, artificial turf, and rubber matting
- walking up and down stairs
- taking an elevator ride
- garbage truck moving and compacting
- cars and motorcycles driving past
- loud music coming from a car

Don't forget there are other creatures in this world, too, and your puppy should meet them. Introduce him to other friendly dogs, dog-friendly cats, rabbits, ferrets, turtles and tortoises, horses, goats, cows, sheep, etc. The more animals he meets, the better.

Maintain Control of the Process

The socialization process should be fun and encouraging so that your Dobe can learn the world is not a scary place. In addition, you want your puppy to learn to look to you for guidance; when you say everything's okay, he will trust that it is.

To accomplish this, you need to maintain control over the entire process. Keep in mind your Doberman Pinscher's adult personality is shaped not just by his breed and genetic heritage, but also by training, socialization, and you.

Don't try to introduce your Dobe to everything all at once. Overwhelming him will only frighten him, which is just as bad as not introducing him to anything at all. Instead, remember this is a process that will take place throughout puppyhood.

Also, don't let groups of people overwhelm your puppy. Let one or two people meet him and pet him at a time. If several people try to crowd around him—especially rowdy kids—just remove your puppy from the situation. Don't let kids get loud around him because it may frighten him. If they become

overstimulated, remove your puppy—even if you have to pick him up and walk away.

Some people also think it's fun to wiggle their hands and fingers in front of a puppy's face, provoking him to play. Please don't allow this behavior to occur either. After all, it's annoying, and should your pup get tired of it and reach out to nip some fingers, offering apologies may not be enough. Wrestling is also not a good idea because it teaches a puppy to fight people. Overall, just ask people to be gentle with your puppy.

CRATE TRAINING YOUR PUPPY

Teaching your puppy to accept—and enjoy—spending time alone in his crate is one of the most important lessons you will ever teach him. A crate can confine him at night when everyone is sleeping, as well as for short periods during the day. However, it is not a cage in which to keep him all the time—that's abusive use of the crate. Far from being punishment, a crate should be seen as a safe, secure den that is your puppy's space and his alone. It is also a useful housetraining tool. By spending brief periods in the crate, he learns to control his bladder and bowels because dogs have an instinct to keep their dens clean. A crate can also be used to train various appropriate behaviors—after all, when confined, a puppy cannot indulge in bad habits such as destructive chewing and trash can raiding. It can also keep your puppy safe when you are unable to supervise him. All in all, a crate should provide a positive and pleasant environment for your puppy throughout his life.

Introducing the Crate

Ideally, when you say, "Puppers, go to bed!" your puppy should run to his crate and dash in with his stub of a tail wiggling like crazy. If your puppy hates his crate and doesn't want to enter it, there's a problem. The crate should be a place your puppy readily accepts as safe and comforting. Convincing him to accept it may take some time and patience, but you'll soon discover that your efforts prove worthwhile.

To begin, set up the crate in a room where people in the house spend a lot of time. This is not going to be a permanent location for it, but your puppy will be more comfortable feeling like he's part of family activity and not isolated and alone.

Introduce the crate gradually. Prop the door open so it won't close accidentally behind him. Provide opportunities for your Dobe to enter it of his own accord; if he chooses to do so, training him to remain in it will be easier on both of you.

For first introductions, have a handful of treats. Let your puppy smell the treats and toss

AKC STAR Puppy Program

The success of the Canine Good Citizen (CGC) Program has led to another related program, the American Kennel Club (AKC)'s STAR Puppy Program. STAR stands for socialization, training, activity, and responsibility. Whereas the CGC program is primarily for adult dogs, this is specifically for young puppies and is designed to teach the owner what the puppy needs, to get the puppy started in life correctly, and to prevent potential problems as much as possible.

Program requirements include that:

- the puppy is healthy and has been started on a vaccination program (as determined by the owner and veterinarian)
- the owner is actively involved with the puppy, including daily play and exercise
- the owner will pick up after her puppy and has a bag or other tools to do so.
- the puppy is wearing identification
- the puppy does not show aggression toward people in the group class
- the puppy is not aggressive toward other puppies in the group class
- the puppy tolerates and wears a collar or harness and accepts a leash
- the puppy accepts hugging and petting from the owner
- the puppy will play with a toy (or treat) and allow the owner to take it away
- the puppy allows petting by someone other than the owner
- the puppy can be groomed, touched, and examined by the owner, and this will include the ears and paws
- the puppy can walk on a leash with the owner without zig-zagging down the sidewalk and without tripping the owner
- the puppy will sit, lie down, and come on leash
- the puppy doesn't panic to visual or sound distractions

Many dog trainers are now incorporating this program into their puppy classes. If you are interested in enrolling with your Dobe, call local trainers and ask if they offer it, or go to the AKC's website at www.akc.org for more information.

one toward but not into the crate. Let him go to it and eat it, then praise him, "Good boy!" Do that a few more times, then toss a treat inside the crate. When your puppy steps into the crate for the treat, praise him with the command you are going to use, "Good to go to bed! Yes!" Repeat a few more times in an upbeat, pleasant voice, and then end the training session on a positive note.

When dinner time comes, put your puppy's food bowl inside the crate, pushing it to the back end. After your puppy enters the crate, quietly close the door. Let him eat in peace, and let him figure out the door is closed. Don't open it immediately after he's finished. If he remains calm and quiet, open the door and praise him. If he begins barking, pawing at the door, and throwing a temper tantrum, don't let him out yet. In fact, walk away and go to another room for a few minutes. You do not want to reinforce this behavior. When he calms down, come back and let him out. At this point, praise him for being good so he associates appropriate behavior (remaining calm) with being rewarded.

After this, begin putting your puppy in his crate every now and then throughout the day, closing the door for a few minutes each time. Always give him a treat or toy when he's inside and never let him out if he's throwing a fit.

Some Dobe puppies can learn this lesson all in one day. If your breeder already introduced the crate to your puppy, he'll switch over to the one at your home in a day. But if your puppy has never been inside a crate before, especially if he's more than 3 months old, it may take several days to get him used to it.

Your Puppy's Bed and Refuge
Once your puppy is used to the crate, put it in the place where you'd like it to remain.

Keeping it in your bedroom is great because then the puppy can sleep in your room, hearing and smelling you, and being close to you even though you're asleep. If you're short of room, move your bedside table out and put the crate there for awhile.

Don't isolate your puppy. If you put him in the laundry room or garage, he will be very unhappy and behavior problems such as barking, howling, chewing, and self-mutilation (excessive licking and flank sucking) can result. Your Dobe puppy misses his pack and needs to be near you.

When your puppy is comfortable with the crate, it will become his bed at night and his refuge when he's tired or stressed. Leave the door to the crate open during the day, and let him run in and out as he wishes. You may find him curled up in it sound asleep with the door wide open and that's wonderful.

You may find you will want a second crate, or even a third. One kept in the car, strapped down with seat belts or tie-downs, will be a safe place for your Dobe to ride. Another crate in the family room or in an area where

Training Tidbit

Crates work well for puppy training because puppies like small, dark places to retreat to and sleep in. That's why you may find your Dobe puppy snoozing under a table that's covered with a tablecloth. Your puppy isn't hiding; instead he's found a secure, safe place to rest where he feels no one will bother him.

When housetraining your puppy, choose a spot in your yard where you want him to eliminate and take him to that same area every time.

the family spends time may also be a good idea. Then, when you want the puppy nearby but you can't supervise him—such as when cooking dinner—he can be close, but safe from making mischief.

Plan on using the crate for quite a while. Most puppies aren't mentally grown up for at least 2 years, but some may be even slower. Mary Swindell says, "Dobes tend to be physically mature between 18 months and 2 years of age. Mentally? Well, the girls tend to be mentally mature between 2 and 3 years of age. The boys are slower and sometimes don't seem to be grown up until closer to 4."

Since one of the biggest benefits of using the crate—besides teaching housetraining skills—is preventing bad behavior from occurring, you don't want to stop using the crate until your dog is mentally grown up and well trained. Even then, many owners leave the crate out as the dog's bed and just take the door off so he can come and go as he pleases.

HOUSETRAINING YOUR DOBE PUPPY

Every Doberman Pinscher needs to be reliably housetrained. This is a basic skill necessary for every dog; after all, indoor mistakes can ruin carpeting and furniture, and constant cleaning up can become a dreaded nuisance.

Housetraining consists of teaching a puppy where it is appropriate to relieve himself. You may have reserved a certain section of the backyard where you want him to go, as well as some spot along your daily walk—like a vacant lot—where it would be convenient. Don't forget to pick up after your dog!

The second part of housetraining is teaching your puppy to try to relieve himself when you ask him to, and this is just as important as teaching him where to go. For example, if you teach your Dobe to relieve himself in one corner of the backyard and in the vacant lot in your neighborhood, you also need to be able to ask him to go on command in other places. For example, if you're traveling, he will need to go during the trip.

Many dog owners feel that housetraining is all about teaching a dog not to relieve himself in the house. That is certainly a part of the lesson, but your dog needs to know what to do elsewhere so that he can be a good canine citizen and member of his community. Besides being ineffective and unfair, yelling at your dog for mistakes that occur in the house won't teach him what to do; it will only teach him that relieving himself makes you angry. Instead, teaching your dog what he should do and where he should do it creates a much more reliably trained and happy dog.

Using a Designated Area

Decide where you want your Dobe to relieve himself. During housetraining, use the same location every time. There doesn't have to be anything special about it; it just needs to be a place to which your puppy has easy access and one you're willing to clean up after each visit.

To teach your Dobe to use his potty area, you're going to have to walk him out to it. For example, when your Dobe puppy needs to relieve himself, such as after waking up first thing in the morning, put a leash on him and walk him to the door as you ask him, "Do you have to get busy?" Then have him go outside with you to the potty area.

Then softly say, "Get busy!" You can use any command you wish. Say it softly so you don't distract your puppy. When he relieves himself, praise him enthusiastically, "Good boy to get busy!"

Never send your Dobe puppy outside all by himself. If you do, you can't teach him where to go, and you can't praise him for doing it. In addition, you really won't know if he's gone or not. He may show up at the door asking to come in and make a mistake on the carpet inside the door. By taking him out, you teach him where to go, teach him a command that means try to go now, and then reward him for doing it at the exact moment he does so in order to reinforce the correct behavior—all of which helps create a reliably housetrained dog.

This process will take several months. Even if your 4-month-old Dobe seems to understand the concept of housetraining and isn't having

Multi-Dog Tip

Well-trained adult dogs are great teachers for a puppy. You may find your Dobe puppy naturally follows your adult dog out to the backyard potty area and relieves himself after your adult dog does so. This is great; however, continue housetraining your puppy as well, and praise the older dog for helping to teach him, too.

Housetraining is easier when your puppy sleeps, eats, plays, and relieves himself on a fairly regular schedule.

any accidents, that doesn't mean you can stop training him. Instead, it means you're doing everything right, and he's learning. If you stop training, he may or may not continue as you began; he may begin relieving himself where he wants rather than where you want him to go. He may get too busy inside to go outside. And your potty command may lose its effectiveness. So continue this housetraining process for several months. By 7 or 8 months of age, your puppy can be considered reliably housetrained if there have been no accidents in several weeks.

Using a Potty Schedule

Housetraining is easier when your puppy sleeps, eats, plays, and relieves himself on a fairly regular schedule. If your personal schedule tends to be erratic, don't worry; an adult Dobe is much more flexible. Puppies, however, need a routine.

The schedule you establish for your puppy needs to work for you, your family, and your puppy. Each individual person and puppy is unique, so combining all the various needs can be challenging. What's most important is getting your puppy outside to his spot as soon as he has to relieve himself. After all, a puppy doesn't have much control, and when he has to go, he's going to go.

Don't be afraid to ask for help with your schedule. If you can't get home from work at lunchtime, for example, perhaps a neighbor would be happy to help take your Dobe outside for a walk. Maybe a neighborhood teenager who loves dogs and is responsible can take your Dobe outside for a potty break and a playtime. Professional pet sitters and dog walkers are also a possibility for busy owners.

Fine-Tuning Housetraining Skills

As your puppy learns what's expected of him, you can begin fine-tuning his housetraining skills. For example, teaching him to tell you when he needs to go outside could come in handy. Whenever you walk your Dobe to the door to go to his potty area and ask him, "Do you have to get busy?" you're already prepping him for this.

To train your puppy to tell you he needs to potty, give the command in a happy, enthusiastic tone of voice. Then, as he responds and looks at you, praise him and ask him again, "Good boy! Do you have to get busy?" If he's dancing and prancing and looking at you, praise him more! Do this every time you take him outside.

Now, for the hard part: Watch for this behavior throughout the day. When your puppy comes to you and makes eye contact with you and dances, ask him if he needs to go potty and praise him as you move quickly to the door. Don't ignore him because he will then feel that his communication with you has failed. Instead, praise him enthusiastically and get him outside right away.

Don't teach your dog to bark when he needs to go outside. Barking can quickly escalate into a problem behavior. However, if you want a cue that's a little more obvious than a dancing dog, teach your Dobe to ring a bell when he needs to potty. Get a bell (or three or four small bells) at a craft store. Tie it on a string so that, when it's hung from the door knob, it's at your Dobe's nose height.

For the first few training sessions, rub the bell lightly with a bit of hot dog or cheese so it smells appealing to your puppy. Also have some pieces of hot dog or cheese in your pocket. Walk your puppy up to the bell hanging from the closed door and point to it. When he sniffs the bell—even if he doesn't ring it—praise him, open the door, go outside, and give him the treat as soon as you step outside. Repeat this three or four times, and then quit. Do it again later.

Each time you need to take your puppy outside to relieve himself, repeat the exercise. When, one day, you hear the bell ringing, respond right away, praise your puppy enthusiastically, and take him outside to do his business.

Doggy Doors and Housetraining

Doggy doors are door flaps that allow a dog to go outside and come back inside at his convenience. Because you don't have to be available to open the door when your dog needs to relieve himself, these can be especially useful for well-trained, adult dogs who are left alone for several hours each day.

Although you can teach your Dobe puppy to use a doggy door, he should be reliably housetrained before being permitted to use one regularly on his own. It's very important that you follow housetraining guidelines even when a doggy door is available. After all, you still need to teach him where to go in the yard. You also want to teach him to reliably respond to the potty command, you need to know that he has actually relieved himself, and it's important to praise him for going to reinforce the training.

Doggy doors can also lead an owner into complacency. You may feel your puppy is well trained because he's going in and out of the doggy door. But when the door is closed one day, you may find your puppy doesn't really know what to do. So teach your Dobe how

Basic obedience commands like the *sit* are the foundation for good manners and all future learning.

to use a doggy door, but follow all the other housetraining guidelines, too, and make sure he's reliably housetrained before letting him potty on his own.

Handling Housetraining Accidents

Accidents will happen, even when a puppy owner is vigilant. A puppy can be playing one second and squatting the next. However, accidents usually occur when the owner gets distracted and is busy with something other than her puppy.

When an accident does occur, how you react is important. If you convey to the puppy that urinating and/or defecating is wrong, he will try to hide it. He may no longer relieve himself in front of you, even outside. You may find puddles or piles behind the drapes or the sofa.

If you catch your puppy in the act, use your voice to interrupt him and calmly but firmly say, "No." Then take him outside. Now, tell him to go using your normal soft voice. Praise him if he has anything left or tries to comply. Then leave him outside while you go back inside to clean up.

Do not yell at your puppy or berate him for what he did. Instead, promise yourself that you will do better next time by making sure he gets outside more quickly and by sticking to the established potty schedule.

If you find an accident after the fact—after your puppy has finished and moved away—do not punish him. Don't drag him to the mess and yell at him, and never stick his nose in it. He should not be punished for a natural biological action. Instead, take him outside and leave him there while you clean up and yell at yourself for allowing this to happen.

Successful housetraining is based on setting the puppy up for success. Maintaining a good schedule, always going outside with your puppy, teaching him a command, and praising him for going in the right areas will all lead to having a well-trained and reliable Doberman.

BASIC OBEDIENCE FOR PUPPIES

Teaching a Dobe puppy to concentrate on much of anything for any period of time is like asking an ocean wave not to hit the beach; it's not going to happen. Dobe puppies are silly, funny, and have the attention span of a gnat. But that doesn't mean training should be ignored.

Having your dog respond reliably to a recall, or *come* command, is good not just for daily living with your dog but also for his safety.

Training helps to teach a puppy what's expected of him. It provides household and social guidelines, and it helps you keep him safe. Most importantly, though, training helps build a bond—a lasting relationship—between you and your puppy.

Obedience training should always be positive—which means lots of praise, petting, treats, and toys offered for good behavior. Punishment of any kind—yelling, hitting, using collars to choke or hurt the dog, etc.— should never be used. You can, however, use a firm voice to interrupt bad behavior, as was suggested earlier to interrupt a puppy in the act of a housetraining accident, for example.

The obedience exercises that follow use a *lure and reward* training technique. This is a positive technique that's easy for most dog owners to understand and sets a puppy up to succeed.

When training all of these exercises, just do three or four repetitions and then take a break. Keep in mind that too much repetition gets boring, and your puppy will learn to dislike training. You want him to learn to listen to you, but you also want him to enjoy the training process. Naturally, if he enjoys it, he's going to be more cooperative.

How to Teach the *Sit*

The *sit* command is one of the first basic obedience commands all puppies learn because by sitting, a puppy learns some self control. He has to sit and hold still for rewards. This lesson is the foundation for all future learning.

Here's how to teach the *sit*:

1. Put your puppy on leash and hold it in one hand. Have a small, tasty treat in the other hand.

2. Show your puppy the treat, and let him sniff it.

3. Move the treat from his nose up and over his head toward his back.

4. As his head comes up to see where the treat has gone and his hips move toward the ground, give him the *sit* command, "Puppers, sit!"

5. As soon as his hips are on the ground, pop the treat into his mouth and praise him, "Good to sit! Yes!"

6. Once your puppy has been sitting for a few seconds, has eaten his treat, and you've praised him for sitting, release him from the *sit* saying, "Puppers, okay," and let him get up and move. Okay is a good release command that means, "You're done for the moment and can get up and move around."

After you've practiced this several times over several days, watch for any occasions when your puppy moves into the *sit* position on his own. At the point his hips touch the ground say, "Puppers, sit," and offer enthusiastic praise. This will begin to reinforce the *sit* using verbal praise instead of treats.

If your puppy has a hard time controlling himself and is moving constantly, practice this exercise holding his collar with one hand, rather than his leash. Then continue holding his collar as he sits so you can help your puppy succeed.

How to Teach the *Down*

The *down* command is practical in many situations. Your dog can lie down when you want him to relax or hold still, such as when you're talking to a neighbor or a guest. You can ask him to lie down and give him a chew toy when he's a little too antsy. When you give him grooming care, it's much easier if he will lie down and be still and calm. It helps when he is being examined by the vet. Once your puppy understands this command, you will find many uses for it.

1. Begin this training exercise by asking your Dobe puppy to sit.

2. Once he's sitting, show him a treat.

3. Hold the treat in front of your puppy's nose and bring it down toward his front paws.

4. As his head begins to follow the treat down, tell him, "Puppers, down."

5. When the elbows of his front legs are on the ground, praise him and give him the treat.

6. After a few seconds, release him by saying, "Puppers, okay!" and encourage him to get up and move around.

How to Teach the *Come*

Having your dog respond reliably to a recall, or *come* command, is good not just for daily living with your dog but also for his safety. For example, if your dog is off leash and decides to chase a squirrel that is dashing past and headed into the street, he could be in danger of getting hit by a car. But if he's well trained and comes when you call him, the disaster is averted. Situations come up every day in which a reliable recall is important.

The easiest way to teach your puppy a reliable recall is with a sound stimulus. For example, you've probably already noticed that your puppy recognizes the sound of his dog food being put in his bowl. He probably also recognizes the sound of the refrigerator door opening, or of the dog treat bag being opening and food being poured into his bowl. Sounds associated with food or a treat are the first ones he learns to listen for and expect.

You can use that same association to teach the *come* command.

1. Find a small plastic container with a lid and put some kibble or broken dog treats inside of it so that, when it is shaken, it makes a distinctive sound.

2. Now, have that "shaker" in one hand, and some really tasty treats—bits of hot dog, chicken, or cheese—in the other hand.

Want to Know More?

For information about intermediate obedience training, see Chapter 9: Doberman Pinscher Training.

3. With your Dobe puppy in front of you, shake the container and, at the same time, pop a treat into his mouth. Don't say anything at this point because you are teaching your dog that acknowledging this sound equals getting a yummy treat.

4. Do this three or four times, then quit. Later in the day, do the exercise again.

5. After two or three days, say, "Puppers, come!" as you shake the container and pop the treat in his mouth. He's still just standing or sitting in front of you, but now you're teaching him that the sound of the shaker is associated with the *come* command, and again he gets a tasty treat for acknowledging both sounds. As before, do this three or four times and then quit. Practice again later in the day.

6. After two or three days of training this exercise, begin backing away from your puppy as you shake the container and call him. Praise him for moving forward as you are backing up. As he becomes more reliable, gradually begin to call him in different situations. For example, call him from across the room, from down the hall, or outside in your fenced backyard. Very slowly and carefully add distractions. Just remember to always set your puppy up to succeed rather than fail.

Continue to use the shaker, your voice, and treats for several months, at least until your puppy is a year old. Then, with this habit firmly entrenched, begin decreasing the use of the shaker and rely solely on the verbal command. Alternate between using the shaker along with the verbal (*come*) command and using only the verbal command when you call your puppy. Then, use the shaker only every third or fourth time you call, gradually fading the shaker from use. As always, use a happy tone of voice and praise your puppy when he comes to you.

How to Teach Walking Nicely on Leash

Walking nicely on the leash is a wonderful skill every dog should know. After all, when a strong dog like an adult Doberman Pinscher pulls on the leash, both dog and owner can be injured; the dog can hurt his trachea, neck, shoulders, and chest, and the owner may end up with hand, arm, and shoulder problems. Luckily, it's not difficult to teach a puppy not to pull. You can use the *let's go* command to cue him to walk nicely when on leash.

1. Put the leash on your puppy and hold it in one hand. Have a pocketful of treats, but keep a few in your other hand.

2. Get your puppy's attention by letting him sniff the treats you are holding in your hand.

3. Back away from your puppy, inviting him to follow you while he is sniffing the treats.

4. After several steps backward, turn and walk forward so your puppy is now walking by your left side, still sniffing the treats in your hand. As you begin walking forward, tell him, "Puppers, let's go! Good boy!"

5. After several steps forward, stop, have your puppy sit, and give him a treat.

6. Repeat this exercise three or four

times, and then take a break. Come back later and do this again.

7. Over several days, gradually walk a little bit farther before stopping. Then add in left turns and right turns, making sure to praise your puppy for his attention.

8. If you go for a walk and your puppy gets too excited, just turn around and go in the opposite direction. Praise him when he catches up with you.

PUPPY TRAINING TIPS

Puppies have very short attention spans, which can make training challenging, but it doesn't mean you shouldn't train—just keep the training sessions short and fun.

Use some really tasty, healthy treats that your puppy likes, but use very small tidbits. Vary your training sessions so neither you nor your puppy gets bored. One day practice sits, the next practice downs, and so forth. Train your puppy at home first, and once he is reliable, take him to new locations, eventually adding some distractions.

Don't get frustrated when your puppy can't seem to concentrate. Instead, look at this as a training challenge for you. How can you help your puppy? Are your training sessions too long? Are you not using enough praise? Should you change treats? Would your puppy be more motivated by a toy?

Last, but certainly not least, remember to set your puppy up to succeed. End all training sessions on a positive note. Never ask your Dobe to do something he's not yet ready to do. And always have fun together!

When training, always set your puppy up to succeed and end sessions on a positive note.

PART II

ADULTHOOD

CHAPTER 5

FINDING YOUR ADULT DOBERMAN PINSCHER

Puppies are adorable. With soft muzzles, round tummies, and wagging tails, it's impossible to resist them. But puppies also require a great deal of time, care, supervision, and training. Mary Swindell, of Dancing Dogs, says, "Training puppies is tedious and high maintenance." They need to be housetrained, taught household rules and social manners, and guided through adolescence. It is definitely a serious responsibility and a 24-hour commitment every day. For these reasons and more, many people prefer to add an adult dog to their family rather than a puppy. Dobes are generally considered adults when they are 2 to 4 years of age.

WHY DO ADULT DOBES NEED NEW HOMES?

Most people would prefer to believe that every dog will find a home as a puppy and live his entire life in one home with a loving, caring, responsible family. That's the ideal and, happily for many dogs, that is their life. However, at times, some of these well-loved dogs end up needing new homes when their owners' circumstances unexpectedly change. For example, when an owner passes away, other family members may not be able to keep the dog. Sometimes a baby grows into a toddler and develops allergies. Economic problems, such as losing a job or home, can make it difficult or no longer possible to properly care for a pet. Bad things can happen to good people and good dogs.

Unfortunately, though, some Dobes lost their homes because their owners didn't understand the breed, or dogs in general. Shanna Gardner, who works with a Doberman Pinscher rescue group, says, "Doberman Pinschers often need help because people don't do their research before getting one. They may have unrealistic expectations of the dog." Many people get a Dobe because they want an intimidating guard dog and then are unhappy when the dog grows up to be a sweet, loving pushover.

Adolescence can also bring problems. When a Dobe is 8 months old, he will test his boundaries and challenge the world, which can be unnerving for someone who has never had a dog and is not experienced in training one—especially a larger, strong breed like the Doberman. Unfortunately, sometimes the dog's owner gives up on him.

Many owners aren't prepared for a young Doberman's activity level. Perhaps they got a dog hoping to become more active themselves, but don't follow through. Then the active healthy young dog becomes destructive when he hasn't gotten enough exercise.

Paulette Bethel, a Doberman breeder, says she can't believe some of the reasons she's been given for a dog's return, "Some of the excuses I've heard for people giving up their dog include, 'We've redecorated, and the dog doesn't match the new sofa.' 'The dog is bigger than we expected.' 'The dog has too much energy.'"

Dobes are indoor dogs who need to be with their family pack, and some owners aren't prepared to deal with a canine shadow. Carol Byrnes, a dog trainer, says, "Some people get a Doberman as an outdoor dog and end up with a dismantled backyard because the dog is upset. Other times, a Dobe left outdoors barks all day long out of frustration, and the neighbors begin complaining." She explained that if people understood the breed better before getting a Dobe, there might be fewer misunderstandings like these and fewer dogs needing help.

IS ADOPTING AN ADULT AN OPTION FOR YOU?

"My husband and I are all about adopting adult Dobermans," Swindell says, "We much prefer dogs who are 4 years old and up because they are more responsible and easier to live with. We adopted Morgan at 7 years old and Jessie at 8. They have both been a dream." The Swindells' reason for adopting mature dogs is not an uncommon one; puppies are a lot of work.

Advantages

When asked why they chose an adult dog who needs a new home, many people say they enjoy saving a dog's life. A Dobe kept in

a home situation in which he can no longer be properly cared for may be in danger of ending up in a shelter, and an adult dog in a shelter can potentially be in danger of losing his life. Many shelters will only keep adults for a limited time and, if not adopted, they may be euthanized. Adopting a dog in such a perilous situation is an act of kindness and compassion—and it feels good.

There are other reasons for choosing an adult Dobe, though. With an adult, you have a pretty good idea of what you're getting:

• You will know the dog's size and build. Although there is a breed standard for Dobes that states the preferred size, not all Dobes conform to these specifications, which describe the ideal dog and one to which only show-quality dogs come close. There are small, medium, large, and super-sized Dobes. Puppies don't always give clues to their adult size.

• You will know his level of training. Most adoptive adults are housetrained or have some concept of what housetraining is, although some may need a refresher course once they join your household. If they do

By the Numbers

Most rescue experts say that it takes dogs about 3 months to adjust to their new home. The first month, the dog feels like a guest and may be tentative about things, but by the end of the third month he's settled in. If a dog has suffered extreme neglect or abuse, however, the adjustment may take even longer.

need retraining, they tend to pick up skills quickly. Some newly adopted adult Dobes will need obedience training; they may pull on the leash or jump on people. But, as with housetraining, adult dogs tend to learn new skills faster and better than you might expect.

- You will get a fairly good idea of what his temperament and personality will be. At the time of adoption, you won't see all of the dog's personality because it will change somewhat as he gets to know you, relaxes into your household, and blossoms with love and good care. But you can still get a pretty good idea of who he is from information the shelter may have gotten from previous owners and from the screening and temperament testing they may have done.

Some people are concerned about adopting an adult dog; they're worried that he might not bond with them. Most adult dogs, including Dobes, are resilient and well able to bond with new owners. It might take some time, and you will need to be patient, but it does happen.

With Dobes in particular, some people are afraid that the dog might not like them or may turn on them. Although the idea of a Doberman Pinscher turning on his owners is rooted in history, probably from when the breed was used by the military and placed in civilian homes after their service in World War I, it still lingers in the public's consciousness. The temperament and personality of the breed today is far different from those dogs, and although any dog can bite given the right provocation, it would be considered highly unusual for a Dobe to turn on his owner.

Disadvantages

The downside of adopting an adult dog is that he may come with some baggage. If people

One significant advantage to adopting an adult is that his personality, temperament, and physical appearance are already established.

have hurt him in the past, through neglect, emotional or physical abuse, or in other ways, he will carry that fear and insecurity with him to his new home. You will need to be prepared to deal with that and help him get past it. Sometimes a dog can't get rid of all his baggage, even with help, and then you will need to find a way to deal with his issues so you and he both can live with them.

At the time of adoption, he may be grieving, too, for his former home and may be somewhat depressed. Even if his former home was less than ideal, it was still his home, and losing it will cause him to be sad. Keep that in mind as you look for an adult dog.

ADOPTING AN ADULT DOBERMAN PINSCHER

If you have now decided that the best dog for you would be an adult Doberman Pinscher, take your time trying to find him. Hopefully, this dog will share your home and life for the remainder of his lifetime, so it's important to find and choose a dog with the characteristics that will make you both happy.

What Qualities Are Important to You?

An adoption that doesn't work out is heartbreaking to all involved, so before looking, it's important to have a good idea what you want in a dog. You want a Doberman Pinscher of course, but what else is important?

• Male or female? Both male and female Dobes can be awesome pets and companions, and choosing one over the other is strictly a personal decision. Males do tend to lift their leg to urinate or mark territory and this bothers some people. Some male Dobes can be aggressive toward other male dogs, but some females can be slightly dog aggressive, too.

• A soft personality or bold? Although more Dobes today tend to be somewhat softer than they were years ago, there are still many with a bolder, more forceful personality. Which will fit your lifestyle best?

• A couch potato or a go-getter? Are you an active person, or a slightly more sedentary one? If you like to get out and about, and enjoy sharing your activities with your dog, then a more active Dobe would fit you better. If you're more sedentary, an active dog would drive you nuts.

• Do you have any training requirements? Do you want your dog to be reliably housetrained or obedience trained before you adopt him? Some people just aren't good dog trainers or don't have any patience for training. If you feel that way, deep down inside, that's okay. Just make sure you choose the right dog, one who has learned basic training skills already.

Now let's take a look at what you plan to do with your dog, which impacts your decision as well:

• Is your Dobe going to be a pet and companion? Do you want him to share your home, go for walks with you, and listen to your secrets? Awesome—many dogs can fill that requirement for you.

• Do you want a jogging partner or a dog who can go hiking and camping with you? To satisfy these needs, you may want to look for a young adult who is healthy, strong, and physically fit.

• Are there kids in your family? Or do children

Training Tidbit

Even if the Dobe you adopt has had some training, don't expect that his behavior will be perfect when you first bring him home. A dog is not like a car that will run perfectly for anyone. Training is something you and your dog do together. So plan on doing some training with your dog even if he's already had some in his first home.

When adopting an adult dog from a rescue or shelter, try to find out as much about your prospective new pet as you can. It's important to choose a dog with the characteristics that will make you both happy.

visit you often? If so, you need a dog who is well socialized with children and comfortable with them.

- Do you plan on participating in canine sports with your new Dobe? If you want to do therapy dog volunteer work, you'll need a softer, affectionate, well-socialized and trained Dobe who loves people. If you want to participate in obedience competition, you will want to find a dog who loves to train. An agility dog is fast, agile, and biddable. A Schutzhund dog needs to be sharper and bolder than the average Doberman Pinscher today.

The fun thing about Dobes is that they are not all identical, and they're versatile. If you have several goals for your new dog, that's okay. You can compete in obedience and agility and go hiking with your Doberman. Your competitive Dobe could be awesome with children, too, and still be your confidante.

Where to Look for a Dobe

There are many ways to find and adopt a dog. Your veterinarian many know that a client is looking to rehome her Dobe because her husband is ill. A friend with a Dobe may have just heard that her breeder is trying to place a retired show dog. Networking—letting friends and family members know you're looking—is a great idea.

A Doberman Pinscher rescue group is also a good place to begin looking for a new dog. Rescues help rehome many dogs who need help. They can do this is a few different ways. Some maintain lists of dogs needing homes and lists of people wanting to adopt dogs. Then people and dogs who match are put in touch with each other. Other groups will physically take in dogs in need, boarding them at kennels or placing them in temporary foster homes until permanent homes can be found for them.

Although it's not common to find Dobes in local shelters or humane societies, it does happen. Some shelters will keep dogs for as long as needed to find them good homes. Other shelters do euthanize dogs after a certain period of time. This can range from hours to days or weeks, depending upon the shelter.

Dogs can also be found via the Internet, although you will want to use reliable sources that have been vetted by professional organizations, as well as meet the dog you are interested in before making a commitment. PetFinder.com is a popular website where rescue groups and shelters post photos and information about dogs needing homes.

All of these organizations will ask you to fill out an adoption application prior to allowing you to adopt one of their dogs. Many will ask some pointed questions about dog ownership,

Dobermans, your family, your home, and your lifestyle. Don't take offense when they do; they just want to make sure one of their dogs doesn't end up in rescue again. They want the dog to find a permanent home.

Search all of these resources if you like. Just be prepared—you may find that many dogs need help, and although you can't save all of them, you can save the life of one dog and bring much joy into his life and your own.

Choosing the Right Dog for You

When searching for your new Dobe, be it at the shelter, at a rescue foster home, or at a private home, don't rush into a commitment. Don't adopt the first dog you see, especially the first time you see him. Don't let someone rush you, either. Adopting a dog is a long-term commitment that requires many considerations, lots of research, and time. Although you will choose your dog with your heart, it's important to use your brain also.

So, when looking for a dog:

1. Observe the dog. What is your first impression of him overall? Does he seem to have a personality and appearance you like? Take a look at some other dogs and then come back for a second look. Is your first impression still valid?

2. Pet the dog. Does he lean into you, or does he try to get away? Watch his body language: Does he appear to be worried, shy, fearful, reserved, and cautious, or friendly, extroverted, outgoing, and silly? Does he appear to be well-socialized?

3. Test his temperament. Toss a ball or play with a rope toy and see how he responds. Then ask him to sit. Can he control himself, or does he become overly excited? What level of training does he appear to have? Is he very responsive, or does he ignore you completely?

Multi-Dog Tip

If you already have a dog or two at home, introduce your new Dobe to your resident dogs in a neutral place. Ask someone to bring your dogs to a neighborhood park and meet you there. Don't force the dogs to greet each other; instead just take them for a relaxing walk. If everything seems okay, then let them greet each other.

Adopting a dog is a long-term commitment that requires many considerations, lots of research, and time.

Talk to the shelter staff, foster volunteer, or the owner of the dog and ask what their opinion is of the dog. Ask what they like about him and what behavior or health issues they see in him. Ask some basic questions such as:

- If he was surrendered, why? If being adopted out by the owner, why?
- Where did he come from? How much of his background is known?
- How old is he?
- Is he neutered? Or, is she spayed?
- Has he been seen by a veterinarian recently? How is his health? Is he up to date on his vaccinations? What health problems does he have?
- Has he had any training? If so, what and how much?
- Has his behavior been formally evaluated by a dog trainer or behaviorist? What were the results of that evaluation?
- How does he act around children?
- Does he show problems around other dogs of the same sex? The opposite sex? With smaller dogs?
- Is he good with cats and other small animals?

Your decision as to whether to adopt this dog will be based on questions such as these, as well as other questions about things that are important to you. So take your time, and get to know the dog a bit; see if you can take him for a walk. Then, you'll be prepared to make a responsible decision.

4. Offer a good treat. Does he take it nicely, or does he try to take half your hand with it?

CHAPTER 6

DOBERMAN PINSCHER GROOMING NEEDS

Doberman Pinschers don't have extensive grooming needs. That doesn't mean grooming can be ignored, though; some grooming tasks should be performed on a regular basis. But beyond making your Dobe look and feel his best, grooming provides one of the most pleasurable bonding opportunities for you and your dog, as well as an opportunity to check him from head to tail.

BRUSHING

The Dobe's shiny, short coat is easy to keep looking great. Good nutrition is a necessary part of maintaining a healthy coat, but so is brushing. Brushing the coat on a regular basis gets rid of the dead hair that's being shed, while also stimulating the production of new skin cells and distributing oils throughout the coat to bring out that well-known glistening shine. Plus, if you keep your Dobe well brushed, there will be fewer hairs floating around the house—and any hair the brush catches is less you need to vacuum up later.

The best brush for a Dobe's coat is a soft natural or synthetic bristle brush. This brush has many bristles grouped close together to catch dead hairs as well as any dirt in the coat. You may also want to have a hound glove on hand. As the name implies, this is worn like a glove and rubbed on the coat to smooth it and catch any remaining loose short hairs. The surface on the palm was originally made of horse hair, but now several different types are available, the most commonly used having small rubber nubs that massage as well as brush. Originally used on hunting hounds (hence its name), this grooming tool works very well on short coats—and your Dobe will enjoy the sensation of being petted as he is groomed.

Don't use a brush with metal teeth or projections or hard bristles. Your Dobe doesn't have enough coat to protect his skin from this type of brush, and you could scratch or even cut him. In addition, because the hard brush will be painful, he'll grow to dislike and resent brushing.

How to Brush Your Dobe

To brush your Dobe, ask him to stand or to lie down. Either position works well; it's a personal preference for you. If you ask him to lie down, here is an easy way to brush him:

1. Sit on the floor and ask your Dobe to lie

Brushing Your Dobe on a regular basis gets rid of debris and dead hair that's being shed, while also distributing oils in the coat to bring out that well-known glistening shine.

down in front of you. Roll him over on one side.

2. Start at his head. Stroke him softly with one hand so you can close his eyes, and then brush in the direction the hair is growing. Continue all over the head, being very gentle.

3. Then move down the neck.

4. Brush in the direction that the hair grows down his neck to his shoulders, down the back to his hips, and then the back of the rear legs.

5. Coming back to his shoulders, brush the shoulders, his side, and down to the abdomen. Brush his chest, and the back of his front legs.

If the brush gets full of hair as you are brushing—and if you're a new owner you may be amazed at how much a shorthaired Dobe can shed—clean the hair out of the brush. When you've finished this side, flip your dog over so you can repeat the process on the other side. Make sure your dog is completely brushed on both sides, from top to bottom.

Grooming As a Health Check

As you brush your Dobe, pay attention to any potential problems:

1. If you find a scratch or cut, wash it with soap and water. A minor wound can be treated with antibiotic ointment. Inspect

it daily. If it doesn't appear to be healing properly, call your veterinarian.

2. If you feel a lump or bump in or under the skin, examine it. Is it new? Or, if not, has it grown? Is it hot and inflamed, or the same temperature as the surrounding skin? Again, if you're worried, give your vet a call and share what you've discovered.

3. If you find a tick, remove it. (See Chapter 8: Doberman Pinscher Health and Wellness.)

4. If you find fleas, take care of them. (See Chapter 8: Doberman Pinscher Health and Wellness.)

5. Look also for changes in the coat, spots where the hair might be thinning, hot spots, or any other potential problems.

Don't hesitate to call your veterinarian should you find a problem. She's not there just for emergencies; she's there to help you keep your dog healthy.

BATHING

Dobes are generally clean dogs. In fact, it's not unusual to see a Dobe lick his paws clean after coming inside off wet grass or dirt. Baths are generally not needed unless your dog actually gets dirty. However, if your dog does get into a mess or smells dirty, then a bath is easy enough to give.

How to Bathe Your Dobe

Dobes don't particularly enjoy a bath outdoors under the hose because it's far too cold for them. A warm bath in the shower or bathtub will be much more enjoyable. Make sure to have all your supplies ready before bringing your dog to the bath.

Use a doggy shampoo because it won't be harsh on the skin or coat (human shampoos and conditioners should not be used). Some shampoos are made specifically for certain coat colors; those made for black coats seems to make dark coats gleam, and you may want to take a look at one. There are also pet shampoos made from natural ingredients. What you use is up to you; just choose a product that's gentle on your dog's skin and coat. Conditioner is optional. You will also need cotton balls, towels, a washcloth, and something with which to rinse the shampoo out, such as a cup or spray hose attachment.

1. To begin, gather all your supplies. Have everything you need before beginning the bath. Then place a rubber mat in the tub so your dog won't slip.

2. Turn the water on until it's the correct temperature. If it's warm and comfortable to you but not hot, it'll be fine for your dog.

3. Put a cotton ball into each of your dog's ears to keep water from running into the ear canal.

4. Place your dog into the tub. Thoroughly wet his coat, starting at the head and rinsing down his body. Do this slowly, and avoid spraying water into your dog's face, which may startle and upset him. Wash his face with a washcloth at the end of the bath.

Dobe Grooming Supplies

You'll need the following basic grooming supplies for your Dobe:
- soft-bristle brush
- fine-toothed flea comb
- hound glove or chamois cloth
- doggy shampoo and conditioner
- canine toothbrush and toothpaste (or baking soda)
- ear cleaner
- nail clippers or grinder
- styptic powder
- cotton balls and swabs
- washcloth and towels
- bath mat and spray hose

Whether your Dobe's ears are cropped or uncropped, weekly grooming is necessary to keep them healthy.

5. Once the entire coat is wet, apply shampoo and lather up the coat. Again, beginning at the head, work the shampoo into your dog's coat until he's thoroughly lathered. Wash the entire dog, including the feet, between the toes, stomach, and genitals. Make sure not to get any soap in his eyes, ears, nose, or mouth. Use a wet, warm washcloth to clean his face.

6. Begin rinsing at the head and then work downward. Make sure all of the soap is completely rinsed out. Rinsing will probably take twice as long as shampooing, but rinsing thoroughly is essential. Soap left on your Dobe's coat can irritate his skin.

7. If you use conditioner, now is the time to apply it. Rub it into the coat, covering all the hair. Wait the amount of time specified by the directions, and then rinse it out.

Again, make sure it's completely rinsed out.

8. Towel dry your dog well, getting as much water out of his coat as you can. You may want to wrap your Dobe in a big, dry towel and let him cuddle up to get warm. Or, if you prefer, carefully blow dry the coat using a hand-held dryer set on a low or warm setting, *never* on hot.

EAR CARE

Cleaning your Dobe's ears on a weekly basis will not only help keep them healthy but will also enable you to spot any potential problems early—such as ear infections—before they turn into bigger problems.

How to Clean the Ears

To clean the ears, you'll need cotton balls and some canine ear cleaner. You can find this at a pet supply store or your veterinarian's clinic.

1. Dampen a few cotton balls with ear cleaner and squeeze out the excess.
2. Gently hold the ear with one hand, slightly opening the ear flap and ear canal.
3. With a dampened cotton ball in the other hand, clean inside the ear, getting all the folds. If the cotton ball gets dirty, use another dampened one.
4. Finish by using a clean cotton ball to wipe the inside of the ear clean and dry.
5. Repeat with the other ear.

If the ear has a bad smell or is red and irritated, your dog may potentially have an ear infection. Call your veterinarian for an appointment.

EYE CARE

Doberman Pinschers have lovely eyes; in fact, it is said that you can see your own soul in your Dobe's eyes. The eyes don't need regular cleaning, other than to perhaps wipe away some minor crustiness first thing in the morning.

How to Clean the Eyes

1. Using a warm, wet washcloth, wipe away any discharge that has gathered in the corners of the eye.
2. To examine the eyes, lift your dog's chin, stroke him on the head, and gently pull back the ears, which will widen and further open the eyes.
3. Inspect both eyes carefully. Healthy eyes should be clear and bright. If there is redness in the whites of the eyes or cloudiness in the pupil, call your veterinarian. Also, if there is more than just morning crustiness or if a yellow or green discharge is present, call your vet. Check the eyelids, too. They also should be clean and free of discharge.

Any apparent changes in your dog's ability to see, even if the eyes look fine, should be reported to your vet immediately.

FOOT CARE

Basic foot care is important in maintaining healthy feet. Inspect your Dobe's paws, pads first. The pads on his feet, which are like the soles of your own feet, need to be kept in good condition. If you notice cracks or cuts, take action because they can eventually become deep and infected. After washing them with warm water, rub them with petroleum jelly or lanolin. Next, inspect the toes and toenails for injuries, treating any problems you may find.

Nail care is another essential part of foot care because growing nails require regular maintenance. Healthy Dobes should have their nails trimmed once a week. Nails that grow too long can deform the foot and cause pain. Plus, long nails are more easily torn when the dog

---

Multi-Dog Tip

When grooming multiple dogs— whether it's brushing, bathing, or cleaning ears or teeth—use your training skills so that you can work on one dog and the others don't interfere. Have one dog with you for grooming, and ask the others to lie down and stay until it's their turn.

Want to Know More?

For more information on eye and ear problems, see Chapter 8: Doberman Pinscher Health and Wellness.

Your Dobe will need to have his nails trimmed on a regular basis.

is running, playing, or working. Dobes ideally have square, boxy toes, rather than sloping ones. The feet are often referred to as "catlike." Because of the shape of the feet, there is a tendency for the nails to grow and not be worn off by normal activity. So it is very important to keep nails trimmed and short at all times.

Nail trimming seems to be one of the hardest grooming chores that dog owners face, but it really doesn't need to be. Perhaps it's because a lot of owners are concerned that they may hurt their dogs by doing it incorrectly. Also, most Dobes have black nails, which makes it difficult to see the quick (the living part of the

nail), so people don't know where and how far to trim. But, as you'll see, there is a trick to it that will make it much easier.

How to Trim the Nails

If you're using nail trimmers, please use heavy, scissors-type clippers. They work best on adult Dobe nails.

1. Sit on the floor, and have your Dobe lie down in front of you.
2. Take one paw in your hand, and separate one toe from the others with your finger.
3. Looking at the nail, you'll see that the top curves downward smoothly. But if you look

underneath the nail, you can see it curves downward at the tip. And, toward the paw, the under part of the nail is flat. Do not cut into the flat part of the nail because it will be painful and it will bleed, as this is where the quick is located.

4. So, with one hand holding the toe and the other holding the nail clippers, trim the outer curved part of the nail.

5. If you do cut the quick and your dog cries, don't worry. You haven't done any lasting harm. If the nail is bleeding, just touch it with some styptic powder or scrape it along a bar of soap. Give the nail time to clot. Rub your dog's tummy in the meantime, and he'll forget all about it.

More and more dog owners are using a nail grinder to trim nails rather than cutting them because it's easier and there's less chance of hitting the quick. A grinder also smoothes rough edges off the nails. Several types of grinders are available specifically for dog toenails. All of them will work for Dobes, so just choose one that's comfortable for your hands.

If you decide to use a nail grinder, get your Dobe used to it first because the noise of the motor and the vibration can worry some dogs.

1. Begin by turning the grinder on. Give your dog a treat, praise him, and then turn it off. Repeat this several times, and then do it again the next day.

2. Next, turn on the grinder, touch the handle (which vibrates) to your dog's paw, and pop a treat in his mouth. Praise him and move the handle away from his paw. Repeat several times, and then do this again the next day.

3. Next, following the directions for the grinder, touch it to your dog's nail. Praise him for being brave, grind a tiny bit, and then move it away. Praise your dog and give

By the Numbers

Most Dobes are born with five toenails on each front paw. There is one nail at the end of each of the four toes, and then one higher up on the inside of the ankle, called a *dewclaw*. There are four toenails on each back paw, one on each of the four toes. Some dogs may be born with a dewclaw on the rear legs as well. However, this isn't as common in Dobes as in some other breeds. Nevertheless, many breeders will remove the dewclaws when the puppy is 3 to 5 days old.

him a treat. Then repeat until one nail is done.

4. Gradually continue the introduction to the nail grinder, doing one nail and then one paw at a time.

When your dog is used to this process, you will be able to do all four paws in a short period of time. That's another reason why so many dog owners really enjoy using the grinder.

However, if your dog is new to having his nails trimmed, do one paw and give him a break. Come back later and do another paw. By keeping the sessions short, he'll be less stressed the next time you try to do them.

If you feel uncomfortable doing this, or if you would like to get instructions, your groomer, breeder, or veterinarian will show you how to properly trim your Dobe's nails. You can also always opt to have them trimmed by your groomer.

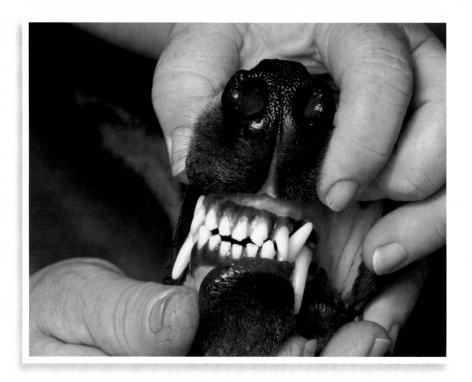

Inspect and clean your Dobe's teeth as part of his regular grooming routine.

DENTAL CARE

Although dogs aren't as prone to cavities as people are, canine gum disease is far too common. In fact, some statistics show that more than 80 percent of all dogs over the age of 3 years have gum disease, broken or cracked teeth, and various other oral health issues. Poor mouth care can lead to health problems in other parts of the body as well, especially when bacteria from the mouth enters the bloodstream, which may lead to chronic inflammation and heart problems.

How to Brush the Teeth

To care for your Dobe's teeth, you'll need either a toothbrush made for dogs or a child's toothbrush. Personally, I use a child's toothbrush with a battery that powers a spinning head. I think it provides just a little more cleaning power. Not all dogs may be comfortable with this. If this sensation makes your dog nervous, stick to a small hand-powered toothbrush.

You will also need toothpaste made for dogs or some baking soda. Do not use toothpaste made for humans because it can make your dog sick. If you use baking soda, add a tiny bit of water to about a teaspoon (5 ml) of baking soda to make a paste.

1. With all supplies gathered next to you, sit with a towel draped over your lap. Have your Dobe sit facing you, so that his head is over the towel.

2. First, let your Dobe sniff the toothbrush. Then, lift one of his lips and touch the toothbrush to his teeth. If he jerks his head

One of the guiding rules of dog training is: "Reward those behaviors that you want to happen again." Although you may not think of teaching your dog to accept a toothbrush as part of dog training, it is. You are teaching him to calmly accept this form of handling. So, to reinforce good behavior during dental care, use praise and petting as rewards when your dog is cooperating with you.

him what a brave dog he is. Then bring him back and do a little more.

Very gradually, over several sessions, increase the time that you brush his teeth. Brush in different parts of the mouth, and don't forget to brush both the front and back sides of the teeth.

If your dog has a lot of tarter on his teeth, his gums are red and sore, or if you see blood when you brush his teeth, take him to the veterinarian. He may decide to do a complete dental cleaning with your dog under anesthesia. Once this is done, you can more easily maintain those nice clean and healthy teeth.

Along with regular brushing, offer your dog safe and durable chews and toys. Many are designed to promote good dental hygiene.

away, just talk to him calmly, then let him sniff it and touch his teeth with it again.

3. Next, place a small amount of toothpaste on your finger, and let your dog sniff it or lick it off.

4. Reapply some toothpaste on your finger, gently lift your dog's lip, and rub one of his teeth for a second or two.

5. Next, spread some toothpaste on the toothbrush and let your dog lick it off.

6. When your dog is comfortable with this, reapply more toothpaste and begin brushing a few teeth. Talk gently to him as you're brushing.

7. After brushing for 15 seconds or so, stop, praise him, and let him move around. Tell

HOW TO FIND A PROFESSIONAL GROOMER

Doberman Pinschers don't need the services of a professional groomer for haircuts, but you might want to have someone else bathe your dog and trim his toenails. To find a professional groomer, start by talking to your dog-owning neighbors to see who they recommend. Then call your veterinarian and find out who she recommends. If a name keeps coming up, stop in and visit the grooming shop. Is it clean? Are the dogs reasonably quiet? Do they seem comfortable with the groomers? What are the prices? If you think the facility meets your needs, then ask if they are willing to take Doberman Pinschers and schedule an appointment.

CHAPTER 7

DOBERMAN PINSCHER NUTRITIONAL NEEDS

Food is life. That may seem simplistic but it's true. Without food, people wouldn't survive and neither would your Doberman Pinscher. Food provides nutrients that help the body function properly, and it creates energy needed for daily activities. But food alone isn't necessarily the key to good health; what's most important is providing your Dobe with a nutritious diet made from the best ingredients possible—whether that diet consists of a commercial food or a home-prepared food, or a combination of both.

THE IMPORTANCE OF GOOD NUTRITION

Foods directly affect an animal's health. Because you are responsible for feeding your dog, it is your job to ensure that he receives complete and balanced servings of carbohydrates, fats, proteins, vitamins, minerals, and water every day. This means giving him a healthy meal based on appropriate canine nutrition. Although there are similarities, your dog's nutritional needs are different from yours.

Dogs Are Carnivores

Dogs are carnivores; they are designed to eat meat. If you look at your Doberman Pinscher's head, you can see that nature has designed it for this purpose; the jaws are strong, and the lower jaw has large teeth and is anchored to the skull with powerful muscles. This is the head of a meat eater.

To make things just a little more complicated, canines—both wild and domestic—can be omnivores when necessity demands it. This means that, although the preferred food is meat, canines will eat fallen fruits or dig up tubers if meat isn't available. The ability to eat a variety of foods is actually an excellent survival skill. Many animals who don't have this ability will often starve to death when faced with a shortage of their primary foods. But canines, having the ability to eat meats and plants, can survive.

Doberman Pinscher owners want their dogs to thrive, however, not just to survive. To thrive, a dog must have all of the nutrients his body needs in a form that can be eaten and metabolized in an efficient and usable manner. Therefore, to provide the healthiest diet possible, it's important to understand all the components of optimum canine nutrition.

THE BUILDING BLOCKS OF NUTRITION

Many elements comprise a proper canine diet, all of which are essential to your dog's overall well-being and longevity.

Proteins, Amino Acids, and Enzymes

Subtract water from a body and the majority of what is left is made up of proteins. Muscles, skin, blood, hair, nails, and all of the internal organs are made up of proteins. Proteins are needed for building antibodies to fight disease, for hormone production, and for many other processes in the body. To say that proteins are an important building block of nutrition is a huge understatement; proteins are necessary for life.

Proteins are made up of a variety of amino acids and come in different forms. When proteins are consumed, they are broken down into individual amino acids or into peptides, which are groups of amino acids. The amino acids are then absorbed into the bloodstream, where they are used by the body.

Dogs can synthesize twelve of the twenty-two amino acids within the body. These are called *nonessential amino acids* because they do not need to be present in the food the dog eats. The remaining ten amino acids are called *essential amino acids* because the dog needs to consume these daily to prevent a protein deficiency.

The Association of American Feed Control

A well-balanced, nutritious diet will help your dog look and feel his best.

Your Dobe's diet should contain the proper amount of proteins, fats, vitamins, minerals, and other essential nutrients.

Officials (AAFCO), the regulatory organization for animal foods, states that the following are essential amino acids for dogs that should be provided by the foods they consume:

- arginine
- histidine
- isoleucine
- leucine
- lysine
- methionine-cystine
- phenylalanine-tyrosine
- tryptophan
- valine

Proteins also contain enzymes. These are catalysts involved in a variety of functions within the body. Enzymes are needed for healing, cell functions, brain functions, and digestion.

The quality of the source of the protein will directly affect how digestible it is for your Doberman Pinscher. Meats, fish, and eggs are all good sources of protein and are very digestible. Plants, such as beans, peas, grains, and potatoes, are also a source of some proteins. However, dogs don't metabolize plant-derived proteins nearly as well as they do meat proteins. Plus, if your Dobe has any food allergies to cereal grains, he will react badly to them.

Carbohydrates

The science of carbohydrates is a complicated one. To simplify it, carbohydrates are sugars and starches found in vegetable matter. Common sources in dog foods are corn, rice, wheat, sorghum, millet, barley, and oats. Carbohydrates are broken down by the body into glucose that is then used as fuel for energy and for a variety of bodily functions. Carbohydrates also provide fiber, which is vital for proper bowel function.

Fats and Fatty Acids

Fats are an important part of your Doberman's diet. They provide him with the most concentrated food energy in his diet. They are also necessary for the absorption of fat-soluble vitamins, for hormonal processes, and for maintaining a healthy skin and coat.

There are three essential fatty acids: omega-3, omega-6, and arachidonic acid. Omega-3 fatty acids can be found in fish such as salmon, mackerel, herring, and halibut, as well as in flaxseeds and walnuts. Omega-6 fatty acids are found in safflower, sunflower, evening primrose oils, and chicken fat. Arachidonic acids are also found in fish and fish oils.

Although too much fat can lead to obesity, that doesn't mean they should be severely curtailed from the diet either. Wendy Volhard and Kerry Brown, DVM, authors of *Holistic Guide for a Healthy Dog* say, "Moderation is the key. The diet needs to have some fat but not too much. Anything between 15 and 18 percent of the diet is okay." Hard-working Dobes, such as those training and competing in vigorous sports, may need slightly more fat.

Minerals

Minerals play a role in almost every function in the body. They work in conjunction with other minerals, vitamins, and enzymes to produce their effects. They aid in the formation of bones and cartilage, the functioning of muscles and nerves, the production of hormones, the oxygenation of blood, and more. Formed in the earth, they find their way into the body via consumed meats or plants that drew the minerals up from the soil.

The following are essential minerals needed in your dog's diet:

• **Calcium and phosphorus:** Calcium is one of the most important minerals your dog can consume. Without calcium, he could not live. It is important for healthy bones and teeth, for muscle and nerve function, healthy blood, and for maintaining correct hormone levels. Calcium is also a coenzyme for many chemical processes in the body. It is found in dairy products,

By the Numbers

A Dobe's nutritional needs stabilize between one and two years of age. At one year of age, he has reached his mature height but will continue to develop for about another year. Transition to an adult dog food between 10 and 12 months of age, and feed meals twice a day. While adult dogs can certainly obtain all the vitamins, nutrients, and calories they need from one feeding per day, there are advantages to feeding twice per day. Eating smaller meals is healthier, helps prevent bloat, and stimulates better elimination patterns.

Fats and fatty acids, which can be derived from certain fish, provide your dog with the most concentrated food energy in his diet.

including cheese, and many dark green vegetables. Phosphorus works with calcium, and one wouldn't be effective without the other; they are needed in a particular ratio to one another. Phosphorus is found in meats and fish.

- **Copper**: Copper pairs with iron in the body to make sure that there is adequate blood cell production. Good sources include meats, including liver, and water that flows through copper pipes. Excess copper is stored in the liver and can damage that organ. Dobermans have a tendency to resist proper assimilation of copper. Be sure to check the label on dog food products to determine that the quantity of copper and other heavy metals is appropriate.
- **Iodine**: Iodine is important for correct thyroid functioning. It can be obtained from fish, liver, and kelp.

- **Iron**: Iron, along with copper, works to maintain adequate red blood cell production. It is also important for proper muscle function. Iron is found in meats, vegetables, and whole grains.
- **Magnesium:** Magnesium works with enzymes to metabolize carbohydrates. It's also important for the functioning of nerves and muscles. It is found in dairy products, vegetables, and whole grains.
- **Manganese**: Manganese works with enzymes to maintain the health of bones and connective tissues. Along with enzymes, it also works to maintain glucose levels within the body. It is found in vegetables and whole grains.
- **Selenium:** Selenium is an antioxidant that, along with fatty acids, supports the immune system. It is found in fish, meats, and whole grains.

Many of the vitamins essential to your dog's diet can be found in meats.

• **Zinc**: This vitally important mineral is a coenzyme for more than 25 different processes during digestion. It also supports the immune system, is important for healthy skin and hair, and aids in promoting healing. It can be found in meats and egg yolks.

Vitamins

Vitamins are organic compounds that perform essential bodily functions. They help the body absorb nutrients and minerals, regulate metabolism, fight disease, and function and grow normally. Dogs derive vitamins from plant- and animal-based foods. There are two types of vitamins: fat soluble (which require fats to be metabolized by the body) and water soluble (which require water to be metabolized by the body). If excess fat-soluble vitamins are consumed, they will be stored in the body's fat cells until needed. Because of this, extreme supplementation can have bad consequences, even to the point of toxicity. On the other hand, excess water-soluble vitamins are excreted from the body in urine and so do not reach toxic levels in the body.

The following are essential vitamins needed in your dog's diet:

• **Vitamin A:** Vitamin A is essential for eye health; it is important for both retinal health and for good night vision. It also keeps mucus membranes healthy in the gastrointestinal and respiratory tracts. To add to its importance, vitamin A is a powerful antioxidant that strengthens the immune system and aids in reproduction. It is a fat-soluble vitamin, so too much can be toxic. When it's obtained from whole food sources, such as egg yolks, fish, and liver, toxicity is rare.

• **Vitamin B_1/Thiamine:** This water-soluble vitamin aids in nerve cell function. Dogs who lack this vitamin generally have difficulty learning. Dogs can easily get enough vitamin B_1 from wheat germ, brewer's yeast, or blackstrap molasses.

• **Vitamin B_2/Riboflavin:** B_2 is a water-soluble vitamin found in meat and whole cereal grains. It helps the body metabolize proteins, carbohydrates, and fats. It's also vital for good vision.

• **Vitamin B_3/Niacin:** B_3 is also a water-soluble vitamin that aids in the metabolism of food. It also aids the blood and circulatory system. It is found in meats, especially liver, and in legumes. The amino acid tryptophan produces niacin within the body.

• **Vitamin B_5/Pantothenic acid:** B_5 is a water-soluble vitamin found in meats and fish. It is important for the proper functioning of the adrenal glands. It also aids in the conversion of food into energy and assists in the metabolism of other vitamins.

- **Vitamin B$_6$/Pyridoxine**: Another water-soluble vitamin, B$_6$ can be found in meats, especially liver. It is important for proper nervous system functioning, and a lack of it can lead to depression. It also aids in red blood cell production.

- **Vitamin B$_9$/Folic acid**: This B-complex water-soluble vitamin is found in many foods, but liver and spinach are good sources. It helps in the manufacture of red blood cells and helps prevent birth defects.

- **Vitamin B$_{12}$/Cyanocobalamin**: A multi-use, water-soluble vitamin, B$_{12}$ is found in liver, kidney, eggs, and cheese. It works with several amino acids to maintain a healthy nervous system, a healthy heart, and good mental health.

- **Vitamin C/Ascorbic acid**: This water-soluble vitamin is produced by your Dobe's body; however, in times of stress, he may not produce enough for his body's needs. There is no recommended amount for dogs, but when fed from whole foods, such as fruits and dark green vegetables, side effects are rare. When given as a supplement, too much vitamin C will cause diarrhea. The ascorbic acid part of this vitamin is often used as a preservative in foods.

- **Vitamin D**: The sunshine vitamin, as it's often called, vitamin D is a fat-soluble vitamin. It maintains healthy bones and teeth, assists in the absorption of calcium and phosphorus, and works with the immune, thyroid, and circulatory systems. Egg yolks are a good source. Over-supplementation (more than 10,000 international units per kilogram of food) can be toxic.

- **Vitamin E**: This fat-soluble vitamin can be found in eggs, fish, and liver. Whole food sources are more effective and more easily metabolized than are supplements. Vitamin E is a powerful antioxidant. It is also important for healthy nerves, assists the muscles during movement, aids the circulatory system, and maintains healthy skin and hair. Toxicity is rarely a problem, especially if the vitamin is obtained from whole foods.

- **Vitamin K**: Vitamin K is a fat-soluble vitamin. It is important for proper functioning of the circulatory system and is especially important for blood clotting. (It is often recommended for Dobes with clotting disorders.) It also assists in maintaining healthy bones and teeth. It is found in dark green vegetables. Vitamin K is best obtained through natural sources; problems have been reported with synthetic versions.

Want to Know More?

For more information on special diets for seniors, see Chapter 13: Care of Your Doberman Pinscher Senior.

Water

All of your dog's bodily functions require water. It is needed for the circulatory system to function, for respiratory processes, and for digestion. It is needed to flush wastes from the body and for temperature regulation. Just about everything that happens within your Dobe's body requires water.

It's almost impossible to determine how much water your Doberman Pinscher needs on a daily basis. Each dog's needs will vary according to his size, health, age, activity level, and other factors. Just make sure there is always fresh, clean water available every day.

CHOOSING THE RIGHT DIET AND FOOD TYPE

For thousands of years, the ancestors of today's dogs ate what their people ate. That included leftover meats, scraps from butchering an animal, eggs, milk, cheese, and other dairy products, leftover fruits, vegetables, and cooked grains. My paternal grandparents lived in the Midwest and always had dogs and cats on the farm. They were given the same foods the family ate, and they thrived. Although this diet wasn't researched as to its nutritional completeness, the variety of foods offered to the dogs probably helped create a reasonably balanced diet, just as it does for people.

Commercial Dog-Food Categories

James Spratt created the first bone-shaped biscuit that was commercially available for dogs, which he introduced in 1890. It was made from wheat, vegetables, beet roots, and beef blood. The next commercially available product was the Milk Bone, created by F. H. Bennett in 1907, and, as all dog owners know, it is still available today. Commercial dog foods became popular after World War II, when convenience was their biggest selling point. Salesmen assured the dog-owning public and veterinarians that these foods were balanced, nutritionally complete, and much better for dogs than the leftover foods that had been previously fed. Unfortunately, though, commercial dog foods vary tremendously in quality.

Generic and Grocery Store Brands

These foods are usually high in cereal grains, especially corn and wheat. The meat ingredients are usually by-products or by-product meals. They contain artificial colors and flavorings, as well as synthetic vitamins and minerals. These foods are designed to be sold at a low price so that many people can afford them.

Premium Foods

These foods are normally not sold in grocery stores but will be found in pet stores and veterinary clinics. The price is generally higher,

Dry foods provide the most popular and diverse meal base for dogs.

but quality is usually higher as well. The foods in this classification will vary, from those with excellent ingredients to those still containing some questionable ingredients.

Super-Premium Foods

The differences between premium foods and super-premium foods are generally the price, the quality of the ingredients, and the choice of ingredients. Super-premium foods often also offer unique ingredients such as bison, duck, or other less commonly available meats.

Natural or Holistic Foods

The guidelines for calling a pet food *natural* or *holistic* are fuzzy. Unfortunately, many consumers buy these foods assuming that the same guidelines for human foods apply to pet foods, but that's not true. Although these foods are not supposed to contain artificial colorings, preservatives, or flavorings, as well as no synthetic vitamins or minerals, that's not always the case. A natural or holistic pet food may be no more natural than any other premium or super-premium food.

Organic Foods

The US Department of Agriculture (USDA) has said, "Pet food regulations are a better fit under the livestock section of the organic rules. Ingredients and additives permitted in pet foods are regulated similarly to livestock feed." That means for a pet food to label itself, "made with organic ingredients" it must be made with a minimum of 70 percent organic ingredients. To be labeled "organic," it must contain 95 percent organic ingredients.

Types of Commercial Foods

To make things more confusing, there are even more choices to consider when selecting what foods to feed your dog. In years past, there

Probiotics

The large intestine, when healthy, contains a flourishing colony of bacteria. Along with aiding in digestion, these beneficial bacteria keep dangerous organisms from taking over the digestive tract, and keep it in balance. However, when something upsets that balance—illness, a poor diet, or a course of antibiotics—then digestion can be affected. Diarrhea is often the first sign that something is wrong.

Probiotics are found in some foods, such as yogurt, and can aid in maintaining or reestablishing those beneficial bacteria. The label on the container should indicate that the yogurt contains *live active cultures*.

were two different types of foods—dry kibble and canned food. Today, there are numerous options on the menu.

Choosing the right commercial food for your Doberman Pinscher can be difficult. Although these foods are convenient, and many companies have large research departments formulating nutritionally balanced recipes for them, the far too common recalls of tainted products can make owners wary. However, there are good, nutritious commercial foods available. Just read the product labels, choose a food with quality ingredients, and watch your dog to make sure he's doing well on the food.

Dry Foods

Dry foods are formed into small dry nuggets and stored in a bag. Fed as-is, these foods can vary tremendously in quality, from less nutritious cereal-grain–based foods to significantly better quality meat-based foods.

Special diets are important to consider if your dog has unique nutritional needs. For example, Dobes who are very active or competing regularly may need higher levels of protein and fat to keep up their weight and energy levels.

Canned Foods

Canned foods are meat-based foods that may be all meat or may be a recipe that includes meats and vegetables. Although, in the past, these foods were all stored in metal cans, some are now sold in foil packages or in single-serving containers.

Semi-Moist Foods

Semi-moist foods were very popular a few years ago because dogs really like to eat them. A huge part of the appeal, unfortunately, is that most of these foods tend to be very high in sugar, salt, and artificial flavors. These can be served as-is.

Frozen Foods

Frozen foods have just been introduced in the past decade because stores were more willing to add a freezer to their pet food section. These products can be frozen cooked recipes or frozen raw foods. These need to be thawed prior to serving.

Dehydrated Foods

Dehydrated foods are generally raw food diets that have been dehydrated to reduce the chance of bacterial contamination. Consumers must add water to rehydrate the foods before serving.

HOMEMADE DIETS

Many dog owners have made the choice not to feed commercial dog foods. Sometimes they make that decision after hearing of too many reports of tainted pet foods, but other times they do so because their dog has a health problem and requires a special diet. Although our dogs ate our leftovers for thousands of years, feeding your dog only leftovers doesn't necessarily mean he's going to be eating a good diet. After all, we aren't necessarily always eating a nutritionally complete diet either.

There are two basic types of homemade diets: raw and cooked. Both have their benefits and drawbacks.

Raw Foods

Proponents of raw food diets say that this is the most natural way for dogs to eat because they evolved hunting and eating raw foods. In addition, they say that some of the ingredients in commercial dog foods—especially cereal grains like wheat and rice—aren't healthy and can sometimes cause allergies.

A good raw food diet is all about the quality of its ingredients. The meat we buy in the grocery store generally comes from animals that were housed in feedlots prior to slaughter. The animals may have been given growth hormones, antibiotics, and who knows what else. The cleanliness of the slaughterhouse isn't to be imagined. When the labels on meat packaging tell us that the meat must be well cooked for safety, you know that meat shouldn't be eaten raw.

However, you can find and purchase quality, clean meats for your dog, such as from a butcher in your area. Ask if he buys local animals because they will likely be well cared for. Ask if he does the butchering himself at his facility. Once you begin feeding, you'll know how much meat you'll need, and he can make sure he has it available for you.

Clean, fresh vegetables and fruits are also an important part of your dog's raw food diet. These can usually be found at local farmers' markets or organic farms. Don't be afraid to ask if the plants have been sprayed with anything and what chemicals were used on the farm.

Homemade Foods

The quality of a homemade diet is also dependent upon the variety, freshness, and cleanliness of the ingredients. Cooking the meats can remove any fear of bacterial contamination. Vegetables must be fresh and

Along with meats, clean, fresh vegetables and fruits are also an important part of your dog's raw food diet.

Training Tidbit

Training treats should be large enough to get your Dobe's attention and serve as a reward, yet small enough so that a training session doesn't upset the nutritional quality of his meals and the amount of food he eats daily. Everything he eats adds up! For most Dobes, treats cut to the size of your finger nail should work fine.

can be lightly steamed, just to make them a little more digestible, but some may also be served raw. And, of course, fruits are served raw.

Nutritional Balance

With any homemade diet—raw or cooked— the key to good nutrition is to make sure the foundation of the diet is protein, which can be provided with beef, chicken, turkey, bison, venison, elk, rabbit, etc. Other animal proteins such as chicken eggs, duck eggs, goose eggs, aged cheeses, yogurt, and goat's milk (no cow's milk) are also good sources. Carbohydrates— fruits and vegetables— are also an important part of a healthy, complete diet.

To make sure your Dobe is getting all the nutrition he needs from his food, vary the ingredients. Feed chicken one day, and beef the next. Vary the other ingredients, too.

Talk to your veterinarian about plans you may have to feed any kind of a homemade diet, raw or cooked, as formulating this diet takes knowledge. A poor homemade diet could drastically affect your dog's health. Many veterinarians recommend that dogs fed a homemade diet be given a multivitamin and

mineral supplement to help ensure they don't suffer any nutritional deficiencies.

SPECIAL NUTRITIONAL NEEDS

No one food and no one diet is right for every Doberman Pinscher. Every dog is unique and will have his own nutritional needs, especially under stressful circumstances.

Doberman Pinschers who are training and working hard, or competing regularly, may need a special diet that provides higher levels of protein and fat to keep up their weight and energy levels. If your dog is training and competing in agility or Schutzhund, and you find that he runs out of steam or is losing weight, then you may want to boost his protein and fat intake slightly.

A Dobe in the later stages of pregnancy may seem like she can never get enough to eat, yet she can't eat much, especially if she's carrying a large litter, because there just isn't room for much food. A pregnant female will need several small meals throughout the day. Once her litter is born, she will need to continue those extra meals so that she can produce enough milk for her growing puppies. Monitoring her weight is also a good idea because many Dobe moms will lose weight while nursing.

Many health problems will also create a need for a special diet, and your veterinarian will provide guidance for you. Several dog food manufacturers produce special diets for everything from weight loss to serious health conditions like diabetes and kidney problems. As with other dog foods, read product labels carefully and talk to your veterinarian before feeding them to your Dobe.

SUPPLEMENTS

A supplement is anything that is added to

your Dobe's normal diet to optimize his nutritional intake. It can be a whole food such as yogurt, or it can be a vitamin or mineral tablet. Again, most veterinarians suggest that dogs fed homemade foods, either raw or cooked, be given a multivitamin and mineral supplement. However, if a premium or super-premium commercial dog food is being fed, a vitamin is not normally needed as these are generally required to be well-balanced and nutritionally complete.

Many nutritional experts recommend supplements made from whole foods rather than synthetic components because whole foods are metabolized more easily by the body. Oversupplementation can be potentially harmful, especially with the fat-soluble vitamins, so always check with your vet before adding any supplement to your Dobe's diet.

TREATS AND BONES

Although a good quality food is the most important thing your Dobe should eat, he will also need good quality treats, especially during training. After all, one of the best rewards for your dog during training—second only to attention from you—is a tasty treat.

Treats

Some commercial dog treats tend to be high in sugar or salt, which makes them tasty and appealing to your dog. However, just as with people, too much salt and sugar is not healthy for your Dobe. So, as with dog foods, read the labels on the treat packaging. If you opt for commercial treats, look for good ones like Nylabone products, which include a range of natural, sugar-, salt-, and preservative-free chews and treats that are healthy and include vitamins, minerals, and omega-3s.

You can also offer food from your refrigerator for training treats. For example, use some bits of cooked chicken or diced cheese, which are tasty and nutritious foods that your dog will enjoy.

Bones

Your Dobe will also appreciate something to chew on. Puppies, adolescents, and even adult dogs all have a need to chew; chewing is satisfying and helps keep teeth clean. Large raw beef bones are favorites for many Dobe owners, especially those who feel homemade foods are best for their dogs. Offer your Dobe sections of large bones, such as the femur, and avoid smaller bones that could be easily swallowed whole. Don't feed cooked bones; those tend to shatter, and your dog could be hurt by a jagged piece of bone if it lodges in his mouth or he swallows a piece.

Safe, durable commercial bones are available as well. Many dogs enjoy Nylabones, which come in a variety of types and flavors. If you offer these, use those sized for large dogs.

Multi-Dog Tip

When there are several dogs in the family, the dominant dog may try to push all the other dogs away from their food bowls so he can have all the food for himself. Or, a dog may guard the bowls, growling at anyone who comes close. Any dog who consistently creates problems during mealtimes should be fed in his crate. By removing him, the other dogs can eat in peace, and, more importantly, receive the nutrition they need to stay healthy.

Although Doberman Pinschers aren't as prone to obesity as many other breeds, even a Dobe can get fat if overfed and not provided with sufficient exercise.

Many dog owners purchase bully sticks, dried beef sticks, cow ears, and other natural animal parts as chew toys. These are usually fine; just supervise your dog while he's eating them just in case there is a problem. Needless to say, your dog should always be supervised when he is given chews and toys.

HOW MUCH TO FEED

The amount you feed your Dobe will vary. Every commercial food provides feeding guidelines on the label. However, this is just a recommendation. Each Doberman Pinscher will have different needs according to his individual metabolism, state of health, activity levels, etc. Also, things can happen throughout the day that will increase or

decrease your dog's dietary needs. Consult your vet about adequate amounts of food for each life stage.

Free Feeding and Obesity

Don't free-feed your Dobe. Not only can he eat an entire day's worth of food at one time, but should he become sick, one of the first questions the veterinarian will ask is, "Did your dog eat normally today?" If you free-feed, it's difficult to answer that question. Also, obesity is a growing problem (no pun intended); far too many dogs eat more than they need without getting enough exercise to burn off the excess calories. Although Doberman Pinschers aren't as prone to obesity as many other breeds, even a Dobe can get fat. If food amounts are supervised, treats are given wisely, and exercise is provided every day, obesity can be prevented.

Keep an eye on your Dobe, and you'll be able to tell if you're feeding the right amount. He should have a waistline between his ribs and hips, and you should also be able to feel his ribs without them appearing too prominent. You'll also know your dog is eating right if his eyes are bright, his is coat shiny, and he has enough energy for work and play.

WHEN AND WHERE TO FEED

It's recommended that adult dogs be fed two small meals per day—morning and evening—rather than one large one. In addition to preventing bloat, feeding twice per day has other benefits. Feeding stimulates bowel movements, which can help reduce the chance of household accidents. Also, a hungry, bored dog is more prone to get into trouble when left to his own devices.

Feed your Dobe in a place that isn't too busy. You may put his bowl in a corner of the kitchen, where people are not always walking past, or in another room. Dobes like to be with their people, and if you feed him away from everyone, he may leave his food uneaten just to be with you. Many dog owners find that feeding a Dobe in his crate works well for them. After all, you want your dog to like his crate and to look at it as a place of security,

so what better way to accomplish this than to have him associate it with mealtime!

Preventing Bloat

Doberman Pinschers, as a breed, can be prone to bloat. This is a situation in which gases build up in the stomach, causing the dog's abdomen to become distended. Quick veterinary care can be life saving; your vet will try to relieve the gas and may need to treat your Dobe for shock. However, if the stomach turns or twists on itself (because of the distention), this can become a life-threatening emergency. Surgery is needed to untwist the stomach and usually to permanently affix it to the abdominal wall so that it won't twist again in the future.

Avoid cheaper, high-fiber foods that release gases during metabolism. An easy test for this is to place some of your dog's food in a small bowl and add warm water. If you see the release of small gas bubbles as the food absorbs the water, change foods. Also don't allow your dog to engage in strenuous exercise for at least an hour after eating or within 30 minutes of exercising as this has also been found to lead to bloating. If you're feeding a dry kibble food, limit your dog's water intake for a couple of hours after eating as this can cause the food to swell, especially if you're feeding a food high in cereal grains. Several small drinks of water are better than one large drink.

CHAPTER 8

DOBERMAN PINSCHER HEALTH AND WELLNESS

Caring for your Doberman Pinscher's health can at times be challenging. Not only can your dog not speak, but dogs often hide symptoms of illness or injury simply because that is nature's way; a hurt or sick animal is vulnerable. Therefore, it's important to observe your dog and recognize signs he may give you that things aren't just right. Luckily, Dobes aren't always the most stoic of dogs—many are quite upfront when they feel bad.

ANNUAL EXAM

One of the more important things you can do for your dog is to schedule a complete veterinary examination each year. Although it may seem like a waste of money to take a healthy dog in for an annual checkup, it really isn't. You see your dog every day and get used to what he looks like, smells like, and how he acts. However, someone who doesn't see your dog often may pick up on things you miss.

- At each exam, the vet will take your Dobe's temperature and weigh him. Because this information is recorded at each visit, she can take note of both good and questionable changes.
- She will take a look at your dog's teeth to check for tarter buildup, inflammation, or breakage.
- She will check the eyes and the ears.
- She will listen to your dog's heart and lungs.
- She will move each leg, stretching it slightly, and then folding it so that she can feel any hesitation or clicking in the joints. She will also want to see what the range of motion is so she can catch any potential problems early.
- She will palpate the abdomen, feeling for masses or anything that feels wrong. While doing this, she'll also be watching your dog's face for flinching or other signs of discomfort.
- The vet will also run her hands over your dog's entire body, feeling for any lumps or bumps, or again, any other signs of problems.

The annual exam is also a good time to discuss any questions you may have about your dog's care with your veterinarian. Do you have any questions about new flea control products? Are you concerned about Lyme disease in your area? Do you need information about proper canine nutrition?

At the same time, the veterinarian may want to discuss certain issues with you. Perhaps your

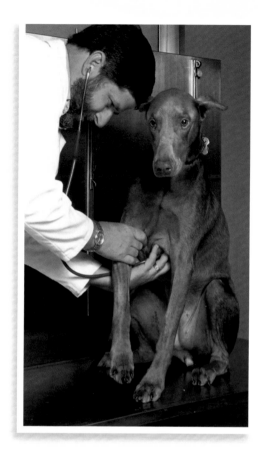

Annual veterinary checkups are essential if you want your dog to stay healthy throughout his life.

If your veterinarian suggests this, please consider it.

PESKY PARASITES

Parasites are organisms that live inside or outside an organism of a different species, called the *host*, feeding on its body in order to survive. Some external parasites, like fleas and ticks, can be found on the skin or in the coat. Others, such as intestinal worms, live inside the host's body and are called, obviously, *internal parasites*. Although it would seem that parasites should live a symbiotic existence with their hosts, taking blood or bodily fluids but doing no harm, those found on dogs can, in fact, cause them a great deal of harm if left untreated.

Internal Parasites

The thought that parasites may be living inside their pet disturbs most owners. Not only does the idea that worms can be harming their dog bother them, but also the fact that they can't be easily seen or detected is worrisome.

Often, a healthy dog won't give any clues that he has parasites until his health is noticeably threatened. A poor coat, unhealthy skin, and soft stools are usually the only symptoms of intestinal parasites. Other internal parasites, such as heartworms, may cause lethargy, difficulty breathing, or coughing. The easiest way to test for internal parasites is to have a small, fresh, stool sample examined under a microscope by your veterinarian, or to have a blood sample drawn and tested. If any signs of parasites are present, testing can identify them so that an appropriate course of treatment can be prescribed.

Heartworms

Heartworms are a type of internal parasite that lives in your dog's heart. They are transmitted

dog needs his teeth cleaned, or he's gained too much weight. She may also want to talk about vaccinations or heartworm preventives.

Many veterinarians recommend a blood panel be run at some point during early adulthood, usually between 4 and 6 years of age. This can serve as a baseline for any future testing done on your dog. For example, if blood is drawn and tested on a healthy 4-year-old Dobe and the results are kept in his records, future blood work can then be compared to the earlier baseline test results.

into the body by mosquitoes, which serve as intermediary hosts. When a mosquito draws blood from a dog already infested with heartworms, it draws into itself heartworm larvae that are circulating in the bloodstream. Then, when the mosquito feeds on another healthy dog, the larvae, called *microfilariae*, are transferred to that dog's bloodstream through the bite. And the infestation cycle continues.

The microfilariae migrate to the heart, where they eventually mature into adult worms. Heartworms can grow to as long as 12 inches (30.5 cm) and continue to live in the heart, as well as in the large blood vessels around it. Symptoms include lethargy, a lack of stamina, and a soft but deep cough. As the disease progresses and the worms grow larger, the dog will lose weight, have more difficulty breathing, and coughing will worsen, sometimes to the point that the dog will lose consciousness. Eventually, the heart will begin to fail.

A blood test is necessary to accurately diagnose heartworm infestation. Preventives can be given to dogs once they've been tested and found to be free of these parasites. These preventives have made a huge difference in preventing infestation by these worms. However, preventives should never be given to a dog who hasn't been tested for heartworms, or one with a positive diagnosis. The dangers of a reaction, including anaphylactic shock, are too great.

A dog with internal parasites will show signs of decreased appetite, lethargy, irregular bowel movements, and weight loss.

External parasites can make your dog uncomfortable and potentially sick. So always check him for fleas, ticks, and mites if he's been playing outdoors.

Hookworms

Hookworms can infest both dogs and people. This parasitic worm lives in the intestinal tract. It grabs onto the tissues of the intestinal wall to feed, causing the host to lose blood. Unfortunately, the worm does this several times a day, causing blood loss each time. A dog with a severe infestation can quickly become anemic, appear sickly, and will fail to thrive. Dogs with anemia will have pale gums, lose weight, and become weak. Other symptoms of hookworm infestation include bloody stools that may be red or dark and tarry in appearance, diarrhea, loss of appetite, nausea, and vomiting.

After diagnosis, via a stool sample, your veterinarian will prescribe medication to eradicate the hookworms. Heartworm preventives will also prevent hookworm infestations. Keeping the yard clean and disposing of feces promptly is the best way to prevent an infestation.

Roundworms

Roundworms (also called ascarids) live in the intestinal tract but can migrate to the lungs, trachea, and even the eyes. Symptoms include vomiting, diarrhea, unhealthy coat, and an enlarged abdomen. It's fairly common for puppies to have roundworms. In fact, most breeders treat the whole litter as a matter of course. These parasites are not limited just to puppies, however, as adult dogs and humans can become infested with them.

Roundworm eggs are passed out of the dog (or other animal's) body via the feces, so cleanliness is the key to preventing infestation. Several heartworm treatments will also prevent roundworm infestations. Usually, if your veterinarian diagnoses roundworms via examination of a stool sample, he will select a specific medication that will eradicate them.

Tapeworms

Just as with heartworms, dogs pick up tapeworms through an intermediate host: the flea. When a dog swallows a flea that contains tapeworm larvae, he becomes infested. The larvae eventually hatch in the intestinal tract and anchor themselves to the intestinal lining to feed. Tapeworms can cause diarrhea and soft stools.

Controlling fleas on your dog, in your home, and in your yard is the key to preventing tapeworm infestation. Monthly topical flea and tick preventive medications are very effective. Also, go over your dog with a flea comb after a romp outdoors, especially in grassy or wooded areas.

Tapeworms are usually diagnosed by seeing a tapeworm segment near the anus or through examination of a stool sample for signs of tapeworm segments or eggs. If tapeworms are present, your veterinarian can prescribe one of several medications to eliminate them.

Whipworms

Whipworms live in the lower part of the intestinal tract, specifically in the cecum (where the small and large intestine meet). Dogs become infested by ingesting food, water, or dirt contaminated with whipworm eggs. When the eggs hatch and mature, the adults burrow into the intestinal wall to feed on blood and lay eggs. Whipworms will cause diarrhea, nausea, and intestinal cramping.

Because the eggs are passed out via the feces and can live in the environment for as long as 5 years, picking up feces regularly is important. Whipworms can live in human hosts as well as canine ones, so care must be used to prevent contamination.

Diagnosing whipworms can be difficult because the eggs are not always shed in the feces; sometimes several stool samples must be examined. Your veterinarian can prescribe one of several medications; however, two or three rounds of the medication is often needed. Some heartworm preventives also prevent whipworm infestations.

External Parasites

Most people, when finding an insect or spider on themselves, will brush it off with a look of horror. If an insect bites, it's going to be smacked and probably killed. This is a survival instinct attributed to the fact that so many insects harbor and pass along diseases and bacteria. Unfortunately, our Dobes need help in fending off external parasites, which are just as harmful to their health and, at the very least, will cause them great discomfort.

Fleas

Fleas are tiny insects, but they can do a great deal of harm, primarily because, where there is one flea, there are likely to be hundreds more. Fleas withdraw blood each time they bite your dog. When they bite, they also inject saliva, to which many dogs are allergic. This causes the dog to bite and scratch, chew on himself, and feel absolutely miserable.

In the past, it was necessary to use powerful insecticides on your dog to control fleas, both on him and in your home and yard. Today, however, there are systemic medications that work even better at preventing infestation without the use of toxic chemicals. These medications vary in how they work. In some, the active ingredient is contained in the subcutaneous tissues, and the flea ingests it when it bites the dog. Others are combined with heartworm preventives. Another type of flea control product is applied to the skin of the dog's back and kills fleas on contact. Talk to your veterinarian about which type will work best for your Dobe.

Mites

Mites are very small arachnids (cousins of ticks and spiders) that live in and on your dog's skin. Most of the time, mites will live symbiotically with your dog, remaining in low numbers and causing no harm. However, sometimes things get out of balance, which enables them to multiply and cause discomfort. The following are the most common types of mites affecting dogs.

Demodex Mites: Demodex mites (*Demodex canis*), when they proliferate, cause demodectic mange. This type of mange occurs most commonly in dogs under 18 months of age due to the immature immune systems of young animals. Although mild cases may resolve themselves without treatment, it's a good idea to take your Dobe in to see your vet if you notice any small hairless spots that appear to get worse, usually on the head or muzzle. Some cases can become serious and even life-threatening.

Skin scrapings will be examined under a microscope to see if demodex mites are present. If they are, a treatment regimen would consist of prescription dips or sprays and diet supplementation to improve your dog's skin and health.

Sarcoptic Mites: A proliferation of sarcoptic mites (*Sarcoptes scabiei*) causes sarcoptic mange, which is very contagious to other dogs, cats, rabbits, and people. This is a persistent and intensely itchy mange that causes red, scaly, inflamed areas on the skin. Many dogs who have it scratch themselves raw, and sores and infections can develop as a result.

Treatment, which consists of prescription dips or sprays to eradicate the mites and the itching, is always needed. Also, because sarcoptic mites are extremely contagious, it is advisable to examine all other pets in the household for possible infection as well.

Ear Mites: Ear mites (*Otodectes cynotis*), as the names conveys, infest the inner ear but can sometimes migrate to the ear flap and on rare occasions to other warm, moist parts of the body. Dark, reddish-brown debris that looks a little like coffee grounds will be visible in the ear canal, causing inflammation and itchiness that will make the dog scratch at the ear constantly. A visit to the vet is needed to diagnose ear mites (a bit of ear wax will be examined under the microscope). The ears may also need to be cleaned by the vet to remove wax and debris that harbor the mites. Medication will then be prescribed, along with a course of treatment that involves cleaning the ears on a regular basis.

Ringworm

Ringworm really isn't a worm at all—and no one seems to know why it's called a worm. Ringworm is actually a fungus, or one of several different related fungi. These are very contagious parasites that can infest people as well as dogs and other animals. They create round, ring-shaped, scaly, itchy spots.

The spores of the fungus that causes ringworm can survive in the environment for up to a year. Therefore, prevention is imperative to avoid reinfection. The dog's bedding should be sealed in a plastic bag and discarded. Anything that can be washed in bleach—toys, grooming tools, and bowls—

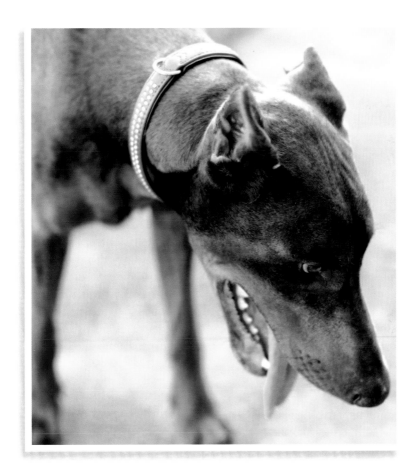

Knowing how to recognize potential health problems and how to handle them is important to your dog's overall well-being.

should be. The house should be vacuumed regularly to pick up shed hair.

Your veterinarian may prescribe a topical antifungal medication if your dog has a mild case of ringworm; however, if there are several spots, an antifungal shampoo or oral medication may be recommended.

Ticks

Ticks also feed on your dog's blood. They live on tall grasses and brush, and attach to your dog as he walks past. Once on him, a tick will bury its head in the skin, inject a bit of saliva to deaden the spot so the dog doesn't feel it, and then will continue to ingest blood until it's swollen. Ticks can pass along some significant diseases, including Lyme disease, Rocky Mountain spotted fever, tick bite paralysis, and several other serious illnesses. The easiest way to control ticks is to check your Dobe daily during the spring and fall, and to remove each tick as it's found. To do this correctly, grab the tick by the head with tweezers or forceps, and slowly pull it out of your dog's skin. After removing it, treat the wound with an antibiotic ointment. Burn the tick to kill it, or drop it in some alcohol.

POTENTIAL PROBLEMS FOR ALL DOGS

Health issues can affect every dog. Some of these can be prevented and/or treated with routine care at home, and others require veterinary care. In any case, regardless of what the health issues are, always seek veterinary advice if you have any concerns.

Allergies

Dogs and people alike can suffer from allergies. However, dogs react differently to allergies than people do. Dogs can get red eyes and a nasal discharge, but there is rarely any sneezing. Most often, dogs tend to become itchy and scratch, lick, or chew on their irritated skin to seek relief. The paws tend to be a focus of licking and chewing, as well as the base of the tail. Some dogs will have red, inflamed skin, especially on the belly, if they have a contact allergy to environmental allergens such as pollens, grasses, household chemicals, or even the carpeting in your house, to name just a few possible irritants. Food allergies can also cause similar symptoms.

Identifying an allergen can be difficult. Your veterinarian can run allergy tests to determine what the offending substances are, but diagnosing and eliminating potential causes of the allergy can take time and patience. A consultation, medication, and follow-ups with your veterinarian are usually required.

Eye Infections

Eye infections can be brought on by many different things. Dirt or sand can get into the eyes, causing irritation. Your Dobe may also come into close contact with another dog who has a contagious infection, such as conjunctivitis. Eye infections usually appear as a sometimes clear but usually yellow or green, thick discharge from the eye.

Keeping the eyes clean is important, especially if your dog is very active outdoors. If you suspect your dog has an eye disorder, he needs veterinary care because some problems can escalate rapidly and cause vision loss.

Ear Infections

Ear infections can be caused by ear mites, but also by allergies, yeast, or bacteria. For example, sometimes a dog who spends a lot of time swimming or playing in the water may have a buildup of bacteria from moisture trapped in the ear, and an infection may be the result.

Keeping the ears clean and dry is important to prevent an infection. If the ear should get hot, red, appear dirty, or have a foul odor, then veterinary care and medication are needed.

ALTERNATIVE THERAPIES

What people today call "alternative therapies" are actually the medical practices that were used for most of mankind's history. When looked at in this perspective, modern

By the Numbers

Normal vital signs for an adult Doberman are as follows:
- normal temperature is between 100° and 102.5°F (38° and 39°C)
- normal heart rate is 90–140 beats per minute
- normal respiration is 15–30 breaths per minute

medicine's introduction occurred quite recently. Also called *allopathic medicine*, modern or conventional medicine consists of a diagnosis followed by the use of drugs, surgery, and other treatments.

Veterinary care for animals and medical care for humans have often followed the same path. In many instances, procedures would be tested and developed on animals first and then offered for use in people. In others, procedures found to be beneficial for people would then be offered to the veterinary world.

Today, alternative therapies have been used successfully without modern medicine, but many are also used in conjunction with it. Many dog owners prefer to use a combination of techniques to provide the best possible treatments for their dogs.

If you choose to use one or more of these therapies, make sure you let your veterinarian know because some herbal supplements or homeopathic remedies can cause negative side effects when used at the same time as prescription drugs. In addition, since your veterinarian is your partner in your Dobe's health care, she should be fully informed so that the two of you can make the best decisions for his overall well-being.

Acupuncture

Acupuncture is a very old healing art that has its roots in ancient China. In fact, acupuncture

Acupuncture may be used as an alternative to traditional medicine to prevent disease and provide support to the immune system, balance energy, relieve pain, reduce muscle spasms, and increase circulation.

needles dating back at least 7,000 years have been found. The Chinese used acupuncture both on people and animals.

For many years, the Western medical community looked upon acupuncture with disdain, considering it "folk medicine." In the past few decades, however, this attitude has changed. Although the spiritual aspects of acupuncture tend to be dismissed in the West, the sound science behind acupuncture cannot be ignored.

Acupuncture is conducted through the placement of very fine needles in specific spots on the body. These spots, called *acupuncture points*, are located along energy lines, or meridians. Physically, acupuncture works because these points contain small blood vessels and nerve endings. The insertion of the needles causes the body to release endorphins, hormones, and other healing and pain-relieving mechanisms, thereby stimulating the healing process. Spiritually, acupuncture strives to balance the opposing forces—the yin and the yang—in the body. Your Doberman Pinscher may not know of or understand the spiritual aspects of acupuncture, but that doesn't make it any less effective.

Acupuncture can be complicated. Knowing where to place the needles along the energy lines or meridians and how many needles to use takes considerable study. With the growing acceptance of acupuncture, however, an increasing number of veterinarians are practicing it.

Acupressure

Acupressure is based on the same principles as acupuncture, except that pressure (through massage) is used rather than needles. Because there is no penetration of the dog's body, many dog owners learn to do this at home.

The points where pressure can be used can be felt as slight depressions or dimples under the dog's skin. You can find them by giving your dog a massage and feeling for those slight depressions. The Dobe's short coat makes this much easier than it is in a heavily coated breed.

The points to be massaged do not necessarily correlate with the body part closest to the pressure point. In fact, sometimes the location may seem somewhat arbitrary. However, if you study acupuncture and the meridian lines, you can learn where to use massage and pressure to promote healing. For example:

- Massaging just under where a dew claw used to be on the front legs helps assist in relieving conditions of the lungs.
- Massaging to the side of the nose helps if your dog is going into shock. (Obviously, this is done as someone else is driving you to the veterinarian's office!)
- Massaging the nose gently helps relieve head congestion and upper respiratory problems.
- Massaging the mid-back on either side of the spine, from just past the withers to just before the hips, helps relieve gastrointestinal upset.

When your dog is having problems with an illness or an injury, the appropriate spot to massage will feel heavy, or as acupuncturists call it, "clogged." A few seconds of massage should release the pressure.

Chiropractic

Chiropractic is a health care treatment that is based on manipulation of the spine and joints. The science behind it says that when the mechanical parts of the body—the skeletal structure and nervous system—are out of alignment, other parts of the body suffer. Founded in the late 1800s, chiropractic is often used in conjunction with exercise, massage, acupuncture, and other alternative remedies.

Veterinary chiropractic is relatively new, and members of the American Veterinary Chiropractic Association (ACVA) study chiropractic care for people applied to canine anatomy to develop guidelines for chiropractic care for dogs.

Physical Therapy

Physical therapy isn't usually considered an ancient healing art or an alternative therapy. However, it has a long history of use. As far back as 460 B.C.E., Hippocrates, the ancient Greek physician who inspired the doctor's well-known oath to practice medicine ethically, wrote about the power of massage, manual therapy, and water therapy, and he promoted their use as healing tools. Then, in the 1700s, physical therapy was introduced in Sweden, and in the 1800s, it was introduced in Britain. It is now commonly used throughout the world.

For your dog, a course of treatment with physical therapy usually begins with a referral from your veterinarian. She may specify what her goals are for your Dobe and what she feels needs to be handled by the physical therapist. The physical therapist will then query the vet regarding your dog's history of illnesses and injuries, if known, or will ask you about your dog's medical history. She'll then examine your dog and plan a course of action. Physical therapy can include massage, stretching exercises, strength training, treadmill work for endurance, ultrasound treatments, swimming, and more.

Not just for injury rehabilitation, physical therapy can enhance the performance of dogs who compete in high-energy sports by increasing flexibility, strength, and range of motion.

TTouch

TTouch is a holistic therapy developed by animal handler Linda Tellington-Jones. This system of massage consists of circular motions performed with the hands moving in one and a quarter circles. In other words, the hand makes a circle but doesn't stop where it began; it goes another quarter of the circle past the starting spot.

The TTouch system uses a variety of different strokes applied at varying pressures:

- The Clouded Leopard stroke uses the pads of the fingers while the hand is cupped or curved.
- The Lying Leopard stroke uses the fingers and palm of the hand.
- The Raccoon stroke uses only the tips of the fingers with very light pressure.

There are many other strokes and techniques. TTouch is said to aid dogs in a variety of ways, from assisting the body in healing to aiding in the elimination of behavior problems.

Flower Remedies

Dr. Edward Bach, a bacteriologist and pathologist, originated what are now known as the Bach flower remedies in the 1930s. Although people all over the world had been using flowers and plants for medicinal purposes for thousands of years, Dr. Bach created these specific flower essence formulas to further a holistic approach to medicine, one that would treat the entire patient by restoring balance between the body and the mind.

Dr. Bach's flower remedies are still very much in use today, both for people and dogs, as well as other animals. Rescue Remedy, which has an immediate calming effect, is probably one of the remedies most often used for pets—even by owners who may not use any other alternative therapies.

Training Tidbit

Dr. Edward Bach, who originated flower remedies in the 1930s, recommended rock rose, mimulus, cherry plum, aspen, and red chestnut as therapies for fear. Amazingly, these are still recommended today by dog trainers and behaviorists when working with a fearful dog.

Herbal Remedies

Herbal remedies are derived from fresh plants and dried plant materials (roots, leaves, stems, or flowers), and are administered in the form of teas, juices, or extracts. Many modern medicines were originally based on ancient herbal preparations. Willow bark, for example, contains a chemical very close to that of aspirin.

Herbal formulations have long been used as both supplements to help maintain good health and as medicines to treat symptoms and support healing. Here are a few examples:

- **Alfalfa**: Widely grown for livestock feed, alfalfa is a very nutritious plant. It contains plant proteins and vitamins A, B complex, C, D, E, and K. It is also high in chlorophyll, acts as a powerful antioxidant, and has anti-inflammatory properties. It can be used as a food supplement every day with no long-term detrimental effects. The leaves and flowers are used medicinally in capsules or in teas.
- **Burdock**: This Eurasian import was introduced to North America years ago and is now growing wild. Burdock is considered a nutritious supplement because it contains

many minerals and trace elements. The root is the part of the plant most commonly used. It is available in capsules.

- **Calendula**: This plant has beautiful flowers and can often be found in garden centers for use as a decorative plant. Calendula has excellent anti-inflammatory properties. When used as a first-aid ointment, a calendula salve can be applied to a cut or scratch and will bring quick relief to pain and swelling, as well act as an aid to healing. Calendula tea is used as a digestive aid.

- **Chamomile**: Chamomile originated in Europe but is now known and grown all over the world. Dried and in capsule form, it is good for digestive upsets and will calm flatulence, intestinal spasms, and stimulate

digestion. Teas can work as a sleep aid.

- **Red clover**: Also from Europe, red clover has invaded North America. The plant's flowers are used medicinally as a general tonic, but are also known to support liver function. For dogs with liver disease, red clover is often used in conjunction with milk thistle and licorice root.

- **Dandelion**: Long considered to be a pest, dandelion provides good nutrition. Its leaves and flowers are rich in vitamins A, B complex, C, D, and K. The plant also contains many minerals, including trace minerals and iron. Several flowers chopped up and added to your Dobe's food will enhance the food's nutritional value. A dandelion tea stimulates digestion.

Now more commonly used with pets, herbal remedies are helpful in alleviating pain, reducing stress, and boosting the immune system.

- **Dill:** Dill's leaves, flowers, and seeds, when made into a tea, are soothing to the digestive system. Dill is also beneficial to nursing mother dogs, aiding in milk production.
- **Flax:** The seeds of the flax plant provide excellent nutrition. They are rich in linoleic acid and omega-3 fatty acids, which are needed for many different actions in the body, including keeping the immune system healthy. The seeds cannot be fed directly to the dog as-is because they will become intestinal irritants; however, when ground up, they can be added to dog food or baked into homemade treats.
- **Licorice:** Having strong antiviral and anti-inflammatory properties, the roots of the licorice plant—given fresh, dried, or in a tea—are used medicinally. When used as a tea, licorice is soothing for dogs with arthritis. It is used in conjunction with milk thistle and red clover for dogs with liver disease.
- **Milk thistle:** This herb has been used for more than 2,000 years to treat liver problems. It is given in capsule form and often used in conjunction with red clover and licorice root to be most effective.
- **Peppermint:** Peppermint is soothing to the digestive tract. It will stop nausea and vomiting, calm an irritable bowel, and expel gas. It is also good for motion sickness. Peppermint tea is most effective, although peppermint oil is also used.
- **Raspberry:** The leaves and berries of this plant, when used as a tea, are soothing to the digestive tract. Raspberry is also calming and is often used to soothe newly adopted dogs,

sound-sensitive dogs, and fearful dogs. It is also used for female dogs in season because it will calm cramps.
- **Sage:** Sage, when made into a tea, can be used as a mouth cleanser or rinse for dogs with dental disease. It can also be used to help prevent infection after a veterinary dental cleaning.
- **St. John's wort:** This flower's medicinal properties have been known for thousands of years. The new leaves and flowers (not the older ones) are dried and used as herbs or in teas. Although St. John's wort has several beneficial properties, it is best known for its ability to soothe depression. It's good for newly adopted dogs, as well as dogs suffering from stress.

As with allopathic medicines, dogs can have side effects from herbal supplements. Just because an herb comes from a plant doesn't mean it's always harmless; side effects, allergies, or other reactions can occur. Do not use supplements and herbal remedies without first consulting with your veterinarian.

Homeopathy

Homeopathy is the practice of treating a disease using very small doses of a remedy that would produce the same symptoms of that disease in healthy animals. It is based on the principle that "like cures like." As counterintuitive as it may seem, many people believe homeopathy truly works. Some compare it to a vaccination. Like herbal remedies and flower essences, it uses plants, minerals, and other natural substances to stimulate the body's natural defenses and to promote healing.

Want to Know More?

If you want to know more about health care as your dog ages, see Chapter 13: Care of Your Doberman Pinscher Senior.

During the 1700s, Dr. Samuel Hahnemann, who developed homeopathic remedies, was unhappy with the state of medicine in Germany at the time, which included the use of blood letting, laxatives, enemas, and emetics. He felt that medicine should cure disease rather than simply treat the symptoms. Dr. Hahnemann studied the effects of many herbs on the human system, kept detailed notes, maintained strict controls, and supervised the people being used as test subjects. He finally published his work, *Organon of Medicine* in 1810.

Today, more than 200 years later, many of these remedies are available commercially, both for use by people and animals. Homeopathic medicine is quite a complex science. If you're interested in using this for your Doberman, find a homeopathic veterinarian who can guide you.

BREED-SPECIFIC HEALTH ISSUES

Doberman Pinschers do, unfortunately, have the potential to develop some fairly significant breed-specific health issues. Some of these conditions can be inherited. Most can be detected through testing. One of the best and most up-to-date resources on Doberman health issues is the Doberman Pinscher Club of America (DPCA)'s website at www.dpca.org; click on the health tab. Your breeder and veterinarian can answer any questions you may have regarding these concerns.

Cardiomyopathy

Dilated cardiomyopathy (DCM) is a disease of the heart in which the heart chambers become enlarged, stretching the heart muscles, which then in turn become thinner and weaker. In the Dobe, this disease affects primarily the left ventricle and atrium. The heart eventually begins to fail.

This is an inherited disease in the breed. Most Dobes are between 2 and 5 years old when symptoms are first seen. They include shortness of breath, coughing, and a lack of energy. Coughing at night is often more common than coughing during the day. As the disease progresses, the abdomen may become distended with retained fluids. Males are affected more often than females.

Research is ongoing at several institutions. In fact, scientists at Washington State University have been able to offer some hope. Mary Swindell says, "The hot discussion now is that one of the DNA markers for DCM has been discovered in Dobermans. It's not the only marker, but a very prevalent one. While this isn't a foolproof sign that the dog will never develop cardio, it's a great step in the right direction to help breed dogs who will not die at a young age." Swindell also says, "Puppy buyers need to insist that they are getting puppies from tested parents. Breeders need to test and share that information."

The treatment for dogs diagnosed early will include controlling arrhythmias, improving the heart's ability to pump blood, and preventing the buildup of fluid in the body, specifically in the lungs and abdomen. Many veterinarians also recommend the addition of carnitine and taurine to the dog's diet. Unfortunately, the prognosis for this disease is always guarded.

Hip Dysplasia

Hip dysplasia is a crippling disease of the hips and the head of the femur. In a healthy dog, the head of the femur and the socket of the acetabulum work as a freely moving ball and socket joint. In a dog with hip dysplasia, the socket may be malformed, shallow, or even barely in existence. When combined with poor muscle tone and stretched connective tissues and muscles, the head of the femur will cause more wear and tear on the joint.

Hip dysplasia is considered a polygenic trait, meaning that more than one gene is involved in the inheritance of the disease. Deb Eldredge, DVM, author of *Dog Owner's Home Veterinary Handbook* says, "Feeding a very high calorie diet to growing dogs can exacerbate a predisposition to hip dysplasia because the rapid weight gain places increased stress on the hips."

The degree of hip dysplasia varies, from mild to severe. Some Dobermans will have mildly dysplastic hips and show no clinical signs at all, while others with severe dysplasia may be crippled. One of the first signs of this disease is a lack of interest in jumping—many dogs will refuse to jump into the car or up onto the furniture. Some dogs may limp on one rear leg and will show sensitivity when the leg is manipulated.

Signs that the dog is suffering from hip dysplasia may appear as early as 6 to 7 months of age, on into adulthood. Some dogs may cope with it until there is an injury and x-rays show the disease.

Treatment may be medical and/or surgical, and what treatment is chosen will depend on the severity of the dysplasia and how the dog is affected by it. Pain relievers, anti-inflammatory medicines, and joint protectants are commonly recommended. Keeping the dog's weight low is also advised. Several surgical options are available, and which one—if any—would be the most effective depends upon the individual dog's condition.

The DPCA recommends that both parents of a litter be evaluated prior to breeding.

Hypothyroidism

Hypothyroidism is a disease in which too few hormones are being produced by the

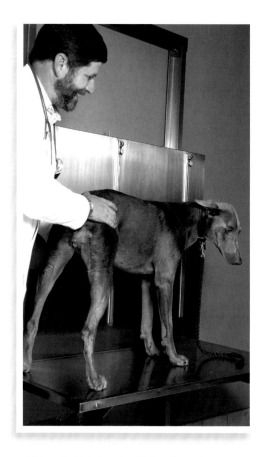

Although fairly healthy, Dobes, like other breeds, are not completely free from certain hereditary health issues and genetic diseases, such as hip dysplasia.

thyroid gland, which controls the body's rate of metabolism. It is usually caused by an autoimmune disorder called *lymphocytic thyroiditis*, a condition known to be inherited.

Symptoms of hypothyroidism include weight gain, intolerance to cold weather, slow heart rate, lack of energy, and, usually, skin and coat changes, including hair loss. If allowed to progress untreated, the dog may develop eye and eyelid problems, deafness, anemia, constipation, infertility, and more. Behavior problems, including aggression, have been seen as well.

Hypothyroidism can be diagnosed through blood work, which tests hormone levels. Treatment consists of a hormone replacement pill, given once or twice a day.

Liver Disease

Chronic active hepatitis (CAH) causes the dog's liver to improperly metabolize copper, causing an accumulation of copper in the liver that becomes toxic. The accumulation may occur because the liver doesn't excrete the copper or because too much is absorbed, or both.

This disease is most commonly seen in female Dobes, although some males have been diagnosed with it. Symptoms are usually seen when the dog is between 4 and 6 years of age and may include poor appetite, weight loss, excessive thirst, jaundice, lethargy, and seizures.

Blood work can test for liver enzyme levels. The only treatment available at this time is a change in diet, paying close attention to copper intake.

Progressive Retinal Atrophy

Progressive retinal atrophy (PRA) causes the degeneration of the retinal cells of the eyes. Initially, there will be a loss of vision in low-light situations, leading to night blindness, and eventual total blindness. The onset may be slow, taking up to a year or more from first impairment to total blindness. In some dogs, it may only be a matter of months before the dog is blind.

There is no treatment for PRA, however, testing by a veterinary ophthalmologist is available to screen out potential breeding dogs.

Vestibular Disease

Vestibular disease, also known as "dings" in Doberman Pinschers, appears in puppyhood. Those puppies who are severely affected may cry inconsolably, may not be able to nurse, and may circle and show a head tilt. Some puppies may not show signs until 3 months of age or so.

Vestibular disease can have many causes, but the inherited condition seen in Dobe puppies appears to be caused by misplacement of nerves in the forward part of the spinal cord. Research to isolate the genetic causes has not yet been done, and as of yet there is no means of screening for the disease.

Von Willebrand's Disease

Von Willebrand's disease (vWD) is an inherited bleeding disorder caused by a deficiency of a plasma protein that is necessary for platelet function in clotting. Although it has been found in a number of breeds of dog, it is often known as a "Doberman disease."

The first signs of vWD may appear when a puppy bleeds more than normal, most commonly when a first tooth is lost. Many cases are diagnosed when an older puppy is spayed or neutered and bleeds too much during and after surgery. More severe cases may also include profuse nosebleeds that don't stop, frequent bruising beneath the skin, and blood in the urine and feces. In severe cases, a dog can bleed to death.

Blood work can provide a definitive diagnosis. Many dogs with vWD also have hypothyroidism. DNA testing can show whether an individual dog is a carrier (has inherited one gene for the disease) or is affected (has inherited two genes).

Wobbler's Syndrome

A devastating disease, wobbler's syndrome is caused by a compression of the spinal cord in the neck. This can be caused by malformed vertebra or a deformed spinal canal. It can also be caused by a ruptured disc. Wobbler's (also known as cervical vertebral instability)

The Doberman breed is known to suffer from a disproportionate number of both skin and pigment disorders.

Treatment varies depending upon the severity of the disease. Medical management, acupuncture, and/or a cervical collar to stabilize the neck may be recommended. Surgery is sometimes recommended; however, the results vary, and some dogs who have had surgery, see a recurrence of the disease.

Because this is thought to be an inherited condition, dogs with wobbler's or those who have produced dogs with wobbler's should not be bred. Both blood tests and DNA tests can confirm the disease in Doberman Pinschers.

The White Factor: Albinism

In 1976, a white, female Doberman Pinscher was born. She was bred to one of her sons, who had normal coloration, in the hope of creating a unique line of Doberman Pinschers. This inbreeding continued and did, in fact, result in a line of related Dobes who are a white/cream color, with whiter markings and blue eyes. The nose, eye rims, pads, and membranes are pink. This type of modified coloration is referred to as *albino*.

However, albinos of any species, including dogs, tend to have significant health problems. Eye defects may include reduced vision, abnormal movements of the eyes, retinal damage, and problems with the optic nerve. The skin, lacking melanin, is prone to sunburn and skin cancers. Those researching white Dobermans are also concerned with temperament issues such as shyness and fearfulness.

White Dobermans cannot compete in conformation competitions because their coat color (or more correctly, the lack of color) is considered a disqualifying fault. The Doberman Pinscher Club of America (DPCA) is concerned about the introduction of white Dobes into the general breeding population

is suspected to be an inherited disorder in the breed, but the means of inheritance has not yet been established.

The first symptom is generally a lack of coordination and most often appears between the ages of 3 and 8, although it has been found in younger dogs. The dog may stumble or have an unsteady gait, a "wobble." There may be some weakness in the legs, and the dog may have pain when he moves his head or neck. Paralysis may result in one, two, or all four legs.

and so, along with the American Kennel Club (AKC), is tracking these dogs. Any individual who is an albino or is white factored (carrying the albino gene) is identified as such with a Z added to his or her AKC registration number.

EMERGENCY FIRST AID

There is nothing scarier than having an emergency and not knowing what to do. Having a plan of action, emergency phone numbers, and an appropriately stocked first-aid kit at hand can help ease some of the stress in these situations.

Emergency Protocols

Before an emergency occurs, know what your vet's recommendations are. Some veterinarians can be paged after hours, while others recommend that their clients contact a local emergency clinic. There is no right or wrong policy, but if you go to an emergency clinic, the veterinarian there won't know your dog's medical history.

If your vet refers you to an emergency clinic, make sure you know where it is located and how to get there. You don't want to get lost should there be a life-threatening emergency. A friend of mine recently had to take her elderly dog to the emergency clinic, and upon arriving discovered it had moved. Although she was able to find the new location, the detour took an additional half hour, causing her to become panic stricken. Luckily, her dog recovered.

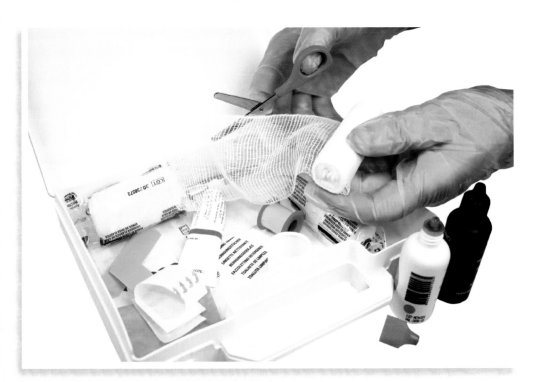

Emergency first-aid measures can increase your dog's chances of a full recovery—and may even save his life—until you can get him to the vet.

Know what your veterinarian and the emergency clinic can provide in an emergency, what forms of payment they accept for emergency services, and whether they accept pet health insurance. Again, ask all these questions before you have to deal with an emergency.

First-Aid Kit

I put a canine first-aid kit together more than 25 years ago, when I was working as a veterinary technician. I have maintained that kit—and enlarged it—ever since then. Here are some supplies you'll want to include in one of your own:

- rectal thermometer
- large and small tweezers
- blunt and pointed scissors, heavy bandage or utility scissors
- disposable razors
- nail clippers
- tape of various sizes, widths, and types, including waterproof tape and duct tape
- butterfly adhesive bandages
- rolls of gauze or fabric of different widths
- gauze pads of various sizes, including eye pads
- elastic wrap for wrapping bandages
- safety pins
- instant cold compresses
- antiseptic cleaning wipes
- sterile saline eye wash
- hydrogen peroxide
- Benadryl tablets
- antibacterial ointment and/or spray
- antidiarrheal tablets
- small flashlight
- mirror
- pen/pencil, marking pen, note paper
- spare leash and collar
- blanket big enough to wrap your dog
- any medications your dog requires on a regular

basis, including prescription drugs (keep copies of prescriptions in the kit as well).

Check these items often. Remove and replace those that have expired and any that have been used. If you keep a list in your first-aid kit, it's easy to check if something is missing.

Training Tidbit

Most Doberman Pinschers panic when it is necessary that they be restrained or muzzled, especially when they are hurt. But if your Dobe is injured or involved in an accident, he may need to be handled in this manner. Teaching your dog to accept restraint before he's hurt, and then practicing it every once in a while, can make the process easier.

Have your Dobe lie down on the floor, then roll him over onto his side as you tell him, "Be still." Gently hold him in place for a few seconds, and then release him and praise him.

Your Dobe should also accept muzzling. A hurt dog may bite, and if you can muzzle him, you can prevent this from happening. A muzzle can be created out of just about anything, from a length of gauze to a leash. Practicing this is also a good idea. Talk to your dog, stroke his head gently, and then take the material and gently wrap it around his muzzle twice. Then cross it under his chin and pull it behind the head. Tie it securely. Praise your dog for accepting this with grace.

CANINE CPR

Cardiopulmonary resuscitation (CPR) is a combination of cardiac massage and assisted breathing that has saved thousands of lives, both in dogs and people. If you see a dog lying still, and he is obviously not sleeping, here's what to do:

- First, check to see if he has a heartbeat. Do *not* perform chest compressions on a dog whose heart is beating; this could cause harm to the beating heart and potentially disrupt the normal rhythm.
- Check to see if he is breathing. Do *not* attempt resuscitation on a dog who is breathing.
- If he is not breathing, clear the mouth of any obstructions.
- Pull the tongue out and to the side of the mouth so it doesn't block the airway.
- Close the mouth and pull the lips down around the teeth to make the mouth airtight.
- Take a large, deep breath (for a Dobe) and exhale into the dog's nose. Watch the chest to make sure it rises. Repeat this every 10 seconds if you can do so without hyperventilating.
- After ten breaths, check again for a heartbeat. If there is no heartbeat, clasp your hands together, one above the other, and press downward on the dog's left side above the heart.
- Compress five times and then go back to the assisted breathing.
- Repeat the cycle: ten breaths and then five chest compressions.

Once you begin CPR, continue until the dog resumes breathing on his own, until someone can help you get the dog to help, or until it's obvious that your efforts are in vain.

Basic First-Aid

I'm a big fan of the emergency pet first-aid classes offered by the American Red Cross. Although the instructions are very basic, they do cover all the common emergency scenarios. After completing the class, you can always find a community college class that will further educate you if you feel you'd like more information.

Often the best emergency response involves simply keeping yourself and your dog calm, assessing the problem, applying basic first aid, and then calling your veterinarian for guidance.

Bleeding

Bleeding that oozes from small cuts and scrapes is rarely an emergency. Clean the wound, apply pressure with a gauze pad, and apply some antibiotic ointment. However, if the oozing continues and the blood doesn't clot, call your veterinarian.

If the bleeding is coming out in spurts, that means a blood vessel has been broken. This is very dangerous because your dog could bleed to death. Although tourniquets used to be recommended to stop this type of bleeding, they can present some hazards also. Instead of using one, call your veterinarian immediately and ask for guidance. If you are a distance from his office, she may recommend you go directly to the closest clinic or give you instructions.

Bleeding under the skin—either in the form of a bruise or hematoma— is not an emergency unless the bleeding doesn't stop. Use an ice pack on the spot for 15 minutes. Let the area warm back up to body temperature and check for additional bleeding. Apply an ice pack again if needed. If it appears that the bleeding is continuing, call your veterinarian.

A dog left outdoors in a parked car or in the heat without adequate shade or water can quickly suffer from heatstroke.

Broken Bones

If your dog appears to have broken a bone, he will show signs of pain, may hold up the affected limb, and the area will begin to swell. Immobilize that limb or area with a splint—anything to hold it still—and call your veterinarian.

Choking

If your dog appears to be choking—coughing and gasping—open his mouth and see if there is anything blocking the airway. If you can reach it, do so and gently pull it out. If you can't reach it, stand above and behind your dog, reach under his belly just below the rib cage, and pull up quickly and sharply several times. If this doesn't work, get him to the closest veterinarian immediately.

Frostbite

Doberman Pinschers are not designed to be outdoor dogs, especially in cold winters. Their short coat leaves them vulnerable to frostbite. Areas most likely to be affected include the tips of the ears, the tail, and paws. In males, the scrotum can also be frostbitten. Frostbitten skin will appear gray and pale, and will feel cold to the touch. Veterinary care is needed right away.

Heatstroke

Dogs don't sweat through pores in the skin, as people do. Instead, they lose heat by panting and sweating through the pads of their feet. Because these are small areas of the body, a dog can overheat quickly. A dog who is overheated will be agitated, may pace back and forth, may bark, or will collapse. He may also go into shock. Cool the dog immediately by wetting him with cool—not cold—water. As soon as he appears cooler, get him to the veterinarian right away.

Insect Stings and Bites

Most insect bites and stings are just an annoyance more than a real problem. However, some dogs may be allergic to bee stings or spider bites. If you suspect your dog has been stung by a bee, remove the stinger. Shave away a little of the dog's hair so you can see the area better. Wash it off, and put an ice pack on it. If you see a growing redness or swelling, or if your Dobe begins to vomit or has diarrhea, call your veterinarian right away. She may want you to give your Dobe a Benadryl and have you bring him in immediately.

Poisoning

Symptoms of poisoning can vary depending upon the type of poison ingested. Some symptoms include drooling, vomiting, diarrhea, muscle tremors, and seizures. Poisoning can become fatal very quickly, so don't hesitate to call your veterinarian right away, give her the name brand and type of poison that was ingested if known, and follow her directions. She may ask you to induce vomiting, depending on what your dog has been exposed to. Or, she may have you feed or give your dog an antidote if something is available.

If you can't reach your vet, you can call the ASPCA National Animal Poison Control Center at (900) 443-0000. The charge is billed directly to the caller's phone. You can also call (888) 4ANI-HELP (888-426-4435). The charge is billed to the caller's credit card; follow-up calls can be made for no additional charge.

Shock

A dog may go into shock after a traumatic injury or during a life-threatening illness. By itself, shock can be life-threatening, but when combined with whatever initiated it, the dog is in serious danger. Symptoms of shock include a fast and often irregular heartbeat, weakness, pale gums, panting or gasping, dilated pupils, or no eye response to movement. Keep the dog warm and get him to the veterinarian right away. There is no time to lose.

Snake Bites

Most snakes are not aggressive; however, they will bite when they perceive themselves to be in danger. The best protection for your dog is to teach him to leave snakes alone. If he gets bitten, try to identify the snake. If your dog is bitten by a nonvenomous snake, just wash the wound and apply an antibiotic ointment. If your dog is bitten by a venomous snake, call your veterinarian right away, keep your dog calm, and get him to the clinic immediately. Do not cut the dog's skin and try to suck out the venom; that's not affective and causes more problems. Obviously, if you can't identify the snake, call your vet right away and ask for guidance.

DISASTER PREPAREDNESS

My husband and I live in southern California. Although people tend to think of this as earthquake country, earthquakes aren't nearly as big a problem as wildfires. When a wildfire begins in rural California and roars toward places where people live, nothing is going to stop it. Several have blazed toward the west, stopping only when they hit the ocean, burning hundreds or even thousands of homes along the way.

After having been evacuated a few times because of fires, I created a disaster preparedness kit for the both of us, as well as for our dogs. I keep this stored in a plastic trash can with wheels that can be grabbed in a heartbeat, rolled to my van, and loaded in.

Here are some of the things I keep in my kit:

- Camping supplies, including a can opener, paper plates, knives and forks, paper towels, garbage bags, etc. We also include sleeping bags, blankets, and a couple of towels.
- Battery-powered radio and extra batteries.
- Cell phone chargers (a plug-in wall charger and a car charger), as well as a list of important phone numbers in case we lose our phones or cell phone service is not available.
- Extra clothing, shoes, toiletries, medications, and copies of health records and prescriptions.
- Extra leashes and collars, licenses, vaccination records, and copies of our dogs'

Have a plan of action and a pet emergency kit prepared in the event of an emergency that requires evacuation from your home.

medical records, and veterinarian contact information.

- Identification for our pets, with our cell phone number on it, as well as photos of each pet, in case we need to identify them.
- A week's worth of bottled water and canned or dried food for both people and dogs.

My first aid kit is also always within easy reach so that it can be grabbed in any emergency. I also keep some tools in my van, not just automobile tools, but a selection of wrenches, sockets, pliers, a hammer, rope, and the ever-handy duct tape.

Check your disaster kit regularly. I do it every 6 months and mark my calendar so I remember to update any information and replace anything expired or used up. I try to do this at the same time that I go update my first aid kit. It's easy to check expiration dates and/or rotate supplies if I do both at the same time.

As we all learned from watching news of the Hurricane Katrina disaster, as well as in numerous other situations, pets left behind are vulnerable and may die. But it only takes experiencing one disaster yourself to teach you valuable lessons. At 3 a.m. one morning, our dogs began barking. My husband and I awoke to a loudspeaker outside our house saying, "Wake up! Wake up! Mandatory evacuation due to wild fire! Wake up!" We didn't question anything; Paul threw on clothes as I did. He called the dogs, grabbed their crates, and ran toward our van. I grabbed the cat, the rabbit, and crates for them. We loaded the animals first, then collected our important papers, disaster kit, first-aid kit, cell phones, wallets, keys, and medications. I drove the van, and he drove his motorcycle. We were off and heading down the driveway within minutes.

It's a good thing, too, because flames had reached one side of our street on the way out and were more than 100 feet high. It was like driving through an inferno. We met at a prearranged spot at a local beach and camped there for several days. But we had everything we needed, and all of us—people and pets—were safe. Our neighbors, who weren't as prepared, weren't nearly as comfortable. When we finally returned home, everything was covered in ash, but, thankfully, unharmed.

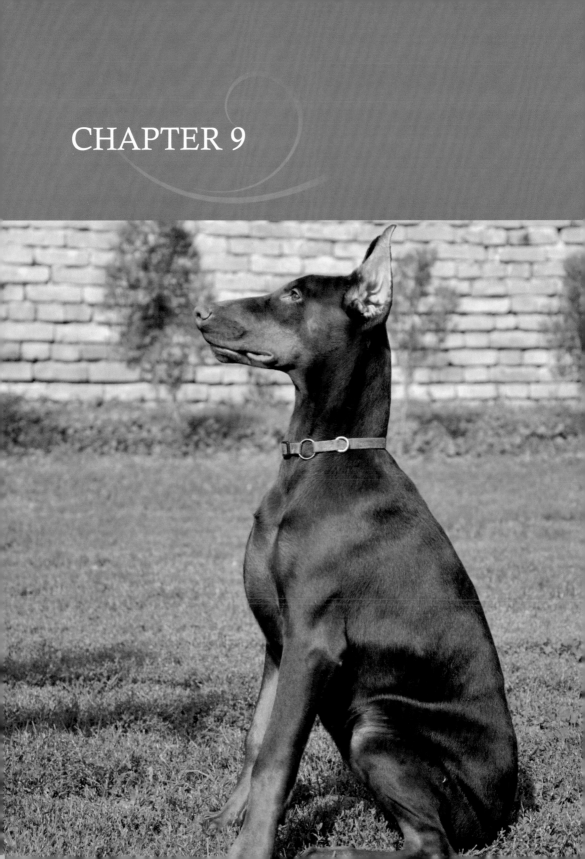

CHAPTER 9

DOBERMAN PINSCHER TRAINING

Training is a lifelong process because reinforcement of basic obedience lessons is necessary to keep compliance reliable. But there are so many additional reasons to continue training, especially with a dog who is intelligent, curious, and has a strong work ethic, such as the Doberman. "Training is very important for this breed," says Kim Somjen, DVM, who competes in performance sports with her Dobes. "This is not important just because the breed has an active mind and a need to work to be fulfilled, but also because an untrained Doberman Pinscher is a poorly behaved one. These dogs like to push their limits and see how much they can get away with. They need boundaries. In addition, they enjoy working with their owners." A well-trained Dobe will know what's expected of him, but even more important, continued training will provide the Dobe with the mental challenges that will keep him happy.

INTERMEDIATE OBEDIENCE TRAINING

Before starting this training, do some refresher training with your dog. Make sure he can do the basic obedience exercises as outlined in

Chapter 4. After all, those exercises are the foundation for everything else you do with your Dobe, and they need to be solid. If you begin this training before those commands are well understood, you and your dog will both be frustrated. So take the time to review and practice the basics.

Teaching the *Heel*

The *heel* teaches your Dobe to walk at your left side, with his neck next to your leg. In this position, he can keep pace with you, watch what you're doing so that he can move with you, and pay attention to you. It also teaches him to ignore distractions. This can be tough; after all, distractions consist of those things that your dog is most interested in and can't ignore. However, when your dog can do this, the *heel* is a wonderfully useful command. Plus, when done nicely, it looks awesome.

Let's work on those attention skills first:

1. Sit your Dobe in front of you. Have his leash in one hand and treats in the other, with more treats in your pocket.
2. Let him sniff one treat and then tell him, "Watch me," as you take the treat from his nose to your chin.
3. When he is looking directly at your face and

Obedience training is necessary for Doberman Pinschers because it is very important for this independent-minded, protective dog to learn self-control and to be thoroughly socialized.

above exercise in the same way for two or three days. Now you're ready to begin with the *heel*:

1. Sit your Dobe by your left side. Have the leash in your left hand, with your arm bent so your hand is at waist level and in front of your tummy.
2. With a treat in your right hand, reach across your body and let your dog sniff the treat as you tell him, "Watch me."
3. Step forward at a normal walking pace as you say, "Heel." Use the treat as a lure to encourage him to walk with you, keeping his head up (no sniffing the ground) and watching you.
4. After ten steps or so, stop, have your Dobe sit, and pop the treat into his mouth as you praise him.
5. Repeat this three or four times, and take a break. Throw a ball for your dog, give him a tummy rub, or do something else that will relax him. Then repeat the exercise a few more times. Do this for a few days, then begin to walk a few steps farther each time.

When your Dobe seems to have the hang of the exercise, add some variety to it. Train it in different places where he might become more distracted, such as at the local park, outside a school, or in the parking lot of the local store.

When he's handling these distractions well, then make the training itself a little different:

1. Instead of walking up and down the block in a straight line, turn corners, both left and right. Zigzag down the sidewalk. Make tight turns around light poles.
2. Act as if you forgot something and make an about-turn to head back home. Then another about-turn to continue on your walk.
3. Take two of your outside trash cans and place them a short distance away from each other and walk in a figure-eight pattern around them.

maintaining eye contact, praise him, "Good boy!" and pop the treat into his mouth.

4. Repeat this three or four times, and then take a break.
5. Repeat the exercise twice a day for two or three days.

When your Dobe has reliably learned to pay attention, have him sit by your left side. Turn your upper body toward him slightly so you can make eye contact with him and repeat the

4. Ask two of the neighborhood kids to stand a short distance apart, and heel around them.

Just remember to use a lot of positive reinforcements, such as your voice, petting, and really tasty treats, so that your dog looks upon this as a fun challenge instead of boring work. You want him to work with you, rather than challenge and fight you.

If your Dobe is having trouble paying attention to you, which is the most important element of this exercise, vary the treats you offer as rewards. Use some smelly treats, like Swiss cheese or hot dogs. Use a toy once in a while, like a tennis ball or a squeaky toy. Keep your voice happy and upbeat when you praise your dog. Varying the reinforcements helps to keep the training fun.

Teaching the *Sit-Stay*

Your Doberman learned the *sit* command in puppy training, so now with the *stay* command added, he can hold a sit for longer periods of time. The *stay* command teaches your dog to hold still and not to walk forward with you. With this command, you can ask your Dobe to sit or lie down, and then remain in that position until you release him. You can walk away from him and fix his dinner without having him under foot. Or, you can have him stay at an open gate rather than dash to the curb as you take the trash cans out. The *stay* is a useful command, but also an important one because it can help keep your Dobe safe.

Always have a leash on your dog as you train him. If he's not on leash and he dashes away while you're trying to teach him, he'll learn that *stay* is an optional command, and that's not what you want him to learn.

1. With your dog on leash, ask him to sit.
2. Wait a few seconds, then praise your dog, pop a treat into his mouth and pat him on the shoulder. Then say, "Okay!," to release him.
3. Repeat this three or four times then take a break.
4. Throw a ball for your dog, scratch behind his ears, and tell him what a smart dog he is. Then repeat the exercise three or four times.

Do this for a few days. Then do the exercise again, but this time, when you tell your dog to stay, take two steps away from him. In a couple more days, take two more steps away from him and so on. When he can *stay* reliably, try making it harder by taking a few steps to the left or a few steps to the right of him. Next, take a few steps away and then turn away from your dog so you aren't looking at him.

When your dog is holding the *stay* reliably on leash in your training sessions, add some variations. Here's an example:

1. With your dog on leash in the house, walk up to the front door. Make sure it is closed.
2. Ask your dog to sit and then tell him stay.
3. Open the door.

All Dogs Can Learn New Tricks

A dog can learn to do anything at any age—whether he's a puppy, adult, or senior. All it takes is time, patience, and commitment. And it's up to you to help your canine companion learn the things that will enhance his life and enable him to live successfully with you. Training is a process that can and should continue throughout your dog's lifetime.

The *sit-stay* command teaches your dog to remain in position until you release him.

4. If your dog dashes for the door, stop him using the leash, and interrupt that behavior with a firm "No." Bring him back to you and have him sit again.
5. Close the door and repeat the exercise.
6. Practice three or four times. When he sits nicely and holds his stay, praise and reward him, close the door, and stop training for a few minutes. Then repeat the exercise.

Do this at the front door, back door (in and out), the gate to the yard, the car door (in and out), and anywhere your dog may prefer to dash ahead rather than control himself. You can even teach him to *sit-stay* at street curbs until you give him permission to move forward.

In several weeks, when your Dobe is able to hold the *sit-stay* well, begin dropping the leash to the ground as you practice. Move your hands around after dropping it so he sees that you're no longer holding it. Walk around, turn circles, do some jumping jacks, and act silly. If he continues to hold the *sit-stay*, go back to him, praise him, and tell him how awesome he is!

Teaching the *Down-Stay*

The *down-stay* is similar to the *sit-stay*, except that the dog is asked to lie down instead of sit. The difference between the two exercises is that the dog can hold the stay longer while lying down because he can relax and be more comfortable.

The *down-stay* has several practical uses. If you don't want your Dobe to beg while the family is eating, have him lie down and stay on a doggy bed away from the table. If you don't want him to bother your guests, ask him to lie down and stay at your feet while you visit with your friends. If, while on a walk, you meet someone you'd like to talk to and your dog is antsy and pulling at the leash to continue the walk, have him lie down, stay, and relax while you talk.

The *down-stay* is also an excellent exercise to help teach your dog self-control. It's impossible to hold the *down-stay* if the dog is wiggling and squirming. However, once he settles down and stays in position, he can be rewarded for it.

Teach the *down-stay* as you did the *sit-stay*:

1. With your dog on leash, ask him to sit and then lie down.

2. Tell him, "Down," and give the *stay* hand signal. Continue standing next to him; don't move anywhere yet.

3. Wait for a few seconds, then praise your dog in the down position, pop a treat into his mouth, pat him on the shoulder, and say, "Okay!," to release him.

4. Repeat this three or four times, then take a break. Throw a ball for your dog, scratch behind his ears, and give him a tummy rub. Then repeat the exercise another three or four times.

5. Do this for a few days. Next, when you tell your dog to *down*, take two more steps away from him and gradually, over a week or more, walk farther away from him each session.

6. When your dog appears reliable, add a challenge, such as walking away and sitting in a chair. This is tough because many dogs will pop up at this point thinking training is over. After all, most training occurs when you are standing, right?

7. If your dog makes a mistake, use your voice to interrupt him as he is making the mistake by asking him to lie down again and telling him to stay. Walk away and sit down again. When he holds the *down-stay*, go back to him quickly and praise him.

Start using the *down-stay* around the house, too. Identify places and times in your routine where asking your dog to be still could help you both. Just remember, when you do ask your dog to lie down and stay, keep the leash on him while he is still training so you can prevent mishaps should your dog be in a position to escape your home or yard.

If you find that your Dobe is consistently making mistakes or seems like he can't hold still, then you may be moving too fast in the training process. Go back to the basic steps, remaining right next to him as you ask him to *down-stay*, and then repeat the training steps more slowly.

By the Numbers

Never ask your dog to hold a *sit-stay* for more than three minutes. If you need him to hold still for a longer period of time, ask him to lie down and stay. A mentally mature, well-trained Dobe can hold a *down-stay* for ten minutes or more. If you find that your Dobe is consistently making mistakes or can't hold still, then you may be moving too fast in the training process. Go back to the basic steps, remaining right next to him as you ask him to *sit-stay*, and then repeat the exercise more slowly.

Teaching the *Stand*

When you teach your Doberman to stand on command, he will stand upright, with all four paws on the floor, and remain still. This is useful when you bathe him, brush him, or when he needs to go to the veterinarian's office. It's also helpful when it's been raining outside and you want to towel him off before he comes in the house.

Teaching the *stand* command is easy:

1. Have your dog sit on your left side in the heel position.
2. Hold a treat in your right hand, and keep your left hand empty.
3. Put the treat in front of your dog's nose and let him smell it. Pull it away from his nose, moving forward, as you tell him, "Stand."
4. As he steps forward to follow the treat, reach over him with your left hand so his body is against your left leg, and place your left hand under his belly so that if he tries to sit you can stop him.
5. Praise him for standing and pop the treat into his mouth. Then release him, "Sweetie, okay, good."
6. Repeat this several times and take a break. Let your dog relax and then try it again.

If your Dobe panics when you place your hand under his belly, work on that as a separate issue. During the day—not necessarily in training sessions—just stop and run your hands over him. Touch his sides, his belly, and all over his back and chest to teach him that your hands are gentle and soft and not a threat. Do this a couple times a day for several days, then go back to teaching the *stand*.

Teaching the *Stand-Stay*

The *stand-stay* command is used in advanced obedience competition, but it still has practical applications for dogs at home. In any of the situations in which the *stand* would be useful, being able to tell your dog, "Sweetie, *stand-stay*," is even more helpful. The *stand* teaches your dog to stand in position, but the *stay* means hold still in that position. Your dog already knows the *stay* command in both the sit and down positions, so it will be easy to teach it in the stand position. But don't start this until he understands the *stand* command well.

1. Ask your dog to stand and praise him for standing.
2. Tell him, "Stand," while giving the *stay* hand signal. Remain at his side.
3. Wait a few seconds (five is plenty), and then praise your dog, give him a treat, and release him.
4. Repeat this three or four times, then take a break. Come back later and do it again.
5. After a few days, when your dog is standing nicely, take one step away. Gradually continue to increase the number of steps you take away from him at each session to ensure his reliability. The *stand* is more

Multi-Dog Tip

If you have more than one dog in the house, using the *down/stay* command can come in handy. For example, when your dogs are overly excited or playing too roughly, ask all of them to lie down and stay. This will calm them down, and help them to relax and be still. You can use this command to manage many behaviors, which can ultimately enable you to include your dogs in many more activities.

When you teach your Doberman to stand on command, he will stand upright, with all four paws on the floor, and remain still. This is useful when you bathe him, brush him, or when he needs to go to the veterinarian's office.

difficult to teach than other commands because it's so easy for your dog to just take one or two steps to follow you. So remain close to your dog when you first teach the *stand-stay*.

In most real-life situations, you aren't going to walk away from your dog in the *stand-stay* anyway. This is a practical exercise you'll most often use when you're near your dog.

KEEP YOUR TRAINING FUN

Many owners train their dogs believing that training should be militaristic and regimented. Although that's the way training used to be, it really doesn't have to be that way. Today, most dog trainers are moving away from that philosophy entirely and employing positive training methods that use reinforcement rather than correction.

When a dog is forced to comply with his owner's wishes, he will be more likely to fight those restrictions and challenge his owner's authority. In a dog's world, aggression begets aggression, and if you're forceful and aggressive toward your dog, he may return that with similar behavior. Other dogs, when faced with aggression and forcefulness, may wilt and become frightened or cowed. But a fearful dog may also bite if pushed too far.

Although training is necessary to set rules and guidelines for behavior, that doesn't mean it can't also be fun. When a dog is taught the rules by being shown what to do (rather than what not to do), and he is rewarded for good behavior with praise from you, treats, and toys, he's going to be much more apt to cooperate with you.

Here are some thoughts to keep in mind as you train:

Whatever your reasons for continuing to train, working regularly with your Dobe will strengthen the bond between you.

- Teach your dog what you want him to do.
- Always reward him for good behavior.
- Interrupt behavior you don't want, but do not punish after the behavior has already happened.
- Teach your dog to cooperate with you rather than fight you.
- Always set your dog up to succeed.

If you find yourself getting frustrated in your training sessions, stop, put your dog in his crate, and give yourself some time alone. Think about what you were doing. Where did things go wrong? Don't blame your dog; instead, look at what you were doing that caused this reaction.

- Were you asking too much of your dog? Was it beyond what he's capable of doing?
- Were you pushing him too fast? For example, were you going too far away from

him on the *stay*, or asking him to do a *watch me* with too many distractions?

- Was your voice beginning to sound like a US Marine Corps drill instructor, which made your dog think he was in trouble? You may find that when your Dobe doesn't understand, he may wilt a little. Dobes can be very sensitive, and a harsh voice or rough training will make him very uneasy.
- Were you giving clear, concise commands?
- Was your timing wrong? Did you not interrupt bad behavior or reward good behavior as soon as it occurred?

Plan your next training session keeping these thoughts in mind so that you can avoid these obstacles. Don't be afraid to return to previous training steps so you can set your Dobe up for success and reward him for good behavior.

TRAINING FOR LIFE

"Training is a constant process that begins the second you get your dog and ends when he dies," says Shanna Gardner. Not only is this because all dogs need training, but also because Dobes were bred to work for their owners—to have jobs and a purpose. Doberman Pinschers weren't bred to be lap dogs, although some may seem to think so!

Before you begin muttering about how you'll find the time and energy to continue training for the next 13 or 14 years, just keep in mind that training doesn't have to be work. Training can be anything you do with your dog, anytime and anywhere. For example, when your Dobe comes up to you and stares at you with those baby browns, willing to do anything for you, ask him to stand, then lie down, and then sit.

◎ Training Tidbit

There are many reasons to keep training fun and rewarding for your dog. However, for your dog to reliably learn what's expected of him, you must always let him know when he's making a mistake. In some cases, you can do that by ignoring the behavior; hence, not rewarding it. You can also use a verbal interruption in a firm (but not loud) voice. What's important is that your dog is shown what to do rather than being punished for bad behavior. He's not trying to misbehave, he just doesn't understand what the rules are yet—and that's your fault, not his.

Want to Know More?

For more information about training for obedience competitions, performance sports, and conformation shows, see Chapter 11: Doberman Pinscher Sports and Activities.

Then release him and tell him how wonderful he is! Or, when your Dobe brings you a ball and wants you to throw it, ask him first to lie down, then sit, then lie down, then sit. Then praise him and throw the ball.

Do some trick training. Teach your Dobe several tricks he can learn easily, but ones that will get him lots of attention and praise too, such as bowing, spinning in a circle, lying down and rolling over, or waving a paw.

Think also about getting involved in obedience competition or performance sports with your Dobe. Mary Swindell is the owner of Casanova, a black Dobe, and they compete in agility together. Casanova, who's registered name is ATCH NATCH Triple B Renejade Casanova, MX, MXJ, RA, SWETT, GM, JM, SM, AAD, AP, WAC, TN-E, WV-E, TN, G-E, holds the record for the 60 weave pole challenge held by *Clean Run* magazine, as well as numerous other honors. Swindell says, "This breed has lots of mental energy and tons of physical energy that needs to be channeled into acceptable outlets. Dobes have strong personalities."

Whatever your reasons for continuing to train, working regularly with your Dobe will strengthen the bond between you, direct his energy in a positive way, and help keep him fit and trim.

CHAPTER 10

DOBERMAN PINSCHER PROBLEM BEHAVIORS

Doberman Pinschers are bright, intelligent, and very aware dogs. They pay attention to what's going on around them, and they are quick to react. Dobes also reason very well and will quickly learn when something works in their favor. All of these traits are wonderful if the owner can keep up. But if the dog gets the upper hand (or paw!), problem behaviors are often the result.

COMMON CAUSES OF PROBLEM BEHAVIORS

Dog trainers and behavior consultants know that an infinite number of things can cause problem behaviors. Paulette Bethel says, "Usually problem behaviors in Dobermans result from not enough exercise or attention. Any dog left alone to his own devices and cut off from his family and pack will resort to some kind of mischief."

At times, it can be difficult to figure out what causes a specific problem; especially because something as simple as being frightened by an object during a very early stage of development can have a lasting impact. But there are some issues that are commonly found in dogs with problem behaviors:

- **Lack of socialization:** Dogs who were not well socialized during puppyhood tend to have behavioral issues later on. Some Dobes will react in a fearful or shy manner when meeting new people or dogs, or when introduced to new things, while others may react aggressively. Socialization is vitally important throughout puppyhood, but especially from 12 to 16 weeks of age.

- **Genetics:** A Doberman puppy born to a pair of adults who are both sharper (more reactive) and/or more aggressive than the general population will produce puppies more like themselves. The same applies to more fearful dogs. Dobermans can sometimes be prone to self-mutilating behaviors.

- **Not enough training:** This has been mentioned throughout the book many times but bears repeating at least once more: Dobes need training, both to teach them household manners and social rules, and to teach them to look to their owner for guidance. Training also provides the dog with necessary mental challenges.

- **Lack of leadership:** The owner of a Dobe must be able to provide him with consistent leadership. This doesn't mean the owner must be forceful or mean; instead, it simply

Most problem behaviors are the result of long-term habits that have been overlooked or tolerated, but some are simply due to lack of enough exercise or attention.

means the owner must teach the dog to look to her for guidance and accept her as pack leader without exception.

- **Poor nutrition:** Many dogs, Dobes included, develop problem behaviors when eating a poor-quality diet, especially one high in cereal grains. These issues generally show up as an excess of uncontrollable energy and poor self-control. These dogs will also have a hard time learning and exhibit poor retention for what has been learned.
- **Not enough exercise:** All dogs need exercise, and Doberman Pinschers are no exception. Dobes need a chance to run, play, stretch their legs, and have some good cardio exercise each and every day. Unless your Dobe has some underlying health issues, this

need will continue on into old age.

- **Not enough time with the owner:** Doberman Pinschers are unhappy—and often naughty—dogs if left home alone for many hours each day, especially if left outside in the backyard. Dobes should only be outside when you are present to supervise them. Dobes need to be close to their people as much as possible. When it's necessary that he be left alone, leave your dog in the house. If you need to be away longer than a few hours, consider hiring a pet sitter or leaving your dog in day care.

Preventing a problem behavior from developing is always preferable to trying to change it after it's already been established. After all, if you've ever tried to change a bad habit, you know it can be tough to do. So concentrate on prevention first.

AGGRESSION

Aggression is a term that's somewhat hard to define, even if we think about it in human terms. For example, if someone cuts you off in traffic, you may get angry, yell, and honk your car horn. Is that aggressive behavior? It would certainly be considered aggressive if you chased the guy down, cut him off in traffic, and fired a gun at him; but what about just honking your horn?

It's just as difficult to define canine aggression, especially because there are so many variables. As a general rule, although many things can cause some kind of an aggressive response from a dog, a Doberman isn't considered dangerously aggressive unless he can't control himself, ignores guidance from you, or is a danger to other dogs or people. Any of these situations would indicate a serious problem that warrants immediate attention.

Here are some common things that can cause a dog to react aggressively, which can range from a mild to somewhat stronger response:

- **Pain:** If a dog is in pain, whether from illness or injury, he may react by growling, snapping, or even biting. This is a defense mechanism because the dog feels he cannot properly defend himself in his weakened state.
- **Protecting puppies:** Many female dogs will actively and aggressively protect their puppies if they feel they are threatened.
- **Being teased or tormented:** If a

dog has been teased, he may well react in an aggressive manner because he feels he is being challenged. For example, kids teasing a dog through the fence may cause him to bark and growl, as well as to jump at the fence and chase them until they pass by out of sight.

- **Violence:** If a dog has been hit or otherwise abused, he may become overly fearful or extremely aggressive toward anyone he mistrusts or does not know.
- **Male aggression:** Some male Dobes older than 3 or 4 years can become aggressive toward other male dogs. Neutering can sometimes curb some of this aggression but rarely stops all of it. Prevention is key here. Do not allow a dog-aggressive Dobe to socialize with other dogs. Likewise, don't allow other male dogs to torment your Dobe, either.
- **Resource guarding:** Some dogs will guard a bone from other dogs, while some may go overboard—crouch over, lower their head over, growl, and even bite—to guard anything they consider to be theirs. This type of problem can have serious consequences, and retraining may require the assistance of a behaviorist.

A certain amount of aggression is normal in this breed. People coming to the house will probably be met by a very watchful dog who will stand at the door waiting for the owner to allow the person in. The dog may bark to alert the owner or may simply keep watch until told not to do so. The dog may react with fierce barking and even more aggression if it

Want to Know More?

Your dog needs to know some basic obedience training cues to help you train him out of certain problem behaviors. For a refresher, see Chapter 4: Training Your Doberman Pinscher Puppy.

appears the owner is being threatened. Ideally, a Doberman will cease all aggression when the owner says everything is fine.

How to Manage It

Never let your Dobe behave in a dominant way toward any human, adult or child. If he does, remove him from the situation and isolate him until he is calm again. Then praise him and give him a reward. Of course, preventing aggression is always the best strategy. Eliminating any situations that may cause aggression is also wise. If you avoid the mistakes listed earlier, and provide proper

If territorial aggression becomes unmanageable and poses a danger to you or others, you may need to seek the help of a professional behaviorist.

socialization, exercise, and set appropriate boundaries through consistent, life-long training, you should not have to deal with aggression problems. Your goal is to have a well-behaved, controlled dog based on positive training, one who will reliably respond to your commands in any situation, especially potentially threatening ones. When your Dobe reliably obeys your commands, it means that he accepts you as pack leader and is less likely to challenge your authority.

However, if you feel your Dobe is showing indiscriminate aggression, too much aggression, or inappropriate aggression, call a behaviorist for help right away. This is not an issue to leave unresolved as it can escalate quickly.

BARKING

Your Doberman Pinscher barks to communicate with others, just as people speak to do the same thing. Your Dobe may simply be barking to say hello and get your attention, or he may be barking to let you know that someone is walking up to your house or that the neighbor's child has jumped over your backyard fence. This type of barking is fine, and probably much appreciated, as long as your dog stops as soon as you ask him to do so.

However, when your Dobe barks at anything and everything, especially if the neighbors are beginning to complain, you have a problem. Boredom, loneliness, and a lack of exercise can all contribute to problem barking. Mary Swindell says, "Dobermans left home alone all day out in the yard will bark because they're lonely, bored, and underemployed." This generally amounts to the dog having no job, no mental challenges, and not enough activity to keep him entertained.

How to Manage It

Ideally, it's wiser (and easier) to prevent barking from turning into a bad habit in the first place. Your ultimate goal is to teach your dog that he can bark to notify you if there's a problem, but then to stop barking at your command.

To do this, ask a family member or neighbor to help you. Here's how:

1. Have your helper go outside and knock on your door or ring the doorbell when you ask her to do so.

2. When your Dobe barks at the doorbell or knocking, follow him to the door and acknowledge his help by thanking him, "Sweetie, thanks!" Then calmly but firmly ask him to stop, "Enough."

3. If your dog stops barking, praise him again, and pop a treat into his mouth. Hook a leash to his collar, ask him to sit, and then open the door to greet your helper.

4. If your dog barks again, tell him that's enough again, and use the *watch me* command to get your dog's attention back on you. Then praise him for paying attention, "Sweetie, good!"

5. Repeat this three or four times, and then invite your helper inside for an iced tea or coffee. Have your Dobe lie down and stay at your feet during the visit.

If you have people who will help you, do this several times over the next few weeks, at least until your Dobe reliably learns the *enough* command. Then teach him to obey the same command when he's at the backyard fence barking at passersby, in the car barking at everything, and any other time he's too noisy.

If this technique is not helping, then contact a dog trainer or behaviorist for some additional help. Do not use the electronic collars made to stop barking without some professional guidance.

By the Numbers

Doberman Pinschers are considered puppies until about a year of age, adolescents until 2 years of age, and adults after that. But just because your Dobe is an adult doesn't mean his behavior will always be perfect; dogs can develop problem behaviors at any age, and even the best-behaved adult dog can get into trouble once in a while. Making training a lifelong commitment will help your Dobe learn the things that will enhance his life and enable him to live successfully with you.

DESTRUCTIVE CHEWING

Destructive chewing is a very common problem with young puppies. They usually begin chewing because they want to play. After all, a shoelace is very intriguing and it smells like you. Then, when the puppies are teething, many puppies seem driven to chew because it helps to soothe sore gums. But, to any dog, chewing is just fun; it's how dog's explore their world, so it becomes a self-rewarding behavior. It's important then to make sure puppy chewing escapades don't turn into a bad habit that lasts into adulthood. Again, prevention is much easier than having to deal with a chewing problem later on.

How to Manage It

The best way to manage chewing is to dog-proof your house by putting away anything that looks even the least bit tempting. That means putting away the kids' toys, keeping personal items out of reach, picking up and

Rather than trying to discourage your dog from chewing, redirect the behavior to suitable objects, such as safe chew toys.

storing clothing and shoes, keeping closet doors closed, tying or taping cords and wires, etc.—basically, prevent the problem from happening by removing all chewing opportunities.

Teach your Dobe what he can and cannot chew on. Provide him with plenty of appropriate, good-quality chew toys, such as the durable nylon bones and edible chews made by Nylabone, which will reinforce correct behavior by channeling it toward safe and acceptable choices. To practice, do the following:

1. Hand your dog one of his toys.
2. When he takes it from you, praise him, "Yes! Good to have your toy! Good boy!"
3. When he picks up the toy on his own,

praise him enthusiastically. Don't ignore him when he's made the right choice; throw him a party instead!

4. Repeat this regularly until your dog appears to have learned what he is allowed to chew on without your direction.
5. If you discover that your dog has chewed on something he shouldn't have, remove the item from his mouth, and redirect the behavior to suitable objects.

If you find out after the damage has already been done, do not punish your dog. Correcting him after the fact will not work because he won't associate the punishment with his earlier behavior. Instead, look at what he's done, think about what was going on when it happened (was he left unsupervised?), and then outline a plan to make sure it doesn't happen again. Keep in mind that dogs can't discriminate between your expensive shoe and the old shoe that you once provided as a chew toy. The solution here is consistency in teaching your Dobe that he is only permitted to chew on his own belongings, the ones you provide, which is tantamount to helping him learn the rules.

Limit your Dobe's freedom until he's trained well enough to have free run of the house. Baby gates can close off hallways so your dog doesn't sneak into another room seeking out things to chew. If baby gates don't work, an exercise pen can confine your dog, as can a crate. Or, you can leash him and keep him close to you.

DIGGING

Dobes are not usually problem diggers. However, they can and do dig—not only because they are strong and athletic, but because they enjoy having fun. But diggers usually do so for a reason. Many working dog breeds are wired to go after gophers or other creatures that live in burrows. Some dogs will dig up things like sprinkler systems. Others like to dig in the dirt to find a nice warm spot in cool weather or for just the opposite reason in hot weather. Many dogs will dig just the right hole to hide a bone or chew toy. Dogs who aren't getting enough exercise will dig so they can use up some excess energy. Bored dogs will dig simply because there's nothing better to do.

How to Manage It

To deal with digging problems, you'll need to try to figure out why your dog digs and then offer better alternatives. There are several ways to prevent problem digging:

- Make sure your Dobe gets plenty of exercise every single day. That doesn't mean just a walk; that's not enough for a young, healthy Dobe. Instead, also include a vigorous run, a game of fetch, or a swim. Or get involved in performance sports—you'll both benefit!
- Do some type of training every day—even if you don't plan to compete—so your dog's mind is busy and challenged. No bored dogs allowed!
- When your dog is left home alone, use a food-dispensing toy to keep him amused and entertained.
- Remove digging temptations. For example, fence off gardens, protect or cover sprinkler heads and drip irrigation lines, etc.
- If your dog is really determined to dig, build him a sand box in an area of the yard where it won't bother you. Dig up the dirt and break it up, then partially bury several dog biscuits and toys. Take your Dobe to the area and tell him, "Get the cookies! Find your toys!" When he starts nosing around and sniffing, praise him. When he digs, praise some more. Let him know he's allowed to dig here.

JUMPING UP

A dog who jumps up on people can easily hurt them without meaning to do so. Dobes are large, muscular dogs and have hard paws with healthy nails. Children and seniors can easily be knocked down, and anyone could have his or her skin scratched or clothes damaged. Jumping up is a bad habit, and it often frightens people.

But this behavior is meant to be somewhat social and a form of invitation. Dogs jump up to get attention, to greet others face to face. Puppies greet adult dogs by licking their muzzle; the adult dogs in turn give the puppies something to eat, some affection, or a chance to play. When people take the place of

The best way to teach a dog not to jump up is to teach and consistently reward an alternative behavior such as sitting or standing calmly to greet you.

then do some refresher training with him; your goal is to have him respond immediately every time you ask him to sit.

Now, you're going to practice this in a situation where he normally jumps up on you.

1. With some treats in your hand, go outside, and then come back inside as you would when you return home from an outing, "Hi, everyone, I'm home!"

2. When your Dobe comes running to you, excited and ready to jump, show him the treat and tell him, "Sweetie, sit!" When he sits, pop the treat into his mouth and then release him, "Okay."

3. If in his excitement, he tries to jump, take hold of his collar with one hand as you show him another treat with the other hand, "Sweetie, no jump. Sit." With the hand on the collar, you can help him sit and then hold still in the sit. Then praise him and give him a treat.

4. Practice this three or four times, then take a break. Have another practice session later on, and then again on subsequent days.

If your dog likes to jump on guests who come to your home, turn visits into a training session or practice with a helper. When someone rings the doorbell or knocks, call out to them, "I'll be right there. Let me leash the dog." Then, with your dog on leash, walk up to the door, have your Dobe sit, and then open the door. If your dog lunges forward as if to jump on the guests as they walk in, use the leash to stop him, bring him back to you, and have him sit. Then praise him. Ask your guests to ignore him until he has himself under control. Then, keep him in a sit while they pet him. Use the leash or a hand on his collar to make sure he continues to sit. Praise him if he behaves appropriately.

adult dogs in a puppy's life, he continues this behavior. Usually, jumping up does get him the attention he seeks; after all, even yelling is a form of attention.

How to Manage It

The best way to teach a dog not to jump up is to teach an alternative behavior. For example, teach your dog to sit instead of jump up. If your Dobe already knows the *sit* command,

You can use this same technique when out on a walk. Just ask your Dobe to sit before people greet him, and use the leash or your hand on his collar to help him control himself. Praise and reward him for sitting.

Several other techniques used to stop jumping aren't at all effective and can, in fact, make the problem worse:

- Don't knee your dog in the chest as he jumps up on you. Although this is a common correction, it could hurt him. Plus, many Dobes will take that as a challenge to overcome.
- Don't grab your Dobe's front paws when he jumps up. If you grab his paws and hold on—as that technique recommends—he will probably start gnawing on your hands so that you let go. Not a good idea.
- Don't turn your back on your dog, hoping that he won't jump up because he can't greet you face to face. He'll just begin jumping even more.

There is one thing that all three of these techniques have in common—besides not being effective—and that is that these techniques don't teach your Dobe what to do instead. After all, he's jumping on people for attention, and if he can't get that attention he's going to continue to jump. When you teach him to sit for petting (and attention), he learns to sit to get what he's craving.

LEASH PULLING

Some dogs seem to feel that going for a walk means pulling the owner's arm out of the shoulder socket. That is not a comfortable way to go for a walk, and it's potentially dangerous for both you and your dog. Dobes are much too strong to behave in this way on a walk. In addition, if your dog is pulling hard on the leash, he's not looking to you for

guidance. A dog who is pulling on the leash is the one in charge.

How to Manage It

The *heel* exercise is a great way to teach your Dobe how to walk nicely on the leash because to do so correctly, he needs to be paying attention to you. Refresh your Dobe's leash skills by practicing that exercise again (see Chapter 9: Doberman Pinscher Training, Teaching the *Heel*). Use the *watch me* exercise to get your Dobe's attention on you, and then make the *heel* exercise fun and challenging. Make right turns, left turns, and about turns

A dog who pulls on leash is difficult to control and poses a danger to himself and the person walking him. The *heel* exercise is a great way to teach your Dobe how to walk nicely on leash.

so it becomes a game to see if you can reliably maintain his attention.

Of course, your Dobe doesn't have to take every walk in the heel position. Sometimes you're going to want to relax on your walk and let your Dobe relax, too. But at the same time, your Dobe needs to be aware enough of the leash to keep some slack in it. After all, if there is slack in the leash, he's not pulling. Practice the following:

1. With your dog on a 4- or 6-foot (1.2- or 2-m) leash, go to an outdoor area where you have some room to move around freely. Hold the leash securely in both hands just in case your dog decides to pull.
2. Without saying anything to your dog, begin walking straight ahead.
3. When your dog forges ahead and tightens the leash, simply turn around and walk the opposite direction. Don't say anything, just hold on to the leash and go.
4. When your dog catches up to you, say, "What happened?" in a surprised but happy tone of voice. Show him you're happy he decided to join you.
5. When he dashes ahead again, repeat the turn-around.
6. When your dog is beginning to get the idea, watching you more than he normally does, praise him. And then turn around anyway, praising him when he follows you.

I like to make a game out of this exercise; I turn right or left, make an about-turn, and then another one. My dogs know it's a game, too, and will dash after me with the stubs of their tails wagging away. As they do, however, that leash is loose!

NIPPING AND BITING

Every puppy is going to use his mouth to manipulate the world around him. It's normal; he doesn't have any hands, and his paws don't have opposable thumbs, so he's going to use his mouth to explore everything. You can teach him not to chew on inappropriate things; we discussed that earlier in this chapter. But puppies also have to learn that using their mouth on people—as they did their littermates—is forbidden.

When any dog uses his mouth to try to get a person to do something or not do something, there is a danger that action could be perceived as a dog bite. For example, perhaps when you're at home you don't mind if your Dobe takes your hand in his mouth to lead you to the doggy treats jar. You know he's not biting you, and he's usually pretty gentle. But what happens if your dog does this when he's more excited and breaks the skin? Or, what if he does it to a guest, particularly a child? Or a worker at the boarding kennel where your Dobe stays once in a while?

Unfortunately, too, many breeds already have a bad reputation, and, sadly, Dobes are one of them. Dobes, Pit Bulls, Rottweilers, and a few other breeds don't need to step very far over the line to have someone labeling them vicious or bad. It's very important then

Multi-Dog Tip

When you have multiple dogs in the household, they can become dependent on each other and show separation anxiety when the family pack is not all present. To prevent this, make sure your dogs go on outings with you and other family members often; taking one or two dogs at a time and leaving the other dogs at home.

To manage nipping behavior, teach your dog to pick up a toy when he becomes overly excited.

that all Dobes are taught that putting their mouth on people is not allowed unless the dog is participating in a working dog sport such as Schutzhund.

How to Manage It

Again, teaching an alternative behavior is the best preventive measure. For example, teach your dog to pick up a toy when he's excited.

1. To start, pick up a toy yourself and hand it to your dog when he begins to mouth or nip, praising him when he takes and holds it, "Sweetie, good to have a toy! Yes!"

2. When he picks up a toy on his own, praise him, "Yes! Good to get a toy!"

3. Then begin to send him for a toy when he's excited, "Sweetie, get a toy!" Walk him to a toy or his toy box initially, but then as he seems to understand, let him go ahead of you to the toy. Always praise him when he gets the toy.

This technique teaches your Dobe an alternative technique; by having a toy in his mouth, his mouth is occupied; he can't do anything inappropriate. This is far more effective—and a positive training technique—

than yelling at your dog every time he uses his mouth.

SELF-REWARDING BEHAVIORS

Doberman Pinschers are elegant, dignified dogs. They look like they belong in the portraits of the Old Masters from Europe centuries ago. That is, until a Dobe decides to raid the kitchen trash can. There is nothing less elegant than to walk into the kitchen and see the trash all over the floor, with your Dobe standing in the middle of it.

Raiding trash cans is what is called a self-rewarding behavior. In most of our training, we provide the rewards for our dog. We praise him in a happy tone of voice, we pop a treat into his mouth, and we have fun with him when he works with us. He continues to work with us because he enjoys it. However, when your Dobe digs in the trash can and finds something good to eat, that becomes the reward. He's going to continue raiding the trash can because he really enjoyed finding those tidbits of food.

Other self-rewarding behaviors include:

- Chasing the family cat. When the cat runs away, even if just down the hall and into another room, the chase itself is exciting: it causes an adrenaline rush, and the dog has fun.
- Stealing food off the kitchen counter.
- Stealing the cat's food or raiding the cat's litter box.
- Chasing birds and other creatures from the back yard. There's an adrenaline rush and the fun of the chase.
- Barking at the postal carrier and other delivery drivers. Your Dobe barks and barks, and then the service person goes away. Now, in this instance, not only did your dog get a rush, but he chased the stranger away—so he won! He chased away a human trespasser,

and for a potentially protective Doberman, that's a big deal.

Because self-rewarding behaviors are so satisfying, training is usually ineffective at changing the unwanted behavior. What's most effective is to prevent the behavior by changing the situation entirely and eliminating the potential for it. For example, put the cat's food and litter box where the dog can't get to it. Make the kitchen off limits, or put the trash can away and out of reach. Keep food off the counters when no one is preparing it.

In other situations, teach your dog to come to you for guidance. When it's time for a mail carrier or delivery driver to come by, have your Dobe on leash. When your dog begins to react, tell him, "Sweetie, watch me!" and use a treat to get his attention. Praise him when he looks at you, and pop a treat into his mouth. When he begins to look to you on his own, enthusiastically praise him.

SELF-MUTILATION

Some Doberman Pinschers will develop problem behaviors when stressed or fearful. They may lick a paw (or paws) repeatedly, nibble on a leg, or suck on their own flank. These self-mutilating behaviors can be repeated so much that the dog will actually cause an open, bleeding wound.

Carol Byrnes, a certified dog trainer, says, "Self-mutilation appears to have a hereditary component." These behaviors are also thought to be caused by boredom, a lack of exercise, and often, the food the dog is eating. Some experts feel that an individual dog may have inherited the tendency for the behavior but something else must supply the cue. A dog with fleas or a tick may begin scratching and then not stop. A bored dog may lick his paws to clean them and then continue on and on. Other experts feel these behaviors may actually be related to obsessive compulsive disorders. Melissa Wilkins, a volunteer with Doberman Rescue, says that it may be caused by a lack of attention from the dog's owners.

In any case, if your dog appears to be hurting himself with repetitive behaviors, call your veterinarian first. Make sure there is no physical reason for the cause of these behaviors, such as fleas or ticks, arthritis in the paws, body soreness, a hormonal imbalance, or anything else.

If you're home with your dog when you see the behavior begin, distract him. Ask him to get you a toy, or to do something else for you. Have him practice a command such as *sit*, *lie down*, *come*, or *stand*, and praise him for working for you.

If you believe these behaviors are occurring when your dog is home alone, make sure he gets plenty of exercise before you go out. Then offer him a food-dispensing toy as you leave. A happy, tired dog will most likely take a nap.

If you try these suggestions and the behavior continues, then it's time to talk to both your veterinarian and a behaviorist. The three of you will have to coordinate a plan that may include medication as well as behavior modification.

WHEN ALL ELSE FAILS

Problem behaviors can be challenging, not just because they can be annoying, but also because there can be so many potential causes for them, some of which you may not be able to pinpoint or handle on your own.

If you're confused, frustrated, or just plain fed up, don't give up. Instead, get some professional help. Start by attending a group obedience class, either to teach your dog basic obedience or to refresh skills learned earlier. If your Dobe's obedience skills are good, perhaps a visit at home from a private dog trainer is the answer. Ask your veterinarian if she can recommend a professional service in your area, or go to the website of the Association of Pet Dog Trainers at www.apdt.com. Your veterinarian might also suggest a behavioral consultant who can delve more deeply into behavior problems. You can find one at the website for the International Association of Animal Behavior Consultants at www.iaabc. org. In any case, get some help so you and your dog aren't fighting each other instead of enjoying each other.

Training Tidbit

Food-dispensing toys are a wonderful addition to every dog owner's training toolbox. These toys dispense kibble or small bits of other types of food when the dog moves them around. Because many problem behaviors stem from loneliness, fear, or stress, this activity can help by keeping your dog occupied and out of trouble, especially when he is left alone.

CHAPTER 11

DOBERMAN PINSCHER SPORTS AND ACTIVITIES

Doberman Pinschers are fast, athletic, and agile. They enjoy working with their owners, love to show off, and appreciate applause. All of these characteristics make them excellent participants in many canine sports and activities. Kim Somjen, DVM, says, "My dogs and I compete in rally, obedience, and agility. I love showing my Dobermans because they do everything with style, and they are so athletic. It's a beautiful thing to see any Doberman working well and happily."

ACTIVITIES TO SHARE WITH YOUR DOBERMAN

Your Doberman Pinscher was not originally bred to be a pet. Although he loves spending time in the house with you, he was designed to be a working dog. Today, he doesn't need to guard the tax collector from bandits, as the earliest Dobes did for Herr Dobermann, but he will be happiest when you and he can do things together. Luckily, there are many activities you can do with your dog that will be fun for both of you, as well as provide exercise for both mind and body.

Camping

We enjoy going camping with our dogs and have done so in tents, cabins, and recreational vehicles. We like to be outside, enjoy hiking in the forest, and just hanging out in the campground. We usually try to introduce our dogs to camping at some point during late puppyhood or adolescence so they get used to it. Watching a puppy explore and discover all these new sights, sounds, and smells is great fun.

It's important to keep your Dobe on leash while camping and hiking, not just because it's usually required by the campground or park department, but also for his safety. Should your Dobe decide to chase a squirrel or deer, he could be out of sight and hearing range in a flash. Even the best-trained dog could easily become lost. Plus, chasing wildlife is illegal in many places.

Make sure your dog isn't disturbing the other campers. Not everyone loves dogs as much as we do. That means no barking or wandering near other campsites or in off-limits areas. It should go without saying, but I'm going to say it anyway: Always pick up after your dog, too.

Exceptionally intelligent, athletic, and agile, Dobes excel at many canine sports and outdoor activities.

Before going on a camping trip, give your veterinarian a call. Make sure that your dog is up to date on any needed vaccinations, especially any special ones recommended for that region. Talk to her, too, about heartworm and flea or tick preventives in case those are needed.

Walking and Hiking

Dog ownership and going for regular walks seem to go hand in hand. Walking your dog is good socialization—your Dobe gets to see, smell, and hear the world around him—but it's also quality time that you and your dog can spend together.

A walk really shouldn't be considered exercise though. Although going for a nice brisk walk might be exercise for you, and is

good exercise for a Dobe puppy or senior, it can't be considered daily exercise for a healthy adult Dobe. For him, a walk is just a pleasant outing.

For healthy exercise, consider leaving the sidewalks and go hiking with your Dobe. Many local, regional, and state parks allow dogs on their hiking trails. Fit your Dobe with a doggy backpack so that he can carry a few bottles of water for both of you, as well as a foldable bowl for his water, some bags to pick up after him, and sunscreen.

With both walking and hiking, begin slowly so your dog's muscles can strengthen and his pads can toughen up. Let him get used to the backpack, too, before you add any weight to it.

Walking and hiking with your Dobe can be a wonderful outing if your Dobe will walk nicely on leash. If he pulls, charges at other dogs, barks at people, or lifts his leg on every vertical object, well, then the walk won't be any fun at all. If your Dobe engages in any of these behaviors, and you cannot successfully train him yourself, contact a dog trainer for some help.

Jogging With a Partner

Doberman Pinschers are bred to run, so if you're athletic and like to go jogging or running, you'll probably enjoy having a Dobe running partner. Not only will both of you get your daily exercise, but your dog will provide companionship and security as you work out together. As with any exercise program, start slowly so your dog can build some endurance and fitness. If your Dobe has any health challenges, talk to your veterinarian before you begin running him.

Teach your Dobe to run by your left side in the heel position. If his neck is next to your left leg, you can pick up speed, slow down,

Multi-Dog Tip

Not all dogs have the same abilities or interests. If you have multiple dogs, experiment with various activities and canine sports to see which ones work best for each of your dogs. You may have one dog who excels at agility and another who is more excited to go hiking and jogging with you. Just remember that keeping the experience fun for both you and your dogs is the most important factor in any type of activity or competition.

and make turns, and he can see you and react appropriately. If he's too far ahead of you, he can't see you and you'll trip over him. You may want to refresh his obedience training before starting a running program.

Running Alongside a Bicycle

If you aren't the jogging type, or can't run fast enough for your Dobe, then you may want to teach him to run alongside your bicycle. Several commercially made hookups are available for this purpose. The one I use everyday fastens to the bar under the bicycle seat and positions the dog at my side, basically in the heel position. My dog is behind the front wheel so there's no problem running into him, and yet he is up far enough so that I can watch him for any problems.

You can introduce your dog to the bike by walking him and the bike together for a few minutes over several days. Bounce the bike, roll it forward, and then side to side, so that your Dobe gets used to it. Then hook him up and begin some slow rides back and forth in front of your house. This gets him used to the bike and, at the same time, gives his pads a chance to toughen.

Gradually increase the time and distance you and your dog ride, watching him for signs of stress, such as panting, wide eyes, and flattened ears. If this occurs, stop, give him a break, give him some water, and let him relax. Take your time getting him used to this activity because sore muscles are no more fun for dogs than they are for people.

Trick Training

While training basic obedience commands is important, there are only so many different ways to practice these exercises. However, trick training can become one of the most enjoyable ways to teach these skills. Although many people think trick training is teaching your dog to shake hands or roll over, there can be much more to it than that. The tricks can range from very simple to much more complicated commands.

For example, a few years ago my husband and I had a black Doberman Pinscher named Inu (EE-new). Inu was tall, handsome, and very regal. He and I were out in the front yard one day while I was talking to a neighbor. Her son had just graduated from the local police academy and was coming by to show his mother his new uniform. When he showed up I congratulated him, but I also wanted to tease him a little since I'd known him since he was a young teenager. I turned to Inu and said, "Inu, would you rather be a police officer or

a dead dog?" Inu dropped to the ground and rolled over to his side, with his head down, looking like a very dead Dobe. The young man sputtered, stammered, and then began to laugh!

This trick worked because Inu's cue was "dead dog." I had taught him to pay attention to those command words so that, when he heard them in conversation, he would react as he'd been trained to do. It was a great trick that always got people to laugh.

A solid foundation in basic obedience is always necessary, but it is essential for trick training as well. By regularly practicing commands, you and your dog will already know how to work together, so that adding tricks to your routine will be easy. A number of

The Canine Good Citizen program encourages owners to foster and encourage good manners in their dogs.

good books that can take you through step-by-step sessions at home are available online and in pet stores. Many dog trainers also offer trick training classes.

You can start trick training when your Dobe is a puppy, but even older dogs will enjoy it. Just tailor the tricks to your dog's skill level.

THERAPY DOGS

Therapy dog work can be one of the most rewarding volunteer activities in which you have ever participated. When you take your Dobe to a nursing home or hospital to visit people, and those people smile, laugh, or even cry when they pet and hug your dog, you will know that you're making a difference in someone's life. And there's nothing better than that.

Therapy dogs are privately owned pets who, along with their owners, visit people in hospitals, nursing homes, and retirement communities. These dogs may also go to day care centers or elementary schools to teach kids how to safely interact with dogs, as well as visit physical therapy facilities to help motivate people. Many dogs participate in reading programs for children. After all, it's a lot more fun to read to a dog than it is to a teacher.

The first requirement for a therapy dog is that he likes people. He doesn't have to be gushingly affectionate toward everyone, but he must be willing to walk up to strangers and allow petting. If the dog is standoffish or aloof, he isn't going to be effective.

The dog must also be well trained in all of the basic obedience commands. He cannot jump on people, paw or scratch them, and obviously cannot put his mouth (and teeth) on them. He should not bark or growl, he cannot lift his leg or have other housetraining lapses, and he must be respectful of other people's belongings when visiting.

Many dog trainers offer therapy dog training to get the dog used to wheelchairs, walkers, and other equipment he may encounter on a visit. The classes also teach visiting skills. Talk to your local trainer and ask if she offers therapy dog training, evaluation, and certification. The Delta Society is one of several organizations that trains and screens volunteers and their pets for assistance programs, and this society can help you find a group in your area offering classes. Visit their website at www. deltasociety.org.

CANINE GOOD CITIZEN PROGRAM

I've been a fan of the American Kennel Club (AKC)'s Canine Good Citizen (CGC) program since it began more than 20 years ago. At the time, my husband and I had German Shepherd Dogs and a Doberman Pinscher, and we knew well what breed discrimination was. Our dogs were prejudged by people to be aggressive and potentially dangerous simply because of their breeds.

The CGC program, though, was designed to recognize responsible dog owners and well-behaved dogs. When the dog is able to pass all ten test exercises, he is awarded the title "Canine Good Citizen" and can have the CGC designation listed after his name. The program is open to all dogs, purebred or mixed-breed, whether registered with the AKC or not.

The test exercises are as follows:

1. The dog will allow a friendly person who is not known to him to walk up and greet his owner.
2. The dog, when approached by a friendly person, will allow that person to pet him.
3. The dog can sit calmly and accept basic grooming procedures.
4. The dog can walk nicely on a loose leash.

5. The dog can walk calmly through a crowd and remain under control.
6. The dog can demonstrate that he can sit, lie down, and stay in place when asked.
7. The dog will come when called.
8. The dog will behave politely around other dogs and will not lunge or bark at them.
9. The dog will react appropriately to distractions, such as visual or sound stimuli.
10. The dog can calmly endure supervised separation from the owner for three minutes.

The CGC title has become so popular that many landlords now require it as a condition of allowing a dog to live in a rental home. Some insurance companies offer discounts for dogs who have passed the CGC test, and many therapy dog organizations use the CGC as a requirement for potential candidates. To find a CGC evaluator in your area, go to the AKC's website at www.akc.org.

CANINE SPORTS

Because of their intelligence and athletic prowess, Doberman Pinschers can excel at a variety of canine sports, making them wonderful competitors. Along with having a good foundation of basic obedience, most of these sports require that the dog be both mentally and physically sound.

Agility

Many agility competitors have said that the sport of agility is like a combination of a working dog's obstacle course, an equine Grand Prix jumping contest, and a thoroughbred race course. To compete in agility, the dog and owner must maneuver through a timed course in which the dog jumps and crosses over or through a variety

By the Numbers

Most canine sports organizations have set age requirements to prevent dogs from competing in sanctioned events before they are physically and mentally mature. Here are a few of the American Kennel Club's age limits for competition:
- agility: 15 months
- Canine Good Citizen: No age limit, but dogs must be old enough to have received their immunizations
- conformation: 6 months
- obedience: 6 months
- rally obedience: 6 months
- tracking: 6 months

of obstacles, all while moving quickly but accurately. A variety of titles can be earned, including championships.

Conformation

At a conformation show, each dog is judged based on how well he meets the specifications of the breed standard, which detail the ideal physical representation of the breed as described by the AKC-sanctioned standard. This competition serves two purposes: First, the best dog of the day wins a coveted title; winning a Best of Breed or Best in Show title is an amazing accomplishment. In addition, in conformation competition, breeders can compare their dogs to the winners and continue to strive to better their breed by producing the best dogs possible.

Obedience Trials

In obedience competition, dogs and their owners compete in different classes, each with its own requirements. The class may ask the dog to heel on and off leash; to come when called off leash; to retrieve a dumbbell, a glove, or a scented article; or to obey the owner's hand signals. As the dog and owner progress from simple exercises to more difficult ones, the dog can earn succeeding obedience titles, and eventually a championship title.

Flyball

Flyball is a fast-paced, exciting team relay sport. Two teams compete against each other as the dogs run from their owners, jump a series of hurdles, bounce on a wall that pops out a tennis ball, and then turn and race back to their owners over the hurdles again. The team that finishes first wins. All dogs can participate.

Freestyle

Freestyle, also called "dancing with dogs" by many people, is exactly that. The dog and owner perform dancing, obedience, and trick-type movements with music. It is challenging and yet great fun. The Dobe's elegant look makes him a perfect partner for freestyle.

Schutzhund

Schutzhund and other working dog competitions developed from the historic jobs that Dobermans, Rottweilers, and other protective breeds were designed to do.

Along with a soild foundation in basic obedience, most canine sports require that the dog be both physically and mentally sound.

Want to Know More?

When participating in canine sports, there is always some risk of physical injury. Taking steps to prevent accidents—and to be prepared if they should occur—allows your dog to continue enjoying the many benefits of being mentally and physically challenged while competing and having fun with you. Always bring a canine first-aid kit with you to any activity or event, and seek veterinary attention immediately if your dog is injured while practicing or competing. For information about first aid and emergency care, see Chapter 8: Doberman Pinscher Health and Wellness.

This activity encompasses protection work, obedience, tracking, endurance, and more.

Search and Rescue

Search and rescue, also called SAR, is an intensive yet rewarding form of volunteer work. The training is for both dog and owner and can include air scenting, tracking, scenting in urban obstacle piles (rubble), scenting in rural settings, orienteering, map and compass and GPS work, and much more. Doberman Pinschers have excelled at SAR work.

If you're interested in any of these sports, talk to a local trainer. She may be able to help you get started in the training needed, or can refer you to someone locally who can.

TRAVELING WITH YOUR DOG

If you decide to participate in dog sports with your Doberman, either in noncompetitive activities or organized sports, some travel may be involved. Many dog owners who go to conformation dog shows, agility trials, or obedience trials will be on the road a couple of weekends a month. Even if you don't participate in these events, you may wonder whether it's a good idea to bring your Dobe along on vacation. Many people travel with their dogs, but there are important things to consider before making any plans.

Should Your Dobe Travel?

Choosing whether you should travel with your dog requires that you take a realistic look at his overall condition and comfort zones. Don't think of your dog as you'd like him to be, but as he really is. Then, too, think about your trip—where you'll be staying, how long the trip will be, and what the weather will be like during the trip.

- Does your Dobe like to ride in the car? If he's a good rider, great. However, if he hates riding in the car, gets carsick, or is a nervous, anxious traveler, don't bring him with you on this year's vacation. Take some time to get him past those issues first, and don't hesitate to talk to a trainer if you need some help.

- Are you flying? Where are you going and when? Many airlines have restrictions on flying animals in cargo during very hot or very cold weather. Shy and fearful dogs shouldn't fly because it can be an unsettling experience. Before making reservations, talk to the airlines about flying your dog. Where are the dogs flown? What conditions do they have in that area? What happens if the plane has to sit on the runway for a while before or after the flight? What are their rules and regulations concerning pets? Only fly your dog if you feel very comfortable about the entire situation. Also, if you are traveling abroad, make sure to check the country's restrictions and vaccination

Before traveling with your Dobe, make sure that dogs will be welcome at your destination.

requirements, then discuss this and your travel plans with your vet to determine if your dog is up to the trip.

- Where will you be staying? Make sure your Doberman Pinscher will be welcome there. Some hotels, motels, and camp grounds have size and/or breed restrictions, or don't allow pets at all. Make reservations ahead of time and tell them you have a large dog. After all, you don't want any surprises when you check in.

- Is your dog healthy? Talk to your veterinarian before traveling with a young puppy, elderly dog, or a dog with an injury or illness. The stress of travel can adversely affect these dogs.

- Is your dog well trained and well behaved? It's much easier to travel with a well-trained Dobe. A poorly behaved dog may lift his leg and

Training Tidbit

If you want to bring your dog along on vacation, it's a good idea do a refresher in basic obedience training in a variety of locations to get him ready for the trip. Practice his obedience skills in unfamiliar places so that he learns to ignore distractions while responding reliably to all commands. Not only will this ensure his safety, but it will make him a pleasant traveling companion who is welcome wherever he goes.

mark the hotel's furniture, or bark in the hotel room, or make people uncomfortable. If his training is not as good as it could be, don't take him this year but spend some time in training so he can accompany you next year.

As you are thinking about whether or not to bring your dog along, keep in mind that during your trip, you'll need to focus some of your energy on your dog. He will need to be walked often, taken outside to relive himself, and he'll need time to play. You'll need to make your plans around your dog, so make sure you really want to bring him along.

When Your Dobe Can't Travel With You

If you've decided it would be better for your dog to remain behind, at least on this trip, several different options are available.

Pet Sitters

Your dog is happiest at home, of course, and many people prefer to leave their pets at home. However, if you leave your Dobe

When dogs are given an adequate amount of recreation time, they are healthier, happier, and better behaved.

at home, who is going to care for him? A neighbor or friend might be busy, or may be unreliable or uncomfortable with your dog. Professional pet sitters can be a better choice because your Dobe won't be stressed by being left home alone most of the day. Some will housesit, living with your dog as you would, while others just come over to feed and walk your dog. Some pet sitters board dogs in their homes. If your Dobe is good with other dogs, this might be an option. You will have the supervision that a boarding kennel provides, yet in a home-like atmosphere. Ask the pet sitter to come over and meet your dog. After all, she must be able to get into the house and yard with your Dobe there alone. If he is protective and she's worried about the dog, he might be better off in a boarding kennel.

Boarding Kennels

A boarding kennel situation may not be like home, but it's more secure and your dog will be well supervised. A growing number of boarding facilities are now run like camps or hotels for dogs, with regular walks and space to run, meals, activities and playtimes, and even special grooming and pampering services.

To find a pet sitter or boarding kennel, talk to dog-owning friends and ask who they've had experience with, who they prefer, and who they don't recommend. Your veterinarian may also make reliable recommendations. Then do some research before your trip.

If you are thinking about leaving your dog in a pet sitter's home or in a boarding kennel, go to visit each one. How secure are the facilities? What provisions are taken to prevent escapes? Does the place look and smell clean? Do you feel comfortable with the caretakers? Do they have experience handling Dobes? Do the dogs there look happy and well attended?

No matter which option you choose, make sure the person responsible for your dog has instructions for his care, your dog's food and some toys, his leash, medications, vaccination and health information, including your vet's contact information, and your cell phone number or vacation contact information. Make sure your dog wears a buckle collar with identification. And then enjoy yourselves!

Your Dobe's Travel Kit

When traveling with your dog—whether near or far—pack a travel kit for him.

For short trips, you don't need too many supplies: a leash, bottled water, portable bowl, treats, a favorite toy, first aid kit, and pickup bags. These items can all be stored in a tote bag or plastic container.

For longer journeys, however, pack the following:

- collar, with ID tags attached (spare)
- leash (spare)
- travel crate
- bedding
- food (enough to last the entire trip)
- bottled water
- medications
- pickup bags
- bowls (one for water, one for food)
- toys
- treats
- grooming supplies
- medications
- first-aid kit
- veterinary records (including vaccination records and contact numbers)

PART III

SENIOR YEARS

CHAPTER 12

FINDING YOUR DOBERMAN PINSCHER SENIOR

When people decide to add a dog to their household, most tend to think of getting a puppy, which has been the traditional choice for generations. More recently, though, people have learned that older puppies or adult dogs can join a household and become family members with few problems. Unfortunately, few think about adding an older dog, and that may be because of some misconceptions about them. That's too bad because older Dobes are a treasure.

OLD DOBERMANS ARE GOLDEN

True, older Dobes are not golden in color; they are black, red, fawn, or blue, but their hearts are made of pure gold. There is nothing quite as special as an old dog. The muzzle may be gray, the eyes might be a little cloudy, and the legs arthritic, but the dog's heart is yours. Old dogs have spent their lives watching us and probably know people better than we do ourselves.

Although it's heartbreaking to think about, older Doberman Pinschers sometimes find themselves in need of new homes. Many people feel that there must be something wrong with the dog; after all, why would an older dog be given up by his owners? However, a dog can lose his home for a variety of reasons, none of which is his fault at all. His owners may be ill and unable to care for him, or an older owner may have passed away. Perhaps a new baby developed allergies to the Dobe, or a military family is transferred overseas and cannot take their beloved pet.

The reasons are many, and it really doesn't matter why. What is important is that an older Doberman who has lost his home is going to

By the Numbers

There is no set age at which a Doberman Pinscher is considered a senior. Often, this is based more upon the dog's overall health. However, veterinarians generally start regarding Dobes as "older" by 7 years of age, even if not yet a senior citizen.

be grieving and is in desperate need of a new loving family.

ADOPTING A SENIOR DOBE CAN BE SPECIAL

Adopting an older Doberman Pinscher can be a wonderful experience. Not only can you gain a nice dog, but you're providing a new home for a dog in need. There are many advantages to adopting an older dog. He is past the housetraining stage of life and isn't going to chew up the sofa. He is no longer rowdy and demanding of play or exercise every hour on the hour. Nor does he need puppy or basic obedience training. There is no guessing how tall, big, or heavy he will be, and you will have a fairly good idea what his temperament and personality will be.

Older dogs are often a wonderful pet for a household with children. The older Dobe, if he was raised with kids, will be patient and kind. The dog should be in good health, however, as dogs with health issues can be grumpy.

People who are growing older themselves don't necessarily want to deal with puppy antics, either. Or, perhaps they don't have the physical ability to deal with a puppy even if they wanted to. And an older dog can provide companionship and security without the hassles of puppyhood.

Misconceptions About Older Dogs

Sometimes older dogs aren't adopted as quickly as younger ones because people have reservations about bringing an older dog into the household. One of the biggest concerns seems to be that the older dog won't fit into the new household, or that an older dog is set in his ways and will find it difficult to adjust. While it's true that an older dog may enjoy his habits—perhaps dinner at a set time every evening, for example—moving to a different location such as a new home will be a cause for change anyway. But an older dog is more than capable of learning a new routine—often more quickly than a young adult. He is more focused and willing to accept your leadership, and he will work hard to please you.

There also seems to be a belief that older dogs will have a hard time bonding with new owners. This, too, is not true. Although Doberman Pinschers do bond very strongly with their people and grieve when they lose their family and home, that doesn't mean they won't become attached to their new owners. In fact, the opposite is true. A dog who has loved and been loved by people, will grieve but will want that closeness again. When given time to get to know his new owners, he will bond tightly to them—as tightly as if he'd live with them all his life.

Potential adopters also have real concerns that the older dog is going to spend less time with them before passing away. Although this is true, the loss of those years is outweighed by the joy of having an older dog and being able to care for him and love him for whatever time he has left, and to be loved unconditionally in return.

Multi-Dog Tip

An older dog can be a great choice for a family who already has a puppy and wants another dog, but doesn't necessarily want the type of commitment raising another puppy demands. The older dog can help raise the younger one and can lead by example.

Doberman Pinscher breed rescues are a good place to look for an older Dobe.

FINDING AND CHOOSING AN OLDER DOBE

There are older Doberman Pinschers who need homes, but it can sometimes be tough to find them. Because most people are looking for a young dog or puppy, many shelters will take in older dogs but will not keep them. The dogs are often euthanized fairly quickly. Although it seems wrong or cruel, it's because most shelters have a limited amount of space and funding and would prefer to give that space to a dog deemed more adoptable. A shelter in your area may maintain a waiting list, though; if they do, ask to be notified when an older Dobe is brought in.

Doberman Pinscher breed rescues are also a good place to look for an older Dobe. If you go to the Doberman Pinscher Club of America's website www.dpca.org, you can click on "rescue." This will provide an e-mail address to contact, or will put you in touch with a rescue group in your area.

Many breeders will know of an older dog needing a new home. A retired show dog, a dog formerly used for breeding, or even a dog of her breeding who has lost his home may be available and waiting for a new home. The breeder may be able to give you quite a bit of information about the dog, and this is always good.

The Internet has become a very useful tool for those working to place dogs in need into good forever homes. PetFinder.com is one of the largest and most reputable sites you may use to locate an adoptable pet. But looking on a website has a few drawbacks. It's tough to search for the dog of your dreams only to find he's in Maine while you're living in San Diego. However, if you're willing to take the time to search through all of the postings, and to keep saying no until you find the right dog for you, then Internet adoption sites can be very useful. Of course, it's always advisable to meet any prospects in person before making a commitment. You don't want to put the dog—or

Your adopted senior will need time to adjust to his new home.

yourself—through the trauma of giving him up and causing him to become homeless yet again.

As you're looking for your new dog, talk to people about your search. It's been said that networking is one of the best ways to find a new job, and it can definitely be one of the best ways to find a new dog. Talk to your veterinarian and his staff. Talk to people at the local pet store, and give them your business card. Talk to coworkers and even the lady at the grocery store. Pass the word!

The Right Dobe for You

When you hear of an older Dobe needing a new home, don't say yes right away. Even if you are tempted to rescue him, he is going to be living with you and your family for a long time, so you must be sure you make the best choice possible.

Ask some questions of the dog's owners or the people who have been caring for him:

- How old is he? Is he neutered (or is she spayed)?
- What health problems does the dog have? Ask for details, including what medications he may be taking. Ask if your veterinarian can examine the dog prior to finalizing the adoption.
- Ask to see the dog walking, running, and moving. How does he look? Is he stiff at first but then limbers up? That's normal—however, if he remains stiff and awkward, you'll definitely want him to be fully examined by your veterinarian.
- Does the dog have any physical limitations? Can he go for walks? Does he like to play? Can he jump in the car? Make sure you'll be comfortable with any limitations the dog has.
- Does the dog have any hearing or vision loss?
- If you sit down next to the dog, how does he react? Does he lean in for petting or does he

pull away? Does he remain next to you but aloof? Or, does he act worried? Remember, older dogs can bond to new owners but a shy or fearful dog will have a harder time doing it.

• Talk to the dog; does he look at you? Or, does he ignore you? If you walk away and call him, will he follow you?

There are no right or wrong answers to any of these questions. Instead, use them as a means to decide what you can or cannot handle and choose accordingly.

BRINGING HOME AN OLDER DOG

Bringing home an older dog is not very different from bringing home a puppy. Any dog will need to learn all about your home and household routine, but the primary difference—and a great advantage— is that an older dog will catch on sooner.

When you arrive home, walk your senior outside to the place where you are going to want him to relieve himself. Try a few common phrases to see what he's used to, "Go potty," or "Get busy." If you can figure out what phrase he's used to, then the adjustment will be easier for him. Praise him when he does relieve himself.

Make all preparations in advance so that your new dog feels welcome and can quickly establish some sense of security in an unfamiliar environment. Decide where he will be sleeping; a large crate in your bedroom is best. Placing the crate in your bedroom gives him a chance to hear you, smell you, and be close to you while you're sleeping. Exiling him to another room where he'll be by himself is never a good idea, especially for a Dobe who prefers to be close to his people as he had always been in the past. The crate gives him a safe and quiet spot of his own, as well as

providing a means to keep him confined when you can't watch him.

Begin teaching the rules of your household right away. If your new dog was previously used to being on the furniture but you don't allow that, stick to your rules and start training him from day one. If he tries to get up on the furniture, instead show him where he can relax and nap by bringing him to a bed of his own in the same room.

Be patient with your older dog as he gets to know you and your household. Keep in mind that he might be grieving for his previous owner; he might be moping and sad. That's okay; don't try to cheer him up. Instead, just give him lots of attention and affection. Get him involved in his new household and the new routine. Take him for walks, ask him to follow you outside while you garden, and introduce him to new people. He'll come around—and he'll soon add lots of joy and love to your life.

Training Tidbit

Train your older dog just as you would a younger dog. Show him what to do, praise and reward him, and teach him a name for each behavior. When he makes a mistake, gently interrupt him, and then show him what to do instead. Never ask him to do anything beyond his capabilities, physically or mentally. Keep training sessions short, fun, and always end on a positive note.

CHAPTER 13

CARE OF YOUR DOBERMAN PINSCHER SENIOR

It's very hard to watch a beloved dog grow old. Your senior Doberman Pinscher probably knows you better than anyone else in the world—better than you know yourself. Yet it seems we just never get enough time with our dogs, and their lifetime passes by in a flash. In addition, a dog's aging can bring with it some challenges; your older Dobe is going to need some special care and assistance. Although it may require more effort and commitment on your part, this is a time in your dog's life to treasure. After all, he gave his all to you throughout his younger years, and now is the time you can give back to him.

SIGNS OF AGING

Susan McCullough, author of *Senior Dogs for Dummies*, says, "Many of the same things that happen to aging humans also happen to aging dogs." As different as people and dogs are from each another, there are many similarities you will recognize in your Dobe's aging process:

- One of the first signs of aging is a graying muzzle. Those first gray or white hairs will begin to appear when your Dobe is anywhere from 6 to 8 years of age. Initially, there may be just a few hairs scattered in among his rust markings, but then those hairs multiply. Eventually, the brilliant rust markings will appear muted.
- Because the metabolism slows during aging, weight gain (and obesity) may occur. Also, carrying too much weight can stress old joints, which in turn causes pain and discomfort. Feeling uncomfortable may make your dog a bit irritable at times.
- Aging bones and muscles can become arthritic and stiff, impeding the ability to participate comfortably in walks and other activities. Your dog may also want to play less and nap more. He may slow down and not move as fast as he once did.
- Changes in vision often occur. Dogs with vision loss may bark because they don't see clearly and are easily startled.
- Partial or total hearing loss may occur. You may notice this when your dog appears to ignore you when you call him or speak to him or ask him to do something.

Just as with humans, dogs don't like these changes either. Growing old can be easier for some dogs and more difficult for others.

FEEDING YOUR OLDER DOBE

If you are feeding your Dobe a high-quality diet, whether commercial or homemade, you may not need to change your senior's food. Growing older is not an ailment; it's a natural process, so if your dog is doing well, he can maintain his feeding regimen perhaps with just a few adjustments.

In the past, it was recommended that older dogs be fed a diet lower in protein because too much protein was thought to stress the kidneys. Unfortunately, these diets have been commonly fed for many years, yet kidney disease continues to escalate. Many experts, including Joan Weiskopf, a veterinary nutritionist, are rethinking this protocol. Weiskopf agrees that senior dogs need proteins that are easily metabolized—such as muscle meats rather than plant proteins—but she doesn't believe that senior dogs should be fed diets lower in protein. When the body ages and becomes less efficient at metabolizing proteins, continuing to feed a very good-quality diet high in animal meat proteins is important.

Dr. Deb Eldredge, DVM, one of the authors of *Dog Owner's Home Veterinary Handbook*, says about geriatric nutrition, "Preventing obesity is the single most important thing you can do to prolong the life of an older dog. Geriatric dogs are less active and may require up to 30 percent fewer calories than do younger dogs." She adds that unless a dog has a problem keeping weight on, he only needs 20 to 30 calories per pound of body weight per day.

Changing to a commercial senior diet is usually not necessary. Instead, simply feed slightly less of the quality food he's used to eating. Dr. Eldredge adds that these senior diet foods are often more expensive than adult or all–life stage foods, and they often have a reduced protein level. Because many older dogs react badly to changes, including changes in diet, feeding less can be more beneficial than changing the food. However, changing the food may be needed in some special cases. Your veterinarian may recommend a special diet for a variety of health reasons—either a commercial food or a change in ingredients. If you are concerned about the change, ask her to explain why she is making that recommendation and present any questions you may have.

How and When to Feed

If you have been feeding your Dobe twice a day, and he is doing well on that feeding schedule, then there's no need to change it.

By the Numbers

With proper care and affection, Doberman Pinschers can live to be 10 to 14 years of age. In 1997, the Doberman Pinscher Club of America (DPCA) started a Longevity Program to identify dogs and lines strong in longevity. Dobes living to 10 years of age or older, or those whose parents live to 10 years or older, are eligible to participate in the program and will be awarded a Longevity Certificate (LC). Recognizing and tracking long-lived Dobermans helps breeders establish longevity as a breeding goal. Visit www.dpca.org/longevity for more information.

Your Dobe's needs will change as he gets older.

One large meal per day is usually not a good idea, though—especially for deep-chested breeds like Dobermans, who can be prone to bloat. Scheduling meals morning and evening works best; in fact, feeding them 12 hours apart is ideal.

Some owners of larger breeds begin elevating food and water bowls as their dogs get older. This is especially beneficial for dogs who have developed arthritis and may be unable to move or bend easily. Lifting the bowl to about elbow height can make it more comfortable for your senior to reach his bowls. Commercially made stands are available at pet store outlets, or you may want to build one yourself. Easier still, just put the bowls on an inverted plastic storage container.

Always feed meals in an area where your dog feels like part of family activity but yet out of the way so people aren't tripping over him; remember he's doing everything at a slower pace now and may take a while to eat all his food. Make sure younger dogs aren't taking advantage of this and trying to steal his meals. It may help to feed your senior at a different time than other pets so he can eat in a stress-free environment.

When the Appetite Lags

As dogs age, it's not uncommon for their taste buds to lose their effectiveness and for their noses to lose some scenting abilities. Because taste and smell are so important for appetite, your Dobe may simply not find his food appealing. You can boost his appetite by adding special ingredients, such as some grated vegetables, grated cheese, or crumbled cooked meat, or you can add some warm water or broth to bring out the smells of the ingredients.

If your older Dobe has shown a preference for becoming a couch potato and his appetite is lagging at the same time, something else may be going on with his health. For example, a dental problem may be making it painful to chew. A broken tooth, infected gums, or other dental issue is usually one of the more common things to cause a dog to not want to eat. If you have any doubts, take your dog to the veterinarian. Have her do a thorough exam to see what's going on. If all is well, get your Dobe outside and moving a little more because some fresh air and activity will usually boost his appetite

Supplements

Seniors may need some nutritional supplementation as they grow older, even if you're feeding a high-quality diet.

As the kidneys become less efficient, and the gastrointestinal tract's ability to metabolize nutrients decreases, additional supplementation can make the difference between good nutrition and possible malnutrition. Many nutrients can be derived from foods, others from commercial vitamin supplements.

- Yogurt is an excellent food supplement for almost all dogs. It can be low-fat to limit calories, and it should contain active live cultures. Those cultures add probiotics to the digestive tract so that it can function better. A tablespoon a day is sufficient for most senior Dobes.

- Antioxidants are also a good addition to your dog's diet. These are naturally produced chemicals that prevent the oxidation, or breakdown, of other substances needed by the body to thrive. Antioxidants grab damaging free radicals caused by oxidation and help prevent damage from occurring. A small handful of blueberries or other foods high in antioxidants can be a great addition to the senior dog's diet.

- An easily digested vitamin and mineral supplement may be helpful to older dogs, even those on a good-quality diet.

- An older dog with arthritis or joint discomfort might benefit from a glucosamine and/or chondroitin supplement as these are known to be beneficial in protecting cartilage and helping it repair itself.

Discuss supplementation with your veterinarian before adding it to your Dobe's regular diet. Dogs with certain health

Want to Know More?

For a refresher on detailed grooming techniques, see Chapter 6: Doberman Pinscher Grooming Needs.

Your senior's grooming needs really won't change much as he grows older, but he will still need to be brushed and have his eyes and ears wiped clean.

conditions may not be able to take particular vitamin supplements.

GROOMING YOUR OLDER DOBE

Your senior Doberman's grooming needs really won't change much as he grows older. He'll still need to be brushed and have his eyes and ears wiped clean.

One difference you may notice is that his nails may need to be trimmed more often. Because most older dogs slow down a little, your Dobe may not be getting the outdoor exercise he used to get, which naturally wears down his nails. If he's healthy and eating well, those nails will continue to grow and will need to be trimmed weekly.

Another change that you want to implement is to make the grooming process more comfortable. Your senior may be more sensitive to being touched in painful areas, or he may not have the stamina to stand for grooming. Instead, ask him to lie in his doggy bed, or invite him up on the sofa for some basic tidying. Regardless of age, all dogs want to look and feel their best, and maintaining a clean coat and healthy eyes, ears, and feet add to your canine companion's overall well-being. This is a chore that should not be neglected at any age.

HEALTH CARE

All dogs—even those of the same breed—age differently. Genetics plays a part here; if your dog's ancestors lived long and active lives, then chances are your Dobe inherited the same good genes. But the food he's eaten all his life also contributes to this, as does his overall state of health, the care he's received, and any illnesses or injuries he's had. All of these factors will determine how well he ages.

Work With Your Veterinarian

As your dog grows older, his annual examination will be more thorough. Dr. Eldredge says, "The geriatric checkup should include a physical examination, complete blood chemistries, urinalysis, and parasite examination."

Your vet will also ask you for information about your Dobe's appetite, activities, and level of exercise, as well as changes in behavior and any other physical changes you've noticed. You see your dog every day, so you can provide her with a considerable amount of information about him. Don't think any detail is insignificant; let your vet worry about whether it's important or not.

As your dog advances in age, and especially if he develops some health problems, your vet may ask that your old dog come in for checkups more often, or she may need to perform sporadic testing to monitor his condition. Feel free to ask your vet any questions you may have and discuss any concerns you may have about providing this level of care. Granted this may add expense, but when your vet sees your dog more often she may be able to prevent problems before they start or treat problems before they turn into even bigger ones.

Looking Out for Potential Danger Signs

Some symptoms need to be taken seriously no matter when you see them. If you see any of these, call your veterinarian right away:
- rapid or labored breathing
- accelerated pulse or pounding heartbeat
- fever (more than 102°F/39°C)
- bloody or pus-like discharge from any orifice or wound
- blood in the feces or urine
- diarrhea or mucus in the feces, or significant changes in bowel habits
- coughing that continues or occurs at certain times of the day, especially at night
- weakness, inability to exercise, or changes in strength or ability to move
- significant weight gain, or appearance of swelling in the abdomen
- significant weight loss
- increased thirst
- increased urination

These are the most common danger signs, but any change should be watched. If things get worse or you're the least bit concerned, call your veterinarian right away.

ILLNESSES OF OLD AGE

Old age is itself not a malady, of course, but it can bring with it some disabilities and illnesses. Not every dog will develop the following problems, but unfortunately, some will.

Cancer

Cancer can be benign (it can grow slowly without invading neighboring tissues) or malignant (it can grow out of control). When cancer cells break off from the original tumor and enter the bloodstream, they can then form new tumors elsewhere in the body. At this point, the cancer is said to have metastasized.

The cause of different types of cancers in dogs is still being researched. Some dog breeds seem to have a genetic predisposition to it, and unfortunately Doberman Pinschers are one of those breeds.

Most cancers are found through a physical examination. Either the owner finds a questionable lump or bump, or a sore spot on the skin, or the veterinarian will see or feel something suspicious during an exam.

Depending on the type of cancer, treatments can include surgery, chemotherapy, radiation, special diets, or immunotherapy.

Cataracts

Many older dogs will develop cataracts, which are opacities on the lens that result in impaired vision. This condition is called *acquired*

Your dog's overall quality of life should be the most important factor you consider as he advances in age.

As dogs get older, they become more susceptible to age-related disabilities and illnesses and will need special care and consideration.

cataracts or *senile cataracts*. It often begins appearing sometime between 6 and 8 years of age, but may not appear until 10 or 11 years, depending on the dog's genetic predisposition to cataracts. If a dog develops cataracts, they often form in both eyes. However, having one affected eye is not unusual.

Generally, senile cataracts are not treated because they usually do not cause complete blindness. However, if the dog is having trouble coping, the cloudy lens can be surgically removed.

Cognitive Dysfunction Syndrome (CDS)

Cognitive dysfunction syndrome (CDS) is also often called canine senility and is sometimes compared to Alzheimer's disease in people. Dogs who are affected lose mental function and may show changes in behavior, from a loss of housetraining to not recognizing their owners. The dog may stare at a wall, pace back and forth, appear confused or lost, forget to eat or drink, and may even withdraw from family members. CDS is a progressive disease for which there is no cure. However, medication started early can sometimes slow the advance of the disease.

Congestive Heart Failure (CHF)

Congestive heart failure (CHF) occurs when the heart can no longer pump enough blood so that the body can function as it should. As the heart muscle weakens, other organs that depend on good blood circulation also begin to fail. Coughing is often one of the first symptoms. The dog will cough at night after having gone to bed, or during excitement or exercise. The dog may also tire quickly or refuse to walk or play. Eventually, he will lose weight but will develop a distended abdomen as fluids in the body accumulate. Medications can help strengthen the heart muscle and help its efficiency. Your veterinarian may recommend a change in diet or other therapies depending upon your Dobe's overall condition.

Cushing's Disease

Cushing's disease, also called hyperadrenocorticism, is a disease of the adrenal glands. Although there can be several causes of this disease, spontaneous Cushing's can occur in middle-aged to older dogs. Symptoms can include hair loss, dry dull hair coat, distended abdomen, and lethargy. Medication is available to treat (but not cure) this disease.

Dental Problems

Problems with the teeth and gums are far too common in older dogs. If your Dobe has bad breath, tartar on his teeth, red, inflamed gums, or other infections in his mouth, he will need veterinary care. Infections in the mouth can also lead to other health issues, including malnutrition and inflammation of the heart.

Diabetes Mellitus

Diabetes results when the pancreas doesn't produce enough insulin for the body's normal functions. Initial symptoms include increased appetite and increased thirst. In advanced cases, the appetite will lessen, the dog will have no energy, he may vomit, and in extreme cases, he may fall into a coma. Diabetes can be treated in much the same way as it is in people, with blood glucose tests, medication, and diet.

Kidney Disease

Kidney disease, also called renal failure, can occur at any time but affects aging dogs more frequently. The kidneys remove wastes from the bloodstream and pass them from the body via urine. As dogs age, the kidneys become less efficient. Other diseases, including diabetes, can also hamper kidney function. One of the first symptoms of renal failure is when the dog appears to be drinking an excessive amount of water. The dog will then urinate more, and housetraining accidents may occur. Treatment may include diet changes, salt and phosphorus restrictions, and medication.

Musculoskeletal Changes

As your Dobe ages, you will see some changes in his physical structure. Sometimes the back sags and becomes somewhat swayback. The elbows may turn out a little. The neck may not have the proud arch it used to have. Most of these changes are due to a lack of muscle tone. This is just one of the reasons why it's so important that older dogs get regular exercise.

Biannual Checkups

To ensure the well-being and longevity of your Dobe, begin biannual veterinary checkups at age 7 or 8 so you and your vet can formulate the best care plan for the future years of your aging canine companion. You can discuss what to expect and what to watch out for as your dog gets older, as well as learn how to best handle his changing physical, nutritional, and emotional needs.

Although some seniors cannot exercise as strenuously as younger dogs, they should walk, run if they can, and play so they can keep their muscles strong.

Osteoarthritis

Osteoarthritis, or as it is commonly called, arthritis, is a degenerative disease that affects the bones and joints. Symptoms include soreness, lameness, difficulty getting up, and a hesitance to move quickly or jump. Diagnosis by x-ray will show bone spurs or irregularities, especially where ligaments attach to the bone at the joints. Although there is no cure for arthritis, treatments can make the dog significantly more comfortable and improve his quality of life. Treatments will include keeping his weight down, adding physical therapy (often swimming), adding a glucosamine-chondroitin supplement, and prescribing medications for inflammation and pain.

Skin and Coat Changes

Small fatty tumors under the skin—called lipomas—are common in old dogs. These are generally regarded as harmless unless they change, grow too large, or inhibit the dog's movement. Some dogs will have dry skin and/or a dull, dry, flaky coat. Some diseases (such as those of the thyroid gland or adrenal glands) can cause these problems, but they are usually a part of aging that occurs when the oil glands in the skin no longer work well. Nutritional deficits or allergies can also cause skin problems.

Old age can bring with it other diseases and conditions. It is imperative to maintain open communication with your veterinarian; don't hesitate to talk to her when you have questions or concerns. With good care and your veterinarian's help, chances are good

your Dobe can live a comfortable old age.

GIVING YOUR SENIOR A HELPING HAND

Dog owners can't stop the aging process but they can help their senior canine family members move through this period of their lives with special care and consideration. As your dog ages and changes, be patient with him and don't get angry. He doesn't understand why he's changing, and if you're upset with him he may become withdrawn and depressed. Old dogs should be treasured and well loved.

There are many ways you can make life easier for your senior. Sometimes just a minor adjustment can make all the difference. For example, there are many ways to help your dog have easier access to the world around him. A ramp or set of stairs can help him get up on to your bed or into the car, or you may have to lift him when a situation warrants it. Also, understand that he will need extra time to do most things now, such as going out to potty or take a walk.

Physical changes may require modifying how you communicate with your dog. Don't get angry when your old dog doesn't respond to your verbal commands; chances are he isn't hearing you. Instead, learn to wave to get his attention, then smile and call him. He may hear a little or recognize your hand signals. If your dog suffers vision loss, try to keep furniture and other things in the same place so your Dobe doesn't run into them. Cushion sharp edges of furniture and other items so your dog doesn't hurt himself.

Also, be careful about what you ask your older Dobe to do. You may ask him to jump into your truck (or out of it) as he's always done, and because he wants to please you, he's going to try. But at this stage of life, it is likely that he may hurt himself—or, at the least, that this will be painful for him. So think twice about those things you do every day as a matter of course and perhaps show your senior new ways to do them.

Protect your senior from himself. He may think he can still take out the bad guy on the Schutzhund training field or jump after a thrown tennis ball. Although keeping his

mind and body busy is important, there comes a time when his activities need to be adapted to his current physical abilities and limitations. Perhaps he should do some trick training or therapy dog work rather than continuing to engage in more strenuous sports.

Training Can Help Seniors Cope

Training is a lifelong endeavor, but it can be especially helpful to older dogs coping with the emotional as well as physical challenges that come with aging.

For example, practicing basic obedience commands can help keep your senior's skills sharp and his mind active. Your Dobe doesn't have to attend a group training class with young dogs—just take him outside with a pocketful of healthy treats and refresh his skills. He'll enjoy the attention.

Trick training can give you something to laugh with your dog about; it provides an opportunity for you and your Dobe to do something fun together. Many easy tricks can be adapted to your dog's physical condition, from shaking paws to playing dead. Just keep the training lighthearted, and don't push your dog to do anything that would be uncomfortable for him.

Therapy dog work is an excellent occupation for older dogs. With a refresher in obedience skills, an older dog can visit people in nursing homes and hospitals, where everyone will appreciate and empathize with his gray muzzle and stiff joints. Many trainers offer therapy dog classes, and these are open to dogs of all ages.

Training Tidbit

Puppies and young dogs, especially adolescents, tend to garner the most attention from dog owners. But this may make your older dog feel left out, alone, and no longer loved or useful—especially if he has been with you for many long years; after all, it is his house and his family. Giving your senior special time with you every day, perhaps training basic skills or learning tricks, can help him feel more a part of things and even a bit special. And it's not true that you can't teach an old dog new tricks. In some ways, training an older dog is easier because he is less excitable than a puppy and has a longer attention span, so he's more likely to learn lessons faster and accept your leadership. Besides, it's important to his overall well-being to make him feel as important as ever, which his success combined with praise and treats will provide. Senior dogs need your love and attention up until the very end.

CHAPTER 14

END-OF-LIFE ISSUES

The worst thing about giving your heart to a dog is that dogs simply do not live as long as we'd like them to live. That adorable puppy you brought home has gone through adolescence, adulthood, and is now a gray-muzzled senior. And as that senior ages and his body begins to fail him, you're going to have to make a few decisions that won't be easy.

WHEN YOUR DOBE'S HEALTH BEGINS TO FAIL

Very few dogs—or people, for that matter— simply go to sleep in their old age and pass away. Those who do are extremely lucky. The reality is, unfortunately, that often in old age the body begins to fail, and illnesses and discomfort begin to take over.

- You may notice that your Dobe wants to move less and less; he may curl up on the sofa or on his bed and ignore any invitations to get up and move.
- He may no longer want to play, or won't show any interest in toys that he previously enjoyed.
- He may whimper when you touch him or handle certain parts of his body.
- His appetite may disappear.

Some dogs tend to detach themselves from the life around them; they prefer to be alone. Although many people say this is more a cat-like than dog-like behavior, dogs do this as well. It's almost as if the dog is preparing himself to leave and so is emotionally detaching himself. Although this appears to be a normal stage of life for some dogs, it upsets many owners who would prefer to spend every remaining second with their beloved pet. Some dogs go the other way, though, and do want to spend every second with their owners. It's as if they want to crawl under your skin if they could.

What is important, though, is to notice any changes in your dog that will let you know the end is approaching. Even though your pet's passing is just as normal as his birth, you will be able to cope better when you understand that your longtime companion is ready to go, and you are prepared to do what is necessary for him.

WHEN IS IT TIME TO LET GO?

It's difficult to say when it's time to let a treasured pet go. In fact, afterward, most dog owners ask themselves questions: "Did I wait too long? Did my dog suffer too much before I made the decision?" "Did I let him go too soon?" Questioning is normal, but unfortunately deciding when the time is right is hard.

Every dog and owner is unique, of course, and only you can make this very important final decision for your pet. Many veterinarians will talk to you and let you know what's going on in your dog's body—whether he appears to be in pain, or whether medication can give him more quality time with you.

The following are some things to take into consideration while making this decision:

- Is your dog in pain? If he is in pain and medication isn't working, or it wears off too soon or too often, then perhaps it's time to end his suffering.
- Is your dog suffering from a terminal illness? If he's ill, uncomfortable, and there's no hope for recovery, then it may be time.
- Has your dog stopped eating and drinking? Some dogs make the decision to go themselves by not eating and drinking.
- Can your dog no longer get up on his feet? Is his back end refusing to cooperate? A Dobe who can't stand or walk is usually a very unhappy Dobe.
- Is he incontinent? Does he realize this? Well housetrained dogs are often very disturbed and unhappy when incontinent.
- Does your dog no longer enjoy the things he used to? Is he inactive and unresponsive? This may be his way of telling you he can no longer cope.

Some dogs will try in a variety of ways to tell their owners the time to leave is approaching. I've seen this both in my own dogs and those of friends. Dax would snap at her owner's hand when he tried to help her. She never bit him, but she discouraged his attention. In her own way, she was telling him she was hurting. Dawn kept trying to stare into her owner's eyes, trying to convey something to her. Unfortunately, our dogs can't tell us verbally that they're ready, and so they try to communicate in other ways.

CANINE HOSPICE CARE

Hospice care is a wonderful option. When my father was dying of cancer, hospice helped us so that he was comfortable and his pain was controlled. It also enabled my mother, sister, and me to get the help we needed. Hospice care for pets is still new but, thankfully, it's become more and more available.

Training Tidbit

At the end of your dog's life, you are probably more in need of training than your dog. It's a good idea to prepare yourself ahead of time, to know how to best help him through his last days and what criteria you will use to make that last hard decision. For example, you should learn:

- how to minimize his pain
- how to administer medications and IV fluids
- how to hand-feed him, if necessary
- how to assess his quality of life
- how to make arrangements for his passing

Train yourself to be courageous and act selflessly, so that in the end you may give your friend the greatest gift and let him go without pain.

It may be time when your Dobe no longer enjoys doing the things he used to do.

Hospice care for your Dobe will be similar to that offered for people. You and your veterinarian will discuss what's going on with your dog and will create a plan for his care. You'll stop all treatments for his illness and will instead focus on providing what is needed to keep him comfortable and pain-free.

EUTHANASIA

Eventually, you will find yourself ready to end your dog's suffering. Although euthanasia is usually performed in the veterinary clinic, some vets will come to the dog's home. The choice is yours.

The procedure is simple and painless. A catheter is put in a vein in the dog's leg. The dog is often given a mild sedative, so that he's sleepy and not afraid. Then, while you talk to him and tell him what a wonderful companion he's been, a solution of the euthanasia drug is given and your dog will slip away. It's usually very quick. Your vet will check for a heartbeat, then let you know when your dog is gone.

For your sake, as well as your Dobe's, spend this time with your dog. Although it may be incredibly difficult, and you may find yourself overwhelmed with sorrow, you will later be glad you did. After all, your dog loves you and trusts you more than anyone else in the world, and your touch and voice will be comforting as he slips away.

THE FINAL RESTING PLACE

Deciding where your dog spends eternity is not easy either. My Grandfather buried his dogs in his apple orchard. When a dog was buried, an apple tree was planted over the grave. Although I love this idea, local laws now prohibit me from doing the same thing.

Cremation is the simplest way to dispose of your dog's remains. The ashes can be returned to you, if you wish, in a small urn or a lovely wooden box. You may decide to spread your dog's ashes under a rose bush or in the woods where you used to walk together.

GRIEF

After your Dobe's death, you may find that you are overwhelmingly sad, close to tears at the oddest moments, and even grumpy. A touching commercial on television may cause you to cry. That's normal; we all grieve after a loss, and the death of a dog is a special one.

You may feel that people don't understand your grief; after all, "It was just a dog!" some may say. But if you talk to others, you'll find that they really do understand and know in their own hearts how important dogs are to our lives.

Grief is generally experienced in stages: denial, anger, bargaining, depression, and acceptance. People feel these in varying degrees, depending upon their individual situation. You may have felt denial when told that your Dobe was ill, for example, and might have felt angry and upset when you found out

the disease was terminal. Bargaining could have come into play when you tried a variety of treatments or perhaps incorporated unusual experimental techniques. Depression may have kicked in when you realized you had to euthanize your dog, and certainly after your dog's death. And then, eventually, after time passed, you learned to accept it.

How you deal with grief is very unique. You will not deal with it the way your sister did when she lost her dog, nor will you feel it as your best friend did. This is about you and your own special relationship with your dog.

Many dog owners also feel guilty, especially if a decision had to be made to euthanize their beloved pet. You may ask yourself questions, "What if I had done this instead of that?" Or, tried a new medication or a different alternative technique? It's important, though, that you not beat yourself up with grief and guilt. You did the best you could, you loved your dog, and you made the best decisions for him that you could make.

CREATE A MEMORIAL

I have always found it comforting to create a memorial for my deceased dogs. For me, this becomes a part of how I handle grief. You may want to do the same thing; after all, just because your dog is gone doesn't mean that

Want to Know More?

Some veterinary hospitals and organizations offer hospice care, which allows pets to be kept comfortable in their own homes during their last days and gives family members time to come to terms with their impending loss. If you are interested in learning more about veterinary home hospice care, ask your vet or contact your closest veterinary school. The American Association of Human-Animal Bond Veterinarians (AAH-ABV) offers information on its website at http://aah-abv.org.

Don't expect grief to last any set period of time. You can't predict whether it will last one week, or one month, or six months. There is no rhyme or reason to the grieving process, so don't place additional pressures on yourself to react in any particular way.

If you find yourself having a hard time dealing with your grief, many counseling services are available for pet owners. Here are just a few hotlines you can call:

- University of California at Davis, Veterinary Students: (530) 752-3602 or (800) 565-1525
- Cornell University, Veterinary Students: (607) 253-3932
- University of Illinois College of Veterinary Medicine: (217) 244-2273

Other veterinary schools offer grief counseling as well. You may want to talk to your veterinarian ahead of time about contacts he recommends.

you will forget him. He's always going to be a part of who you are.

As a writer, I like to write about my dogs. These essays may never be seen by anyone else but me, but by writing about them I can express my feelings of grief in their passing, as well as my joys in having shared a life with them.

A friend of mine loves to scrapbook, and so when she lost a beloved dog, she went through her photos of that dog, from puppyhood through old age, and created a photo album and scrapbook. She included his registration papers, Canine Good Citizen certificate, obedience titles, and everything else that documented his life.

You may want to make a monetary donation in your Dobe's name. You could do this at the local shelter, a Doberman Pinscher rescue group, or a local spay and neuter program.

Just remember, the best memorial for your Doberman Pinscher is in your heart and mind. You'll never forget him, and so, in that manner, he will continue to live on. Eventually, when grief passes, you'll be able to talk about him without tears. You'll even be able to laugh again, perhaps when talking about his puppy antics in years past. And those who listen to your stories about him will remember him, too.

50 FACTS EVERY DOBERMAN PINSCHER OWNER SHOULD KNOW

1. Karl Friedrich Louis Dobermann, the creator of Doberman Pinschers, lived in Apolda, Thuringa, Germany, where one of his jobs was that of tax collector.

2. Herr Dobermann wanted a dog who would be easy to care for and yet imposing enough to ward off would-be robbers to accompany him when he made his official rounds.

3. Herr Dobermann has often been critiqued by today's breed historians for his lack of record keeping. Although his choices of breeds for the development of the Doberman Pinscher were made carefully and some facts are known, the complete breeding crosses are unknown.

4. When Louis Dobermann's health was failing, he turned his breed over to Otto Goeller. Goeller shared Dobermann's vision for the breed and continued its development.

5. Breeds used to create the Doberman Pinscher included German Pinschers, Manchester Terriers, Beaucerons, Weimeraners, Rottweilers, an old German herding dog that is now extinct, and later, Greyhounds.

6. The German Pinscher was chosen for its alertness, aggressiveness, and persistence.

7. The Manchester Terrier was chosen for its short, shiny coat, elegant appearance, refinement, and black and tan coloring.

8. The Beauceron was chosen to give the breed size, substance, intelligence, working ability, and a desire to work with people.

9. The Weimaraner (then known as the Weimer Pointer) added retrieving and scenting abilities.

10. The Rottweiler was chosen because of its intelligence, stamina, and working ability.

11. An old German sheep herding dog (not the German Shepherd of today) was chosen to provide working instinct, intelligence, physical soundness, and a strong work ethic.

12. Long after Louis Dobermann's death, it is said that Greyhounds were added to the breed to improve the breed's appearance, creating the elegant sleek look, as well as adding the quickness of movement that Greyhounds are so famous for.

13. The first name for the breed was Dobermann's Dogs. Later the breed was called Thuringian Pinschers and Soldatenhunds (Soldier Dogs).

14. The breed was recognized in England in 1948 and called, simply, Dobermann.

15. No one knows when the second "n" was dropped from the breed's name.

16. The Doberman Pinscher of today is a lean, clean looking, symmetrical dog with an elegant appearance.

17. Although the breed is most recognizable with a short, docked tail, at times they have been born with a natural bobbed (or short) tail. Dobes are normally born with a long whip-like tail that often has a big curl in it.

18. Although cropping has become a controversial issue, cropped ears are representative of Louis Dobermann's vision of the perfect guard dog because they give the impression of keen alertness and sharpness.

19. Dobes are medium sized, between 24 and 28 inches (61 to 71 cm) tall and 70 to 95 pounds (32 to 43 kg), with males being larger than females.

20. The Dobe has a very sleek coat with short, close-lying hair that is smooth and shiny.

21. The Dobe comes in a variety of colors: black, red, blue, and fawn (a shade of tan also referred to as Isabella).

22. Albinism in Dobermans is a genetic mutation (a hereditary condition) that causes a lack of pigmentation in the skin, coat, and iris of the eye.

23. Dobes are born athletes, with a strong yet not bulky build, and an inborn agility and athleticism that enable them to work and play hard.

24. Dobes are loyal, intelligent, intuitive, watchful, and protective. They are also known for their sense of humor and love of play.

25. Numerous tests and studies have shown the breed to rank among the top five breeds of dog for trainability.

26. The Doberman Pinscher was first registered with the American Kennel Club (AKC) in 1908.

27. The first champion Doberman was Intelectus. He was imported from Germany.

28. The Doberman Pinscher Club of America was founded in 1921.

29. The first American-bred champion was Doberman Dix, bred by Theodore Jager, from his Doberman Kennels.

30. The first American-bred Best in Show Doberman was Carlo of Rhinegold. He was from F. F. H. Fleitman's Westphalia Kennels.

31. During World War I, the breed almost disappeared in Europe. With food shortages and starvation facing many people, dogs starved to death or were put to death because their owners could no longer feed them.

32. Although dogs have been used in war time in Europe for centuries, World War II saw the first official use of military dogs in the US. Doberman Pinschers were one of the chosen breeds.

33. Sydney Moss, then President of the Doberman Pinscher Club of America, promised to help recruit Doberman's for the US Marine Corps. Richard Webster, of the DPCA, headed up the recruitment efforts. The Marines called their war dogs Devil Dogs.

34. To honor all the Doberman Pinschers (and other war dogs) who served and gave their lives to protect their human partners, Dr William W. Putney, a retired vet who served with the Marines in World War II, was instrumental in creating a war dog memorial in Guam.

35. The United Doberman Club (UDC) was founded in 1990 to preserve and protect the breed, and to promote the breed's working abilities.

36. A long-standing myth is that Dobermans turn on their owners. This may have resulted from when dogs used by the military were rehomed with civilian families after the conclusion of the war. However, today's properly bred, raised, and socialized Dobermans will not turn on their owners.

37. The Doberman Pinscher's character today is that of an intelligent, courageous, extremely loyal, and devoted companion.

38. Dobermans have served admirably as assistance and service dogs for people with a variety of disabilities, including blindness and mobility issues.

39. All Dobes need training, both in puppyhood and on into adult hood. This teaches manners, but also helps keep the breed's intelligent mind challenged.

40. Learning how to train your Dobe is a valuable skill. Not only does it teach him what's expected of him, but as his owner you also learn how to communicate with him so you can continue his education throughout his life.

41. Behavior problems in Doberman Pinschers can have many causes, including a lack of socialization, genetics, too little training, a lack of leadership, poor nutrition, and more.

42. Dobes are naturally protective, so meeting a variety of people during puppyhood, and learning that people of all sizes, ages, and ethnic backgrounds are okay, is vitally important.

43. Doberman Pinschers were originally bred to be working dogs—not pets—so these dogs are happiest when doing something with their owner. Training can satisfy this need, as can participating in canine performance sports.

44. Dobes are generally very good with children and make excellent family dogs, especially when raised in a family environment.

45. Dobes are usually very good with other household pets, provided that they receive positive experiences with them and are properly introduced.

46. There is only one size for Doberman Pinschers and that is of a medium-sized dog. The terms Warlock or King have been used to label larger than normal dogs but there is no breed standard or official recognition for large, extra-large, or giant-sized Dobes.

47. There is no such breed as the Miniature Doberman. The dog many people mistake as a Miniature Doberman is actually a Miniature Pinscher; a unique breed in its own right.

48. The Dobe's nasty reputation continues to be perpetuated by Hollywood's portrayal of him as a villain dog. For example, in the movie, Beverly Hills Chihuahua, one of the bad guy characters was an evil Doberman Pinscher named El Diablo. Typical typecasting!

49. Celebrity ownership has encouraged a change in the public's perception of the breed. William Shatner—actor and famous Star Trek starship captain, director, and avid horseman—has owned several Doberman Pinschers. Mariah Carey owned Princess, a Dobe, who was prominent in one of her videos and accompanied her to interviews.

50. In 2010, Dobes were the 14th most popular breed registered with the American Kennel Club (AKC).

RESOURCES

ASSOCIATIONS AND ORGANIZATIONS

Doberman Pinscher Clubs

Doberman Pinscher Club of America (DPCA)
9821 Dunbar Lane
El Cajon, CA 92021-2623
www.dpca.org

Doberman Pinscher Club of Canada (DPCC)
1140 Rock Street
Victoria, BC V8P 2B8
Canada
Telephone: (250) 995-1675
www.dpcc.ca

The Dobermann Club
United Kingdom
Telephone: 01205 821583
info@thedobermannclub.co.uk

United Doberman Club (UDC)
P.O. Box 58455
Renton, WA 98058-1455
www.uniteddobermanclub.com

Breed Clubs

American Kennel Club (AKC)
5580 Centerview Drive
Raleigh, NC 27606
Telephone: (919) 233-9767
Fax: (919) 233-3627
E-mail: info@akc.org
www.akc.org

Canadian Kennel Club (CKC)
200 Ronson Drive, Suite 400
Etobicoke, Ontario
M9W 6R4
Canada
Telephone: (416) 675-5511
Fax: (416) 675-6506
E-mail: information@ckc.ca
www.ckc.ca

Fédération Cynologique Internationale (FCI)
13 Place Albert 1er
B-6530 Thuin
Belgium
Telephone: 32 71 59 12 38
Fax: 32 71 59 22 29
E-mail: info@fci.be
www.fci.be

The Kennel Club
1-5 Clarges Street
Picadilly, London
W1J 8AB
United Kingdom
Telephone: 0844 463 3980
Fax: 020 7518 1058
www.thekennelclub.org.uk

United Kennel Club (UKC)
100 E. Kilgore Road
Kalamazoo, MI 49002-5584
Telephone: (269) 343-9020
Fax: (269) 343-7037
www.ukcdogs.com

Grooming

The International Society of Canine Cosmetologists (ISCC)
2702 Covington Drive
Garland, TX 75040
Fax: (972) 530-3313
E-mail: iscc@petstylist.com
www.petstylist.com

National Dog Groomers Association of America, Inc. (NDGAA)
P.O. Box 101
Clark, PA 16113
Telephone: (724) 962-2711
Fax: (724) 962-1919
E-mail: ndgaa@
nationaldoggroomers.com
www.nationaldoggroomers.com

Pet Sitters

National Association of Professional Pet Sitters (NAPPS)
15000 Commerce Parkway,
Suite C
Mt. Laurel, NJ 08054
Telephone: (856) 439-0324
E-mail: NAPPS@ahint.com
www.petsitters.org

Pet Sitters International
201 East King Street
King, NC 27021
Telephone: (336) 983-9222
Fax: (336) 983-5266
E-mail: info@petsit.com
www.petsit.com

Rescue Organizations and Animal Welfare Groups

American Humane Association (AHA)
63 Inverness Drive East
Englewood, CO 80112
Telephone: (800) 227-4645
Fax: (303) 792-5333
www.americanhumane.org

American Society for the Prevention of Cruelty to Animals (ASPCA)
424 E. 92nd Street
New York, NY 10128-6804
Telephone: (212) 876-7700
www.aspca.org

Canadian Federation of Humane Societies (CFHS)
102-30 Concourse Gate
Ottawa, ON K2E 7V7
Canada
Telephone: (888) 678-CFHS
Fax: (613)723-0252
E-mail: info@cfhs.ca
www.cfhs.ca

The Humane Society of the United States (HSUS)
2100 L Street, NW
Washington, DC 20037
Telephone: (202) 452-1100
www.humanesociety.org

Partnership for Animal Welfare
P.O. Box 1074
Greenbelt, MD 20768
Telephone: (301) 572-4729
E-mail: dogs@paw-rescue.org
www.paw-rescue.org

Royal Society for the Prevention of Cruelty to Animals (RSPCA)
Wilberforce Way
Southwater, Horsham,
West Sussex RH13 9R
United Kingdom
Telephone: 0300 123 4555
Fax: 0303 123 0100
vetfone: 0906 500 5500
www.rspca.org.uk

Sports
Agility Association of Canada (AAC)
RR#2
Lucan, Ontario N0N 2J0
Canada
Telephone: (519) 657-7636
www.aac.ca

North American Dog Agility Council (NADAC)
P.O. Box 1206
Colbert, OK 74733
E-mail: info@nadac.com
www.nadac.com

North American Flyball Association (NAFA)
1400 West Devon Avenue, #512
Chicago, IL 60660
Telephone/Fax: (800) 318-6312
E-mail: flyball@flyball.org
www.flyball.org

United States Dog Agility Association (USDAA)
P.O. Box 850955
Richardson, TX 75085-0955
Telephone: (972) 487-2200
Fax: (972) 231-9700
E-mail: info@usdaa.com
www.usdaa.com

The World Canine Freestyle Organization, Inc.
P.O. Box 350122
Brooklyn, NY 11235
Telephone: (718) 332-8336
Fax: (718) 646-2686
E-mail: WCFODOGS@aol.com
www.worldcaninefreestyle.org

Therapy
Delta Society Pet Partners Program
875 124th Ave. NE, Suite 101
Bellevue, WA 98005
Telephone: (425) 679-5500
Fax: (425) 679-5539
E-mail: info@deltasociety.org
www.deltasociety.org

Therapy Dogs Incorporated
P.O. Box 20227
Cheyenne, WY 82003
Telephone: (877) 843-7364
E-mail: therapydogsinc@qwestoffice.net
www.therapydogs.com

Therapy Dogs International
88 Bartley Square
Flanders, NJ 07836
Telephone: (973) 252-9800
Fax: (973) 252-7171
E-mail: tdi@gti.net
www.tdi-dog.org

Training
American College of Veterinary Behaviorists (ACVB)
Dr. Bonnie V. Beaver, ACVB
Executive Director
Texas A&M University
College Station, TX 77843-4474
E-mail: info@dacvb.org
www.veterinarybehaviorists.org

Animal Behavior Society (ABS)
Indiana University
402 N. Park Ave.
Bloomington, IN 47408-2603
Telephone: (812) 856-5541
Fax: (812) 856-5542
E-mail: aboffice@indiana.edu
www.animalbehaviorsociety.org

Association of Pet Dog Trainers (APDT)
101 North Main St., Suite 610
Greenville, SC 29601
Telephone: (800) PET-DOGS
Fax: (864) 331-0767
E-mail: information@apdt.com
www.apdt.com

Certification Council for Pet Dog Trainers (CCPDT)
1350 Broadway, 17th Floor
New York, NY 10018
Telephone: (212) 356-0682
E-mail: administrator@ccpdt.org
www.ccpdt.org

International Association of Animal Behavior Consultants (IAABC)
565 Callery Road
Cranberry Township, PA 16066
E-mail: info@iaabc.org
www.iaabc.org

International Association of Canine Professionals (IACP)
P.O. Box 560156
Montverde, FL 34756-0156
Telephone: (877) THE-IACP
www.canineprofessionals.com

National Association of
Dog Obedience Instructors
(NADOI)
PMB 369
729 Grapevine Hwy.
Hurst, TX 76054-2085
www.nadoi.org

Veterinary and Health Resources

American Veterinary Dental Society (AVDS)
P.O. Box 803
Fayetteville, TN 37334
Telephone: (800) 332-AVDS
Fax: (931) 433-6289
E-mail: avds@avds-online.org
www.avds-online.org

Academy of Veterinary Homeopathy (AVH)
P.O. Box 232282
Leucadia, CA 92023-2282
Telephone/Fax: (866) 652-1590
www.theavh.com/contact/index.php

American Academy of Veterinary Acupuncture (AAVA)
P.O. Box 1058
Glastonbury, CT 06033
Telephone: (860) 632-9911
Fax: (860) 659-8772
www.aava.org

American Animal Hospital Association (AAHA)
12575 W. Bayaud Ave.
Lakewood, CO 80228
Telephone: (303) 986-2800
Fax: (303) 986-1700
E-mail: info@aahanet.org
www.aahanet.org

American Kennel Club Canine Health Foundation (AKCCHF)
P.O. Box 37941
Raleigh, NC 27627-7941
Telephone: (888) 682-9696
E-mail: caninehealth@akcchf.org
www.akcchf.org

American College of Veterinary Internal Medicine (ACVIM)
1997 Wadsworth Blvd., Suite A
Lakewood, CO 80214-5293
Telephone: (800) 245-9081
Fax: (303) 231-0880
Email: ACVIM@ACVIM.org
www.acvim.org

American College of Veterinary Ophthalmologists (ACVO)
P.O. Box 1311
Meridian, ID 83860
Telephone: (208) 466-7624
Fax: (208) 466-7693
E-mail: office10@acvo.com
www.acvo.com

American Holistic Veterinary Medical Association (AHVMA)
2218 Old Emmorton Road
Bel Air, MD 21015
Telephone: (410) 569-0795
Fax: (410) 569-2346
E-mail: office@ahvma.org
www.ahvma.org

American Veterinary Medical Association (AVMA)
1931 North Meacham Road, Suite 100
Schaumburg, IL 60173-4360
Telephone: (800) 248-2862
Fax: (847) 925-1329
E-mail: avmainfo@avma.org
www.avma.org

ASPCA Animal Poison Control Center
Telephone: (888) 426-4435
www.aspca.org

British Veterinary Association (BVA)
7 Mansfield Street
London
United Kingdom
W1G 9NQ
Telephone: 0207 636 6541
Fax: 0207 908 6349
E-mail: bvahq@bva.co.uk
www.bva.co.uk

Canine Eye Registration Foundation (CERF)
VMDB/CERF
1248 Lynn Hall
625 Harrison St.
Purdue University
W. Lafayette, IN 47907-2026
Telephone: (765) 494-8179
E-mail: CERF@vmdb.org
www.vmdb.org/cerf.html

Orthopedic Foundation for Animals, Inc. (OFA)
2300 E. Nifong Blvd.
Columbia, MO 65201-3806
Phone: (800) 442-0418
E-mail: chic@offa.org
www.offa.org

US Food & Drug Administration's Center for Veterinary Medicine (CVM)
Communications Staff (CVM)
Food and Drug Administration
7519 Standish Place, HFV-12
Rockville, MD 20855
Telephone: (240) 276-9300
E-mail: ASKCVM@fda.hhs.gov
www.fda.gov/cvm/default.htm

Veterinary Pet Insurance
P.O. Box 2344
Brea, CA 92822-2344
Telephone: (800) USA-PETS
www.petinsurance.com

PUBLICATIONS

Books

Anderson, Teoti. *Puppy Care & Training. Neptune City: TFH Publications, Inc., 2007.*

Anderson, Teoti. *The Super Simple Guide to Housetraining.* Neptune City: TFH Publications, 2004.

Anne, Jonna, with Mary Straus. *The Healthy Dog Cookbook: 50 Nutritious and Delicious Recipes Your Dog Will Love.* UK: Ivy Press Limited, 2008.

Biniok, Janice. *The Doberman Pinscher.* Neptune City: TFH Publications, 2010.

Boneham, Sheila Webster, Ph.D. *The Multiple-Dog Family.* Neptune City: TFH Publications, Inc., 2009.

Boneham, Sheila Webster, Ph.D. *Training Your Dog for Life.* Neptune City: TFH Publications, Inc., 2008.

Dainty, Suellen. *50 Games to Play With Your Dog.* UK: Ivy Press Limited, 2007.

DeVito, Russell-Revesz, Fornino. *World Atlas of Dog Breeds, 6th Ed.* Neptune City: TFH Publications, Inc., 2009.

King, Trish. *Parenting Your Dog: Complete Care and Training for Every Life Stage.* Neptune City: TFH Publications, Inc., 2010.

Knueven, Doug, DVM. *The Holistic Health Guide for Dogs.* Neptune City: TFH Publications, Inc., 2008.

Morgan, Diane. *Good Dogkeeping.* Neptune City: TFH Publications, 2005.

Morgan, Diane. *The Living Well Guide for Senior Dogs.* Neptune City: TFH Publications, Inc., 2007.

Magazines

AKC *Family Dog*
American Kennel Club
260 Madison Avenue
New York, NY 10016
Telephone: (800) 490-5675
E-mail: familydog@akc.org
www.akc.org/pubs/familydog

AKC *Gazette*
American Kennel Club
260 Madison Avenue
New York, NY 10016
Telephone: (800) 533-7323
E-mail: gazette@akc.org
www.akc.org/pubs/gazette

Dog Fancy
P.O. Box 6050
Mission Viejo, CA 92690-6050
Telephone: (800) 365-4421
E-mail: barkback@dogfancy.com
www.dogfancy.com

Dog & Kennel
Pet Publishing, Inc.
7-L Dundas Circle
Greensboro, NC 27407
Telephone: (336) 292-4047
Fax: (336) 292-4272
E-mail: info@petpublishing.com
www.dogandkennel.com

Dogs Monthly
Ascot House
High Street, Ascot,
Berkshire, SL5 7JG
United Kingdom
Telephone: 1344 628 269
Fax: 1344 622 771
E-mail: admin@rtc-associates.
freeserve.co.uk
www.corsini.co.uk/dogsmonthly

Websites
Nylabone

www.nylabone.com

TFH Publications, Inc.

www.tfh.com

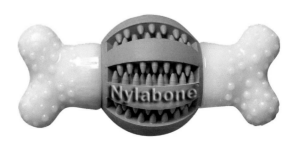

INDEX

Boldfaced numbers indicate illustrations.

PHOTO CREDITS

ABOUT THE AUTHOR

Liz Palika is an award-winning writer with more than 70 books and 1,000 magazine articles published. Her work has received numerous awards from the Dog Writers Association of America (DWAA), Cat Writers' Association, San Diego Book Writers, and other organizations. A Certified Dog Trainer and Certified Animal Behavior Consultant (CABC), Liz is also the owner of Kindred Spirits Dog Training in Vista, California. Liz and her three dogs participate in obedience, agility, carting, flying disc, trick training, lure coursing, and therapy dog work. For more on Liz's writing, go to www.lizpalika.com, and for her training services, go to www.kindredspiritsk9.com. Listen to Liz's podcasts on Pet Life Radio at "It's a Doggy Dog World."

VETERINARY ADVISOR

Wayne Hunthausen, D.V.M., consulting veterinary editor and pet behavior consultant, is the director of Animal Behavior Consultations in the Kansas City area and currently serves on the Practitioner Board for *Veterinary Medicine* and the Behavior Advisory Board for *Veterinary Forum*.

BREEDER ADVISOR

Paulette Bethel has been an animal lover all her life. She got her first Doberman in 1971 and currently lives with Sara and Usher, her ninth and tenth.

Paulette bred her first litter of purebred Dobermans in 1974. By the early 1990s, along with Mary Rodgers of Marienburg Kennel, she bred Gravin Onyx v Neerland Stamm, Sch III, CDX, ThD, VC, WH, GHC, TDI to Am. Ch. Bruda Teller of Tales, Sch III and produced Am Ch Marienburg's Coral Pendant, mother to Ch Marienburg's Repo Man, winner of 55 All Breed Best in Shows, DPCA National Specialty Winner 2002 and Number One Working Dog 2002. Temperament, health, and correct conformation have been the cornerstones of her breeding program.

Paulette is also a Master Instructor and Team Evaluator for the Delta Society and was a Pet Partner with three different Dobermans. She co-founded Intermountain Therapy Animals, a not-for-profit 501(c)3 animal therapy organization based in Salt Lake City, Utah, renowned for its outstanding and innovative therapeutic techniques and highly regarded as a model for animal therapy organizations. She served as training director there for 10 years. Paulette also hosted a live radio show to expand knowledge about animals and their care and has been featured in numerous publications about animal therapy training. She is also a competitor with her Dobermans in various dog sports, including Schutzhund, in which she and her Doberman, Gravin Onyx v Neerland Stamm acquired the coveted Schutzhund III level, as well as numerous AKC High in Trial awards in Obedience.

A native San Diegan and published author, Paulette lives in Fallbrook, California, where she owns an editing business and writes about dog training, self improvement, and dragons. Follow her on her blogging website, TherapyDogTrainingTips.com.